The Church
and the Older Person

by

Robert M. Gray   and   **David O. Moberg**
University of Utah,   Marquette University,
Salt Lake City   Milwaukee, Wisconsin

with a Foreword by
the late ERNEST W. BURGESS
Professor of Sociology, University of Chicago

REVISED EDITION

William B. Eerdmans Publishing Company

Library of Congress Cataloging in Publication Data

Gray, Robert M.
　　The church and the older person.

　　Bibliography: p. 215.
　　Includes index.
　　1. Church work with the aged.　2. Aged — Religious life.
I. Moberg, David O., joint author.　　II. Title.
BV4435.G7　1977　259　76-51286
ISBN 0-8028-1091-8

Foreword

This book on the place and function of religion in the lives of older persons is the first to be solidly based on the findings of social science research. Dr. Gray and Dr. Moberg present the known facts about aging and the religious behavior and experiences of older persons. They also include their own original contributions which measurably advance our knowledge of the meaning of religion in the lives of the aging.

Certain findings of the authors furnish guideposts to ministers and to all others interested in the welfare of older persons. Church membership in and of itself seems not to be related to good personal adjustments, but religious beliefs and activities probably are. Interviews reveal concretely how religion and the church function in satisfying the basic needs of older persons and in enabling them to face and meet the problems of old age such as fear of death, loneliness, the loss of the spouse and other crises.

These interviews also disclosed the conflict in roles between the older and the younger church members and the feeling of the former that they are being rejected. The older members are also dissatisfied with their inability to contribute to the church, to dress appropriately, to meet the cost of transportation to services and with the changes in the church from the good old ways of the past.

The recommendations made by the authors will be of value to ministers, other religious workers and older people. Suggestions are made of ways in which the church can fulfill its obligations to its older members; but also, and of equal if not greater importance, are specifications indicating how older people can be of help to the church.

One puzzling question is not conclusively answered by this volume. It is the explanation of the greater religiosity of older people than of middle-aged and younger people in this country. The experiences associated with aging as described in this book may be sufficient reason. But this consideration does not rule out cultural survivals in the present generation of older persons of the religious beliefs and convictions of their childhood and youth.

A valuable appendix contains suggestions for further research. They cover a wide range — church members compared with non-members, evaluation of existing types of church programs, differences between church members by social class, impact of urbanization upon the church and its older members, religious conflict and personal adjustment in old age, personal satisfaction derived from religion and the church, self-selection of religious faith and activity, non-Christian religions and personal adjustment in old age, religious and personal adjustment in the stages of the cycle of adjustment, adaptability in old age, the pervasiveness of religion in old age, the "faith of our fathers" and personal adjustment, church leadership and personal adjustment, church participation compared with other social participation, the status of older persons in the church, the church and the needs of older people, religious conversions of older people, fluctuations in their personal adjustment, religious beliefs of older people, and international comparisons. These suggestions may well stimulate research which will throw new light upon the many ways in which religion makes its distinctive contribution to the welfare and happiness of older persons.

ERNEST W. BURGESS (1886-1966)

Preface

This book surveys present knowledge about the church and aging people in contemporary American society as seen by two sociologists who have for some time been aware of both relevant research and programs of various religious organizations. It coordinates and integrates research data and practical experience concerning the subject.

Since the first edition of this work was published in 1962, there has been a great deal of research and a large number of new programs dealing with religion and older people. Although these changes have altered some of the perspectives in the first edition, they have not radically changed any of our basic orientations and recommendations.

Perhaps this volume can most accurately be thought of as a work in applied social science. The authors believe that they are not circumventing their professional role as social scientists by stepping into the position of suggesting and recommending certain types of activity. Rather they are helping to implement the cooperation between science and the practicing professions which is increasingly recognized as essential to the welfare of society. Not only is empirical knowledge presented, but suggestions which flow out of that knowledge are given to churches and to older people. An attempt is made to present the material in a way that will interest them as well as social scientists. Suggestions for further research proposed by this study have therefore been placed in an appendix. Technical details have been simplified or referred to in footnotes through which the interested scholar may find them.

It is obvious from the footnotes in the text that certain

chapters are more the work of one author than the other. This book is nevertheless an outgrowth of cooperative planning and true collaboration in which each has critiqued the work of the other.

The revision has brought the materials up to date. Because many of the detailed references in the original footnotes now are old and have been incorporated into the "general knowledge" of Social Gerontology, we have eliminated many old footnote references, while adding notes to the most pertinent recent resources. We have not attempted to make this book a bibliographic guide by incorporating all of the pertinent research references upon which the generalizations are based. Nevertheless, in addition to the recommended reading in Appendix III, readers can find a wealth of resources through the footnotes and current issues of the journals mentioned in them. Hence, although exhaustive coverage of all pertinent resources is impossible (and more is being published every month), the sources used can be interpreted in part as constituting a guide to both present and future resources on the topics which are covered.

A new chapter, "The Clergy and Older People," has been added because of the pivotal role played by the clergy in churches and synagogues. The working definition of Spiritual Well-Being developed by the National Interfaith Coalition on Aging is presented in Appendix I, and the suggestions for further research in Appendix II have been extended.

A large number of people have contributed to the development of this book in various ways. It is not possible to mention here all those who aided, in one way or another, in its preparation. Special gratitude is due to the readers of preliminary manuscripts of this work who have given many valuable suggestions for its improvement. They are the Reverend Warren R. Magnuson, then Pastor of the Central Baptist Church in St. Paul, Minnesota, and now General Secretary of the Baptist General Conference; the late Reverend Joseph E. Tanquist, retired missionary to Assam, India; the Reverend Lynn S. Lyon, Pastor of Salt Lake City's Central Christian Church and past President of the Salt Lake Ministerial Association; Dr. Lloyd Wilcox, Chairman, Department of Social Science, Westminster College, Salt Lake City, Utah; Dr. Rex A.

Skidmore, Dean, Graduate School of Social Work, the late Dr. Henry Frost, former Chairman, Department of Sociology, and Dr. Anthon Cannon, Professor of Sociology, all of the University of Utah.

We are also grateful to many other friends and colleagues who have contributed directly or indirectly to this work. Among those to whom special recognition is due are Dr. Clifford E. Larson, former Dean of Bethel College; the late Dr. F. Stuart Chapin, Professor Emeritus of the University of Minnesota; the late Dr. Ernest W. Burgess, Professor Emeritus of the University of Chicago; John K. Edmunds, President of the Chicago Stake, Church of Jesus Christ of Latter-day Saints; the Reverend Adolph Bohn of the Edgewater Beach Presbyterian Church, Chicago, Illinois; the Reverend Virgil Lowder, formerly of the Church Federation of Greater Chicago; and Dr. Lauris B. Whitman and the late Dr. Benson Y. Landis, who then were in the Bureau of Research and Survey of the National Council of Churches in New York City. Miss Karen Moore, Research Assistant at Marquette University, contributed significantly to the revisions, and our secretaries, particularly Dinah Landfried, made the all-important technical contributions without which there could be no book.

Finally, our sincere appreciation is extended to our wives, Helen Hale Gray and Helen H. Moberg, for their generous sympathy and understanding during the course of the study. Without their comfort and hard work this book would not have been possible.

Contents

ONE

Introduction

Expressions like "the problem of old age," "the deprivations of aging," "the declining years," and "aging as a social problem" are often heard in contemporary society. Partly to counteract their negative impact and partly to reflect the great variety of people and circumstances in the later years of life, other descriptive expressions also are used. These include "senior citizens," "golden agers," "the harvest years," "older Americans," and "late life." Because of growing recognition of both the negative and positive aspects of aging, attention frequently is turned to questions of the social, material, psychological, and spiritual well-being of older people. It is a relevant subject for the church, as well as for social and recreational organizations, educational institutions, business, industry, and government.

Many experiences and circumstances associated with old age tend to undermine the dignity and sense of personal worth of older people. Whether they consider themselves "old" or only "aging," mature Americans are increasingly aware that the economic, social, and psychological consequences of their circumstances affect everybody at all ages. The growing sensitivity to the fact that the widespread practice of relegating the elderly to a place of disrespect and contempt is inconsistent with both democratic ideals and Christian and Jewish ethics has helped to focus attention on the aging.

The number of people affected by the problems of old age and retirement in America is far greater than the number directly affected by the traditional types of social problems — crime, juvenile delinquency, and others — that have been the

subject matter of many college and university courses. In the
United States there are about three times as many persons
past their sixty-fifth birthday as college students. The aged
greatly outnumber most of the ethnic and racial minority
groups that receive considerable attention from scholars. Yet
only a small proportion of social scientists have turned their
attention to the systematic study of aging.

Both the increasing number of older people and the fact
that religion plays an important part in society and in the
lives of individuals make an examination of relationships between older people and the church pertinent and appropriate.
Alone and in cooperation with other agencies, churches are
helping to meet many needs of older people. This book surveys
this vast subject, presenting some of the problems of older
people, what we know about their religion, relationships between religion and their personal adjustment, ways in which
churches contribute both to good adjustment and to problems
of the aging, practical suggestions about what churches can
do for older people and what they, in turn, can do for the
church, and the leadership role of the clergy.

Pollak noted a generation ago that the impact of the
various aspects of religious life on the adjustment problems
of old age had almost completely escaped the attention of
social scientists. "This neglect," he said, "is surprising because
phenomena associated with old age always have aroused the
anxiety of man and thus created a special need for comfort
and reassurance, which throughout the ages have come from
the sources of religion."[1] The questions he and the Social
Science Research Council's Committee on Social Adjustment in
Old Age asked have stimulated research; action programs have
provided experience; and conferences, workshops, churches,
and other agencies have discussed the subject. Today, with
knowledge gathered from all of these, we can give at least
tentative answers to many of the questions.

WHO IS AN OLDER PERSON?

To say that an older person is "one who has reached old

1. Otto Pollak, *Social Adjustment in Old Age,* Social Science Research
Council, Bulletin 59, 1948, p. 161.

age" seems a simple, uncontroversial statement. In fact, however, it is only a tautology which confuses the issue. The term "old age" is often used very loosely. One must know the context of a communication in order to interpret the definition correctly.

There are at least three reasons for the lack of a clear-cut definition of what constitutes old age. One is the relativity of old age. Professional baseball players, boxers, and football stars are "old" by the age of 30 or 35 years, but President Eisenhower at the age of 65 in 1956 was not considered too old for election to a second term as President of the United States. Sir Winston Churchill did not retire as Prime Minister in England until he had passed his eightieth birthday. Members of Congress and the Supreme Court often continue to work well into their seventies and eighties. Yet many an American clergyman has been prematurely "laid on the shelf" at the age of 50 or 55. The "older worker" in industry is one who has passed the age of 45.[2] The profession or occupation of an individual often dictates the age at which he becomes "old"; this age varies tremendously from one occupation to another.

Difficulties of defining "old age" also result from the relative positions from which judgments are made. The grade school child is likely to consider high school students to be old and mature. The college student often regards married persons who have children as old. Even upon arrival at the "ripe old age" of 70 or more, others of the same age appear young to the person making the comparison. Residents of retirement homes who are in their seventies often refer to people in their eighties and nineties as "the old people" while considering themselves to be "young."

A third source of differences among definitions of old age is the tremendous variation in individual characteristics. The superintendent of a home for retired and disabled veterans once told one of the authors about a man aged 30 who looked as old as certain other residents in his institution who were over 100 years of age. Many people at the age of 65 or 70 can pass among strangers as being 20 years younger, while others

2. Bonnie Greene, "Obsolete at 45?" *The Guide,* Christian Labour Association of Canada, 21(10): 5-7, Nov. 1973.

in their fifties or sixties could pass for 85 or 90. The process of aging does not affect all alike. One person is "old" at 50, while another is still "young" at 75. Many a rural church has grayhaired members in its young people's society!

For most purposes, precise definition of "old age" is unimportant. At times, however, it becomes necessary to assign older persons to, or to remove them from, certain positions. Retirement policies even for church-related jobs are often based in part upon definitions of old age. Scientists also need precise definitions as they conduct their research. There are four major types of potentially usable definitions: the physiological, psychological, sociological and chronological.

Physiologically a person is old when signs of the wearing out of the body appear. There is disagreement among biological and medical authorities as to the time at which this senescence[3] normally begins. There is no one age when all physical functions of a given individual begin to show a decline. Deterioration of the various parts of the body proceeds at different rates of change and generally is so slow that it cannot be measured accurately at weekly, monthly, or even yearly intervals. Not all indications of age appear with equal severity in a given individual. Except for certain limited purposes it is therefore not yet practicable to use physiological criteria as a basis for determining whether or not an individual is "old."[4]

Psychological definitions of old age are based on changes in mental abilities, such as memory, intelligence, personality, attitudes, and emotional reactions. Here again there is no one age when all individuals begin to show the signs of aging. The rate of change is very slow and difficult to measure, and there are internal differences for a given individual in the appearance of the various signs of aging as well as in the rate at which

3. *Senescence* refers to normal old age in which the physical condition of gradual deterioration of the body is apparent; in contrast, *senility* refers primarily to the abnormal mental conditions that sometimes occur in old age.

4. For a brief summary of physiological changes during old age, interpreted as beginning at 60, see W. A. Marshall, "The Body," chap. 19 in Robert R. Sears and S. Shirley Feldman, eds., *The Seven Ages of Man*, William Kaufman, Inc., 1973, pp. 117-122. See also R. B. Weg, "Changing Physiology of Aging," in R. H. David, ed., *Aging: Prospects and Issues*, University of Southern California, 1973; and Marion D. Meyerson, "The Effects of Aging on Communication," *Journal of Gerontology*, 31(1): 29-38, Jan. 1976.

they proceed. It is not feasible at present to use psychological criteria as a practical basis for determining who is old because the problems of measurement have not yet been surmounted, and all the traits overlap with those of other age groups.[5]

From a *sociological* viewpoint, a person is old when he or she has relinquished the social relationships, roles, and statuses which are typical of middle-aged adulthood and has accepted those which are more typical of persons in the later years of life. One of the most impressive efforts to define aging objectively for personnel policy is based on sociological criteria. It attempts to determine the ability of workers to continue on the job by a yardstick for functional age constructed in a multi-disciplinary research project that began in 1962.[6] This kind of definition of old age is an exception to the general pattern and is far from widespread acceptance in our society. In "primitive" societies it is relatively easy to classify persons functionally, for definite active roles, such as preparation of food and clothing, midwifery, ceremonial leadership, and the like, are assigned to older people. In modern urbanized America, however, no definite place is established for the aged; as a result, we cannot define old age precisely on the basis of sociological criteria.[7]

The experiences of success and failure during earlier periods of life greatly affect the attitudes of older people toward particular activities. Success tends to breed further success; failure leads to failure. Although studies of abilities have shown that persons in their sixties and beyond are at least as capable as the average of persons in their twenties in the

---

5. For discussions of psychological criteria and definitions of old age see Felix Post, "Personality," chap. 20 in Sears and Feldman, *op. cit.*, pp. 123-127; Lawrence F. Greenleigh, *Changing Psychological Concepts of Aging,* National Institute of Health, U.S. Dept. of Health, Education, and Welfare, 1953; Richard A. Kalish, *Late Adulthood: Perspectives on Human Development,* Brooks/Cole Publishing Co., 1975.

6. J. N. Dirken, *Functional Age of Industrial Workers,* International Scholarly Book Services, 1972.

7. Leo W. Simmons, *The Role of the Aged in Primitive Society,* Yale University Press, 1945; Edward Nelson Palmer, "Toward a Sociological Definition of Old Age: A Research Note," *American Journal of Sociology,* 59: 28-29, July 1953; Esther H. Penchef, "The Concept of Social Age," *Sociology and Social Research,* 34: 177-183, Jan.-Feb. 1950; Zena Smith Blau, *Old Age in a Changing Society,* New Viewpoints, 1973; Irving Rosow, *Socialization to Old Age,* University of California Press, 1974.

performance of certain tasks and functions, there is doubtless a certain amount of relinquishing of social roles among older persons. For example, an attempt to master quickly new skills or knowledge, even if such mastery would have taken many hours or days in earlier life, can lead to feelings of defeat and lack of further effort.[8] Some relinquishing of social roles does reflect diminished physical or other abilities; but some reflects the consequences of changes in self-concept as a result of experiences in the middle or later years of the life cycle.

Because of the difficulties of using these definitions, *chronological* age is the standard used by most who speak or write about aging. Although age in years has varying significance for different individuals, many positions people fill in society are determined in part by their chronological age. A person's physiological, psychological, and sociological old age are related to his or her chronological age, yet many persons who are advanced in years are "young" in body, mind, and social relationships. Old age in any one sphere of life is not necessarily accompanied by old age in the others.

In this book the term *older person* refers to one who is chronologically "up in years."[9] It applies primarily to individuals who are experiencing "normal" old age, but reference will be made also to those who are physically, mentally, or socially incompetent and infirm.

Although everyone begins aging at the moment of conception, it has become customary to refer to persons in their sixties and older as "the aging." In similar manner, while life lasts, all people are growing older; everybody is older today than yesterday. There is no terminal point in life that can be called "old" as if it is the end of the life cycle, but people aged 65 and over commonly are considered to be elderly or in the period of "old age." Differences between older persons under the age of 75 and those who have passed that landmark sometimes are reflected in a differentiation between the "young old" and the "old old."

8. See A. T. Welford, "Ability," chap. 21 in Sears and Feldman, *op. cit.*, pp. 128-134.
9. E. Fritz Schmerl, "In the Name of the Elder—An Essay," *The Gerontologist,* 15(5): 386, Oct. 1975, points out that we lack a convenient, common, and correctly used noun to designate an old person, in contrast to other age groups which have precise nouns. He recommends using "elder."

It is important to remember that aging is a natural phenomenon.[10] It is characteristic of all living things. Those who have attained the status of old age have survived numerous hazards in the earlier periods of life. They will continue to develop and to change, for to live means to experience continual changes, both internally and externally, in relationships to one's self, other people, and one's environment. In this respect, as well as in recognition of the wide variety of cultural reactions to aging and the roles provided for older people, old age is very clearly a social concept. Evaluations in society of the proper and improper behavior for persons of advanced years are more significant in differentiating old age from middle age and youth than are the biological processes associated with advancing years in the life cycle. Social controls in the form of retirement rules, pension systems, and pressures to conform to expectations generally make people act in a manner consistent with the imposed societal definitions.[11] As we shall see, these expectations are more likely to involve the stigma of prejudice, discrimination, and deprivation in our culture than they are to bring praise, prestige, and status, as has been true in many pre-industrial societies.

THE CHURCH AND THE OLDER PERSON

The local church, whether called a congregation, parish, stake, assembly, or some other name, is the chief subject of this book's discussion of the church. Although oriented primarily toward the Christian religion, much of the content applies directly to Judaism and other religions in America as well. This is particularly true of the recommendations summarized in chapters 8, 9, and 10.

The specific activities a church can undertake for older people are related to its theological and philosophical orientation, the age-structure of the community it serves, activities in the community on behalf of the aged, the value-judgments of its members, and numerous other factors.

10. James E. Birren, "Research on Aging: A Frontier of Science and Social Gain," in Virginia M. Brantl and Sr. Marie R. Brown, eds., *Readings in Gerontology*, C.V. Mosby Co., 1973, pp. 20-30.

11. Leo Miller, "A Concept of Social Aging," paper presented at the annual meeting of the Gerontological Society, Nov. 5-9, 1973, Miami Beach, Florida.

The historical traditions of some churches prevent them from putting certain methods of serving older people into practice. In some cases, doctrinal interpretations may prevent the application of recommended activities. For example, if Holy Communion is looked upon as a sacrament that imparts a measure of special grace to those who partake of it, serving Communion to the ill and the shut-in is likely to be considered an essential part of the clergy's ministry. If, on the other hand, the Lord's Supper is believed to be an ordinance of the church with only symbolic significance, or if it can be served only in the presence of the local body of believers, then the administration of Communion to an older person who is alone at home or in the hospital and not in the literal presence of fellowshiping members may be considered unnecessary or even improper.

The church that is located in a community where *all* the social, recreational, economic, and similar needs of older people are already being met effectively through special clubs, recreational centers, counseling facilities, and other agencies may not need to do much more for older people than to continue its traditional program of worship and Christian teaching. Such communities, needless to say, are very rare, if not nonexistent!

Biased opinions of a church's members (such as some we shall examine in later chapters) may limit the scope of its activities for the aged. Wise leadership over an extended period of time can do much to modify these biases in a direction consistent with the basic values of the religious faith the church represents. These prejudices must not be ignored when planning programs to meet the challenge of older people; failure to deal with them may prove to be the downfall of an otherwise excellent plan.

Coordination and integration of the efforts of churchmen and representatives of various scientific disciplines interested in the church and the older person hold great promise for better theoretical understanding and improved programs of action. Among the many subjects about which increased knowledge is needed are the problems of specific types or categories of older people, their religious beliefs and practices, actual and potential contributions of the church to the aged, and contributions of older people to the church. Additional information about the effects of each of these upon older people is especially needed. (See Appendix II for more research needs.)

Tentative answers for numerous questions which may be asked about the relationships between the church and the older person are found in this book. Our excursion into these answers begins with a brief survey of the problems typically faced by older people in American society.

TWO

Problems of Older People

A revolution in population characteristics closely followed the industrial revolution in western Europe and the United States. One of the outstanding results of this demographic revolution was a shift in the age composition of the population. During the century following 1850 the proportion of persons aged 50 to 59 years in the U.S. more than doubled, those from 60 to 69 nearly tripled, and the proportion of people aged 70 and over increased more than three times.[1]

During the half century from 1900 to 1950 the population of the United States doubled, but the number of persons past age 65 quadrupled. In 1900 only one in every 25 persons in our total population was aged 65 years or over; in 1950 the ratio was one in 12 and steadily decreasing.[2] In the single decade 1940 to 1950 the population above age 65 increased by 37% while the number under 65 increased by only 13%.[3]

That the proportion and numbers of older persons in this country (21,800,000 aged 65 and over in July 1974) has continued to increase and will most likely continue to do so in the future is documented in this statistical summary:

1. Clark Tibbitts and Henry D. Sheldon, "Introduction: A Philosophy of Aging," *Annals of the American Academy of Political and Social Science,* 279:1-10, Jan. 1952.

2. Committee on Aging and Geriatrics, Federal Security Agency, *Fact Book on Aging,* U.S. Government Printing Office, 1952, p. 4.

3. "Our Aged and What They Do," *Statistical Bulletin,* Metropolitan Life Insurance Co., 32 (7):5, July 1951. From 1950 to 1960 the population aged 65 and over increased by 34.7% to a total of 16,559,580, of whom 55% were women. Special Staff on Aging, Dept. of Health, Education, and Welfare, *New Population Facts on Older Americans, 1960,* U.S. Government Printing Office, pp. 2-4.

By 1980 the population of these ages [65 and over] is expected to increase to more than 24.5 million and by 1985 may reach 26.7 million. Such persons constituted 10.3 percent of the total population of the United States in July 1974, and it is likely that the proportion will rise to 11.0 percent in 1980 and may reach 11.4 percent in 1985.[4]

This trend is not limited to the United States. "Today there are in the world 200 million men and women who have reached or passed the retirement age of 65. By 1985 that figure will have climbed to 270 million, and in some developed nations old people will make up 20 percent of the population."[5] Of further pertinence is the disclosure that "the problem of the isolated oldster is present in most of the world's developed nations, whatever their system of government."[6] It is thus apparent that survival to old age is increasingly common throughout the world. This blessing is not without problems, which one would do well to view from this broader worldwide perspective rather than to seek singularly for causes and explanations within the American system. Notwithstanding this caution, it is obvious that social problems associated with old age will become greater in the future unless much more is done to alleviate them.

It is in part a realization of these population trends that has made churchmen, social scientists, and others hold many conferences on the needs of the aged. Special courses on geriatrics and gerontology have been introduced to the curricula of colleges and universities, research has been done on the subject, books have been written, a host of articles have appeared in both popular and scholarly journals, and new popular magazines for older people as well as scholarly journals in the fields of geriatrics and gerontology have been issued. It is universally recognized by those who have devoted careful attention to the subject that older people have numerous problems

4. "Profile of Elders in the United States," *Statistical Bulletin*, Metropolitan Life Insurance Co., 56(4): 8-10, April 1975. See also D.G. Fowles, "U.S. 60+ Population May Rise 31% to 41 Million by Year 2000," *Aging*, No. 248-249, pp. 14-17, 1975.

5. Margaret H. and S. Allen Bacon, "Time to Retire?" *The Christian Century*, 90(7): 201, Feb. 14, 1974.

6. *Ibid.*

even in the most prosperous large nation on earth, the United States.

Some of the problems faced by the aged are an almost inevitable result of the physiological and psychological changes that result from the aging process. Others are largely a result of man's dealings with his fellows; these can be alleviated most readily by wise and considerate programs of the church, the government, and other social institutions and organizations.

The older person in the United States typically faces problems that are more numerous, more serious, and more strange than any he or she has faced since adolescence and early adulthood. The stereotyped picture of grandmother sitting at ease in her rocking chair all day with no worries or cares whatever is not characteristic of the majority of American grandmothers. For most people, old age is a period of development and adjustment "rather than a period of nirvana — of blissful and unstriving ease leading to a quiet and peaceful passing out of this life."[7]

"While there is some wisdom in the observation that a person is as old or young as he feels, our social security legislation, our retirement policies, and our statistics on morbidity and mortality suggest another way of determining who is old."[8] This method is that of stereotyping, for example, everyone over 55 years of age as being old. The main problem with this approach is that people of this age are not all alike, and certainly not all of them are old at this age. Nonetheless, such stereotyping does provide a useful mechanism for dealing with the old age problem, particularly if the matter of differentiation within such grouping is kept in mind.

The picture of the aged man drawn in *As You Like It* by William Shakespeare was no doubt a conception typical of the pictures of the aged citizen in the minds of many of his countrymen:

---

7. Robert J. Havighurst, "Old Age—An American Problem," *Journal of Gerontology*, 4: 300, Oct. 1949.

8. George L. Maddox, "Growing Old: Getting Beyond the Stereotypes," in *Foundations of Practical Gerontology*, ed. by Rosamonde R. Boyd and Charles G. Oakes, University of South Carolina Press, 1972, p. 7.

All the world's a stage,
And all the men and women merely players;
They have their exits and their entrances,
And one man in his time plays many parts,
His acts being seven ages. . . .
The sixth age shifts
Into the lean and slippered pantaloon,
With spectacles on nose, and pouch on side;
His youthful hose well saved, a world too wide
For his shrunk shanks; and his big manly voice,
Turning again towards childish treble, pipes
And whistles in his sound. Last scene of all
That ends this strange eventful history,
Is second childishness, and mere oblivion:
Sans teeth, sans eyes, sans taste, sans everything.

Perhaps in Shakespeare's day, just as today, the stereotyped picture of the old man did not fit the majority of older people; yet there are some elements of truth in the physical and mental characteristics implied in his statement. The physical and mental changes which often accompany old age, whether first apparent at the age of 40 or 80, take place within a cultural setting which determines their significance and which, in our country, decrees almost inevitably that there shall be economic and social problems as well. We shall, therefore, examine briefly some of the typical physical, economic, psychological, social, and spiritual problems faced by older persons here and in other nations with similar cultures. All of these problems have distinct implications, implicitly or explicitly, for the church and its work.

PHYSICAL PROBLEMS[9]

Both the belief that old age is necessarily a period of de-

9. The factual details in this section, except where otherwise noted, are based upon the report of The President's Commission on the Health Needs of the Nation, *Building America's Health,* U.S. Government Printing Office, 1953, vol. II, "America's Health Status, Needs and Resources," pp. 89ff., and vol. III, "America's Health Status, Needs and Resources—A Statistical Appendix," pp. 125ff. Cf. the Hearings Before the Subcommittee on Problems of the Aged and Aging of the Committee on Labor and Public Welfare, U.S. Senate, 86th Congress, Second Session, *Health Needs of the Aged and Aging,* U.S. Government Printing Office, 1960, and U.S. Department of Commerce, *Statistical Abstract of the United States, 1974,* 95th Annual Edition, U.S. Government Printing Office, 1975.

terioration and that there are certain diseases which are the special province of old age alone are false. It is true, however, that the effects of many diseases upon older people differ radically from the effects of the same diseases upon the young. Although health problems continue to be extensive among older people in this country, it is encouraging that the health of all Americans has been steadily increasing over the past several years. Of saliency in the present context is the fact that the overall health status of older persons is much better than it was several years ago, as is indicated by the following excerpt from a government report on health in the later years of life:

> Average length of life is a traditional measure of the health status of people of all ages. By this standard, the health status of older Americans of the 1970's is markedly better than that of earlier generations. People who are 45, for example, have already lived almost as long as the average person born in 1900 could have expected to live, and today, they have about 30 more years of life remaining.
>
> In only a few countries in the world does the life expectancy of women at ages 45 to 65 exceed that of American women. However, there are many countries in which older men have a longer life expectancy than do American men.[10]

Another important health fact is that the gap in death rates for men and women at the older ages is becoming more pronounced rather than decreasing.

> For example, among white men at ages 45-64, the death rate in 1940 was about 50 percent higher than for white women. In 1950, it was about 80 percent higher; and by 1968, it was more than double the rate for women. A similar but narrower divergence characterizes the rates for men and women of races other than white.[11]

Although almost everyone who lives to the age of 60 has acquired some more or less permanent disability or disease, only between 10% and 15% of the elderly are actually incapacitated at any one time. However, "about two-fifths of all persons 65 years and over suffer some limitation of activity because of chronic conditions — a high rate indeed when com-

10. U.S. Department of Health, Education and Welfare, Public Health Service, *Health In the Later Years of Life*, National Center for Health Statistics, Rockville, Maryland, Oct. 1971, p. 1.

11. *Ibid.*, p. 7.

pared with those under 17 years of age, of whom only 2 percent are limited in activity."[12] Further emphasizing the extent of chronic diseases among older persons are the findings of the National Health Survey which disclosed that 86% of Americans aged 65 or older are afflicted with one or more chronic diseases as compared to 71.6% of those aged 45 to 64.[13]

Commenting on the amount of disablement and concomitant limitation of activity among the aged suffering chronic conditions in this country, Loether writes:

> Activity limitations are much more prevalent among older persons. Fewer than 1 out of 100 of those under 45 are subject to activity limitations compared to 1 out of 20 of those between 45 and 64, and almost 1 out of 5 of those 65 years of age or older.[14]

The four major chronic diseases are arthritis, heart disease, hypertension, and diabetes.[15] The most common chronic disease is arthritis, which affects 20,250,000 Americans;[16] one form, osteoarthritis, afflicts 80% of the older persons in this country.[17]

Many elderly people are faced with the problem of adjustment to their own or their spouse's disability, and frequently they are invalids for prolonged periods of time before death relieves them of their suffering. As Havighurst has indicated, half of all who live to be over the age of 50 die of heart disease or its complications; this comes on slowly and, in many cases, first makes one an invalid. Equally significant is the fact that a sizable proportion of those who reach the age of 70 can expect several years of invalidism before death.[18]

A large proportion of the deaths in the United States today occurs among persons over the age of 65. In 1900 about one-fourth of all deaths occurred among the 4% of the popu-

12. *Health In the Later Years of Life, ibid.,* p. 32.

13. U.S. Public Health Service, *Working With Older People: A Guide to Practice,* vol. II, Pub. No. 1459 (U.S. Government Printing Office, April 1970), p. i.

14. Herman J. Loether, *Problems of Aging,* 2nd ed. (Dickenson Publishing Company, 1975), p. 30.

15. *Health In the Later Years of Life, op. cit.,* p. 18.

16. The Arthritis Foundation 1974 Annual Report, *We Don't Like Being No. 1* (The Arthritis Foundation National Office, New York, 1975), p. 4.

17. *Health In the Later Years of Life, op. cit.,* p. 20.

18. Havighurst, *op. cit.,* pp. 298-304.

lation in the older years, while in 1950 over half of all deaths were among the 8% in the same age group.[19] The death rate of persons 65 to 74 was 35.5 per 1000 population in 1972 while persons aged 75 to 84 had a death rate of 79.0 per 1000 for the same year.[20] The advances of the medical sciences have made it possible for thousands to avoid being stricken by or to survive the results of diseases that would otherwise have taken their lives at an earlier age.

In the U.S. in 1975, as a reflection chiefly of the high death rates of the aged together with the tendency of men to marry younger mates and to die at an earlier age than women, over half (52.5%) of all women aged 65 and over were widowed, 37.6% were married and living with their husbands, and 9.9% were of other marital status.[21]

With increasing age there is a general reduction in strength, endurance, and skill. Hearing and vision adversely affected by the aging process encourage increased isolation. Fears of ill health, chronic invalidism, and death often contribute to mental illnesses and may contribute significantly to the many psychosomatic ailments of which the medical profession is becoming increasingly aware.

Decreased metabolic efficiency of the older person makes it difficult to keep warm; decreased ability to masticate food makes watchful care over the diet more important than in earlier life; decreased physical strength and vigor undermine energy and contribute to short-windedness and to other limitations upon physical exertion.

The increasing emphasis upon health maintenance as opposed to disease medicine will no doubt have a major impact on health delivery systems in this country. The main implica-

---

19. In 1957, 938,294 or 57.05% of all deaths in continental U.S. occurred to persons aged 65 and over. "Mortality from Selected Causes . . . , 1957," *Vital Statistics—Special Reports, National Summaries,* 50 (5), Apr. 24, 1959. The overall death rate in the United States was 9.4 per 1000 population in 1972; the overall death rate of persons aged 65 to 74 was 36.7, and for those between ages 75 and 84 it was 77.7 per 1000 population. U.S. Bureau of the Census, *Statistical Abstract of the United States, 1972,* U.S. Government Printing Office, 1972, p. 56.

20. *Statistical Abstract of the United States,* 1974, *op. cit.,* p. 60.

21. Donald G. Fowles, "Elderly Widows," Statistical Memo No. 33, U.S. Dept. of Health, Education, and Welfare Publication No. OHD 77-20015, July 1976.

tion of this change in orientation will be the demand for more preventive and health maintenance services by older citizens who will need more care than younger persons. This point is succinctly made by Verwoerdt:

> Aging individuals are more likely to have multiple chronic conditions. In order to prevent undue disability, chronic conditions such as arthritis, heart disease, and high blood pressure will require continuous medical attention.[22]

Medicine, in an attempt to meet the increasing demands for service, is currently in the throes of a move to expand and refine existing medical services. One result of this development is the trend toward getting more persons involved in providing medical and related services, such as allied health personnel and community agency leaders. A concomitant of this development is that many persons are turning to the church for assistance in maintaining health and coping with serious illness.

Since all the physiological changes of older people affect their pattern of living, it is often necessary to work out new patterns of adjustment. All of these adjustments influence the type of work the church can do on behalf of the older person.

ECONOMIC PROBLEMS

Only brief investigation of the incomes of older people is needed to bring one to a realization that many of the elderly have serious economic problems. In 1970 the median family income in the United States was $9,715 while the median income for families with heads aged 65 and over was $5,032.[23] "In 1973 the Bureau of Labor Statistics set budgets for an intermediate standard of living at $5,200 for elderly couples and $2,860 for single persons."[24] An estimated 11 million aged persons had incomes below these levels.[25] A report of the Special Committee on Aging of the U.S. Senate disclosed that in this country one out of every four persons 65 or over was im-

22. Adrian Verwoerdt, "Biological Characteristics of the Elderly," in Boyd and Oakes, eds., *Foundations of Practical Gerontology, op. cit.,* p. 57.

23. *Statistical Abstract,* 1972, *op. cit.,* p. 326.

24. Loether, *Problems of Aging, op. cit.,* p. 69.

25. Special Committee on Aging, United States Senate, *Developments in Aging: 1972 and Jan.-March 1973,* U.S. Government Printing Office, 1973, p. 15.

poverished.[26] Even though their incomes may be supplemented by income in kind gained from home-grown food, free housing, and contributions of food and clothing, it is obvious that thousands of senior citizens in the U.S. are seriously handicapped economically.

Adding to the magnitude of the problem is the fact that, except for the World War II years, the proportion of older persons in the work force in this country has been steadily declining.[27] The proportion of older persons not in the labor force today ranges from 75% for males 65 and over to 88% for those 75 and over.[28]

Reduced income often reduces social contacts at a time in life when these are needed more than for several earlier decades of life. It limits the medical care sought by those who are most in need of it. It may lead to deficient diets and malnutrition, and, at worst, housing in dwellings unfit for human habitation.

Since 1890 the proportion of men aged 65 and over who are in the labor force has decreased from over two out of three (68.2%) to less than one out of four (23.3%).[29] The proportion of working women in the same age group decreased until 1940 (to 6.8% from 7.6% in 1890)[30] and in the following decades increased to almost one out of ten (8.8% in 1972).[31] This may indicate that older women are increasingly compelled to seek work outside the home or that they are receiving somewhat better treatment when they seek jobs while men are increasingly forced to retire from the labor force because of old age.

With the increasing emphasis upon mechanization in farming and in many other occupations, the tendency is to place a premium upon certain characteristics and capacities of workers; this often operates to the detriment of the older

26. *Ibid.*, p. 14.

27. U.S. Bureau of the Census, *Historical Statistics of the United States, Colonial Times to 1957* (U.S. Government Printing Office, 1960), Series D 13-25, p. 71.

28. "Profile of Elders in the United States," *op. cit.*, pp. 8-9.

29. *Statistical Abstract*, 1974, *op. cit.*, p. 337.

30. *The Aged and Aging in the United States: A National Problem*, U.S. Government Printing Office, Senate Report No. 1121, 86th Congress, 2nd Session, 1960.

31. *Statistical Abstract*, 1974, *op. cit.*, p. 337.

worker. Recent developments in job-breakdown and speciali-
zation have resulted in a relative growth of the number of
semi-skilled workers and in a decline in the number of skilled
workers. This has made it more difficult for older workers to
retain prominent positions in the labor force. Mechanization
has made it possible to hire unskilled or semi-skilled workers to
do the work formerly done by skilled workers, many of whom
have been of an older generation trained specifically for certain
precise types of work. The increasing speed of industrial
processes also handicaps the older worker, while rapid technological changes make it impossible for most workers to use the
same skills throughout their working lives.[32]

With the increasing automation of industry and business,
many jobs and occupations are declining, and some are even
disappearing. Older workers often are less flexible and adaptable and have a shorter working span remaining; they often
become unemployed as younger workers are trained for the
new positions created by this trend.[33]

Most older people do not wish to retire as long as they are
physically and mentally able to work. Yet compulsory retirement policies in many places of employment lay many people
on the shelf prematurely. Private pensions, old age and sur-
vivor's insurance, supplementary social insurance, and savings
provide their main sources of income after retirement. As we
have already seen, for large numbers of them that income is
insufficient to meet the demands of the American standard of
living. Because of the Puritan tradition of work for its own
sake and of personal independence, and because home conditions have changed from what they were a century ago,
retirement is often a major disintegrating factor for the older
person.[34]

---

32. William H. Stead, "Trends of Employment in Relation to the Problems of the Aging," *Journal of Gerontology*, 4:290-297, Oct. 1949.

33. George Thomas, "Mechanized Industry Presents New Employment
Hazards for Our Increasing Older Population," *The Railway Clerk*, 53
(23):8, Dec. 1, 1954.

34. Michael T. Wermel and Selma Gelbaum, "Work and Retirement in
Old Age," *American Journal of Sociology*, 51:16-21, July 1945. A good
discussion of the pros and cons of a fixed retirement age is found in four
articles in *Annals of the American Academy of Political and Social Science*,
279:72-83, Jan. 1952.

One of the effects of reduced income and related factors that accompany old age is that millions of older persons are forced to depend upon public assistance for a livelihood. The economic plight of older persons and the dependency of many upon public assistance is a well-established fact.[35] That this dependency often contributes to problems of personal adjustment has been documented by several researchers, including Wells in his well-conceived study:

> ... making public one's need for Old Age Assistance is not merely an admission of immediate financial need. In a society quick to stereotype, it can be seen as a reflection of a more general, age-related deterioration as well. At this level, ... the need for public assistance marks yet another event which certifies the aging individual's changing status within the social structure.[36]

Wells discloses that a sizable proportion of the public assistance recipients in his study were embarrassed by their dependency status. A large proportion of the embarrassed males were so affected that they expressed themselves in a manner symptomatic of low morale.[37]

The housing facilities in which the aged are compelled by economic pressures to live are often unsuitable for them.[38] Stairways to climb to bedroom or bathroom, large areas to keep clean and in order, kitchen facilities that require much stooping and stretching for use, and other undesirable features create serious problems for thousands of the aged. In addition, serious inadequacies of plumbing, heating, and electricity are found in many substandard dwellings occupied by older people because they are the only facilities available within their limited economic means.[39]

---

35. L. E. Bixby, "Income of People Aged 65 and Older," *Social Security Bulletin*, 33:3-34, 1970.

36. Larry L. Wells, "Welfare Embarrassment," *The Gerontologist*, 12 (2, Part I): 197-200, 1972.

37. *Ibid.*

38. For an insightful study of older persons' long-range satisfaction with new housing see Frances M. Carp, "Long Range Satisfaction with Housing," *The Gerontologist*, 15(1): 68-72, Feb. 1975.

39. For a discussion of problems of housing older people see the report of the Committee on the Hygiene of Housing, *Housing An Aging Population*, American Public Health Association, 1953, and Special Committee on Aging, U.S. Government Printing Office, 1973, p. 1.

Growing old in America thus presents one of the most difficult adjustment problems for millions of persons. Because of conditions such as those described above, many Americans have a difficult time growing old gracefully and coping with their circumstances during later maturity. Unfortunately, much of the problem with respect to this adjustment process results from the low esteem in which our older persons are held, a problem not found in many other countries. For example, one authority has reported:

> The prestige and the respected status of the elderly have a long tradition in Japan. As one of their neo-Confucian scholars put it: "Filial piety is what distinguishes men from birds and beasts."[40]

In sum, the lack of respect for our senior citizens, the growing emphasis upon youth, and the substitution of technology for manpower has left tens of thousands of older Americans with no role in society. These, along with the numerous other problems alluded to in this book and elsewhere, contribute to the despair that is found so frequently among the elderly. Faced with disappointment and disillusionment at reaching the "harvest years"; finding the "golden years" to be a period of relative poverty; feeling themselves to be on the shelf and not permitted to make the contributions they still are able to make to the economic life of our nation; frustrated with the reduction of income which usually comes with retirement, and living in unpleasant, inconvenient, and unhealthful dwellings; it is no wonder that so many older persons are seriously maladjusted. The church has a tremendous challenge to face in the problems related to the economic plight of so many of our older citizens.

PROBLEMS OF SOCIAL RELATIONSHIPS

Since many older people do not know "their place" in society, it is no wonder that they cannot fill it. This is largely due to the fact that we have no institutionalized roles for the

---

40. Alfons Deeken, "Growing Old—And How to Cope With It," *America*, 124: 315, March 27, 1971.

elderly, so people cannot be effectively socialized to old age.[41] As a result, society has failed to provide meaningful roles and opportunities for many older persons who now find themselves unable to fit into American society.

The older individual is compelled to make choices, but he has no assurance that he has chosen "correctly" because no definite patterns of behavior are laid down for him. When his actions involve other people, he must assume certain anticipated reciprocal behavior by them. When the expected behavior is not forthcoming, there often is disappointment. He has no definite place in the contemporary social structure, as elders in most preliterate societies have. He tends to become isolated from the occupational world when he is forced to retire from his work, and he is isolated from social affairs because he is in a small conjugal family as contrasted to the large kinship groups of many other cultures. This social isolation may be a major source of senility and of the low level of personal adjustment common to so many persons who are not mentally ill.[42]

That social isolation both contributes to premature deaths of older citizens and frequently results in their being alone when they die is well attested to by many observers.[43] That old people often are alone even when they die is underscored by Kastenbaum and Mishara in their insightful paper:

41. Irving Rosow, *Socialization to Old Age*, University of California Press, 1974. See also Anne Foner, "Age in Society: Structure and Change," *American Behavioral Scientist*, 19(2): 144-165. Nov./Dec. 1975.

42. For a more complete discussion of this problem see Ralph Linton, "Concepts of Role and Status," in Theodore M. Newcomb and Eugene L. Hartley, eds., *Readings in Social Psychology*, Henry Holt and Co., 1947, pp. 367-370; Ralph Linton, "Age and Sex Categories," *American Sociological Review*, 7:589-603, Oct. 1942; Leo W. Simmons, *The Role of the Aged in Primitive Society*, Yale University Press, 1945; Leo W. Simmons, "Attitudes Toward Aging and the Aged: Primitive Societies," *Journal of Gerontology*, 1:72-95, Jan. 1946; Elaine Cumming, *et al.*, "Disengagement—A Tentative Theory of Aging," *Sociometry*, 23:23-35, March 1960; Raymond Payne, "Some Theoretical Approaches to the Sociology of Aging," *Social Forces*, 38:359-362, May 1960; Susan K. Gordon, "The Phenomenon of Depression in Old Age," *The Gerontologist*, 13(1):100-104, Spring 1973.

43. B. G. Glaser and A. Strauss, *Awareness of Dying*, Aldine, 1965; D. Sudnow, *Passing On*, Prentice-Hall, 1967; and R. A. Kalish, "The Aged and the Dying Process: The Inevitable Decisions," *Journal of Social Issues*, 21:87-96, 1965.

Even when the death of an old person is expected, we are not likely to be at his side. We have more important duties to perform elsewhere, anywhere else. The dying elder is to be screened off from the world of the living — at least in this regard his existence receives a negative sort of acknowledgment.[44]

Many conditions in America rob the aged of definite responsibilities; without responsibilities they tend to feel useless and unwanted, having lost a distinct place of respect and prestige. One of these conditions is the temporary nature of the typical American family. The family lasts from marriage until death (or in an increasing number of cases, desertion or divorce) separates the couple. Years before that time the children typically have left to establish their own homes. In contrast, the older, traditional type of rural family tended to outlive its elderly members because it included three or more generations of people.

A major problem for many older persons is that of adjusting to the death of the spouse. More than half of all American women aged 65 and over, and more than two-thirds of those past their seventy-fifth birthday are widowed. This compares to just under one-fifth and one-third, respectively, of the men at corresponding ages. (The figures for males are lower because men, on the average, marry women younger than themselves, die at a younger age, and are more likely to remarry after widowhood.) The man who becomes a widower may have to learn how to cook, keep house, keep his own clothes in order, and care for many other details new to him. In addition, he will have to face the major problem of learning how to live alone. More often, however, this is a woman's problem. She may be forced to move to a smaller home, learn about business matters, economize severely because of reduced income, and reconcile herself to living alone.

The aged have many problems associated with their friendships. Friends die, one by one, so the very persons who could do the most to bolster morale may be gone. This problem is accentuated when mobility is great, as it is in our nation today. Old friends not only depart by death; they also move away. The older person himself may move to some distant

---

44. Robert Kastenbaum and Brian L. Mishara, "Premature Death and Self-Injurious Behavior in Old Age," *Geriatrics*, 26:71-81, July 1971.

place where he must make new friends — if he is to have any
friends at all. Older people who remain in the home community are left socially isolated in all too many instances as
newcomers fill the occupational, social, and residential gaps
vacated by those who have departed.[45]

Compulsory retirement is often a complete and sudden
shock — even when it is expected. This makes the individual
feel unwanted and gives him the feeling that he is living as a
parasite on the efforts and energy expended by others. One
day a man works his eight hours; the next he is "on the shelf"
for the rest of his life just because he has reached his sixty-fifth
birthday. Society thus creates an ambiguity for the older person, who must face reduced prestige, problems of status, increased free time, etc.[46] If he has no religion and no hobby or
other avocation, he will face serious problems in the use of
his time and undergo other stressful experiences as described
above.

If the older citizen turns to civic affairs or to increased
activity in social organizations, he may sense the need for major
changes and desirable reforms in traditional practices. All too
often, however, the suggestions he makes will not be evaluated
fairly by others, for the immediate impression of far too many
people is that aged persons are "old fogies" whose suggested
reforms would only take the nation back half a century
or more.

For these and other reasons, many older persons start dis-
engaging themselves from societal relationships; the degree of
disengagement is dependent upon many factors, including personality, economic status, and social setting. According to Barrett, this gradual withdrawal from societal roles frequently
continues until the older person assumes a role position similar
to that he played in early childhood:

45. Zena Smith Blau, *Old Age in a Changing Society*, New Viewpoints,
1973; and G. V. Laury, "Some Reflections on Aging in the United States,"
Geriatrics, 28(5): 178-182, May 1973.

46. Kurt W. Back, "The Ambiguity of Retirement," chapter 5 in Ewald
W. Busse and Eric Pfeiffer, eds., *Behavior and Adaptation in Late Life*,
Little Brown and Co., 1969, pp. 93-114. See also Marion P. Crawford,
"Retirement: A Rite de Passage," *Sociological Review*, 21(3): 447-461,
Aug. 1973.

Social and church associations together with fraternal membership are maintained for many years — probably as long as one
remains fairly mobile — but even these disappear in time. This
returns the geronto to the life he knew as a child — a very simple
primary, social, usually face-to-face existence.[47]

This withdrawal from societal roles which is typical of so
many old people contributes to difficulty in maintaining wholesome relationships with other persons, most of whom are so
busy coping with their own life problems that they do not
have the time or resources to seek out older persons.

The stereotype of old people also contributes to their
problems. This is the idea that all of them have certain definite
characteristics, usually emphasizing the undesirable traits found
in a few individuals. They thus are looked upon as living in
the past, hopeful of getting back into the pleasant circumstances of an age gone by but forgetting the many unpleasant
conditions of that same age. They are considered to be past
the age of usefulness — except when a babysitter is needed —
and are thought to desire only a final period of life at ease in
the rocking chair.

The negative aspects of being classified as "old" and hence
of presumably possessing the characteristics which are alleged
to apply to all "old people" can result in detrimental self-
images. These, in turn, can contribute to impaired mental
health and social relationships in a self-perpetuating cycle of deterioration. On the other hand, positive images of the elderly
also are present in our society and are becoming a part of the
stereotype of old age. Persons who accept for themselves the
positive personalized stereotype of "old" are likely to have much
better social and emotional health than those who adopt the
negative stereotype for themselves.[48]

Cumming and Henry provide an insightful presentation
of the important position taken by many gerontologists that
human aging involves an inevitable withdrawal from relationships with other persons. For most people, they argue, this

---

47. James H. Barrett, *Gerontological Psychology*, Charles C Thomas, 1972,
p. 17.
48. Timothy H. Brubaker and Edward A. Powers, "The Stereotype of
'Old': A Review and Alternative Approach," *Journal of Gerontology*, 31(4):
441-441, July 1976.

is not only an inevitable process, but a healthy one as well.[49] Rose and Peterson, on the other hand, argue that disengagement is not only not inevitable, but also that it is very disruptive for most elderly persons.[50] Particularly disruptive is the process elderly people typically undergo when they enter institutions. They may lose many of the possessions which pertain to their own identity. What they are allowed to keep, indeed, is the fact that every older person has a history in a family. Family is all that most institutionalized older persons have left.[51]

The present authors agree with Rose and Peterson that forced disengagement is unhealthy and personally disturbing to many older persons. The consensus of most authorities on aging is that thousands of elderly persons are quite content to disengage from some societal roles as they grow older and should have that privilege. Our chief concern is for those for whom disengagement is hurtful and those who are not content to be shelved by the disengagement process. The conflicts and stresses encountered as a result of forced disengagement hamper wholesome interpersonal relations with other members of society.

Problems of social relationships are similarly increased by the tendency to emphasize individual accomplishment and individual competition to such an extent that the aged are sometimes actively competing with younger adults for recognition. With our emphasis upon speed, vigor, youthful beauty, and similar values, older people usually lose out in the competition.

Compounding these problems for older persons are the profound social changes in the world and this nation that are making an impact on the lives of all Americans. The close connection between societal processes and personal relationships is well established; as an eminent authority on the social psychology of old age notes,

> ... the interplay between the individual and the social system is a constantly unfolding process, reflecting developmental and

49. E. Cumming and W. E. Henry, *Growing Old*, Basic Books, 1961.

50. A. M. Rose and W. A. Peterson, eds., *Older People and Their Social World*, F. A. Davis, 1965.

51. Dean Black, "The Older Person and the Family," chap. 7 in Richard H. Davis, ed., *Aging: Prospects and Issues*, University of Southern California, 1973.

historical events as the individual moves through time.... the social system — as the person experiences it — is not a static entity, but reflects both continuity and change.[52]

Because of this close interplay between a person and his social structure, the elderly, like others, are vitally affected by what is happening in this nation today. Thus national events, such as the Watergate fiasco, economic depression, rising crime rates, and increasing mobility have had their effect. These, together with empirical evidence that general despair and disillusionment are widespread, document the negative impact of social forces on the mental health of older persons by disrupting their lives and threatening what little security many of them have in the rapidly changing social scene.

These problems reflect basic characteristics of our society. To remove the problems it would be necessary to make wholesale changes in our culture that are entirely out of the question. These changes would include the complete overhaul of our family pattern, modification of retirement policies, discontinuation of population mobility, departure in whole or in part from our competitive economic and social order, decreased emphasis upon the person as an individual, return to a rural type of community life in which relationships in all social institutions and organizations closely coincide and overlap, decreased freedom of individuals to live as they please, an accompanying increased insistence that the various age groups play distinct roles in everyday living, and increased importance of government in many areas of life which are now considered to be purely "private."

It is probable that no one would want all the changes that would be necessary, if it were possible to spell them all out in detail, in order to remove the problem conditions of the aged. Desirable changes would undoubtedly include modification of cultural values and institutional practices to give older people a more satisfactory place in society and to help them continue living wholesome, productive lives that are beneficial to themselves and to others. The church can contribute significantly to such changes.

---

52. Vern L. Bengtson, *The Social Psychology of Aging*, Bobbs-Merrill, 1973, p. 18.

EMOTIONAL AND MENTAL PROBLEMS[53]

A high prevalence of mental illness among the aged and a large number of border-line mental conditions are both a result of previously discussed problems and a partial cause of some of them. Commenting on mental health problems among older persons in this country, Butler and Lewis state: "The extent of mental disorders in old age is considerable. It has been estimated by the American Psychological Association in 1971 that at least 3 million, 15% of the older population, need help services."[54] Further specifying the seriousness of this problem is the disclosure that "A million older persons are at this moment in institutional settings, for a variety of reasons."[55] Drawing attention to the severity of this problem are the results of recent studies which indicate that the majority of residents in nursing homes have serious mental health problems.[56] Worry that one's partner may become ill or die, fear of the possibility of prolonged physical illness or disability, anxiety about financial problems, a sense of worthlessness at not contributing anything recognized as worthwhile to society, and feelings of disgrace because of dependence upon others for a livelihood all contribute to the emotional ailments of older people.

Bored by the inactivity of retirement, a man may daydream about the past until he reconstructs it much more flatteringly than he ever actually experienced. No longer able to perform the deeds which will bring him recognition, he may spin long tales of yesterday's exploits to those who will listen sympathetically. Fantasies often serve as escape mechanisms. The present is uncomfortable and the future offers little, so it is natural for the senior adult to dwell upon his past pleasures and triumphs. If the reality of the past was not rosy enough,

---

53. Much of the material in this section was suggested by Robert J. Havighurst, "Social and Psychological Needs of the Aging," *Annals of the American Academy of Political and Social Science*, 279: 11-17, Jan. 1952; also see Robert N. Butler and Myrna I. Lewis, *Aging and Mental Health: Positive Psychosocial Approaches*, C. V. Mosby Co., 1973.

54. Butler and Lewis, *ibid.*, p. 46.

55. *Ibid.*

56. E. M. Brody, "Congregate Care Facilities and the Elderly," *Aging and Human Development*, 1: 279-321, 1970.

he can add color by exaggerating the favorable details. Thus the retired businessman who actually was always on the verge of bankruptcy may talk about his large and prosperous business, and the mother of disobedient and unruly children may tell during her senescence how well-behaved her little "angels" were when they were children. Giving advice is usually associated with this practice.

Some older persons regress to infancy and actually experience a second childhood to gain much-desired attention; they thus escape emotionally from the stark realities of life. This is manifest in various ways; it sometimes reaches such extreme forms as dependence upon others for feeding and dressing or complete retirement to bed "because of illness" so that others will wait upon them.

The loss of hearing, sight, or memory that is characteristic of so many older persons similarly is often not due solely to the actual degeneration of bodily faculties. The older individual is sometimes hard of hearing except when others talk about him, forgetful of unpleasant appointments he has found it necessary to make but not of the pleasant ones, and in other ways psychosomatically afflicted.

Another common escape mechanism is found in hallucinations. Some aged persons speak to absent persons or loved ones long since departed from this life, and they may engage in other forms of deviant behavior. When adults do this, we become alarmed, but when small children do the very same thing, we praise them for being "cute" or having exceptionally good imaginations.

The self-confidence of aged and middle-aged persons is daily undermined by others who allege that they are too old to do useful work, to make their own decisions, to learn new ways, and to go out alone.[57] These adverse influences may seriously injure the aged and middle-aged.

The memory of many older persons for distant events is sharp, but their memory for yesterday is obscure and distorted. The humiliation of today's events may obliterate recollection of the depressing and debasing occurrences of these later years of life and make one live in the past — a past that is recon-

---

57. Helen Hardy Brunot, *Old Age in New York City*, Welfare Council of New York City, 1943, p. 14.

structed into an even more successful and happy life than it actually was. For the memory tends to select pleasant events and magnify them while it gradually drops unpleasant and painful ones.

Resenting segregation and isolation from social and economic activities in which he has previously played an active part, the senior citizen may be filled with indignation that leads him to become defiant and to spurn the very acts of kindness that are shown him in his need. Many of the ill manners and disgusting actions of certain older persons may result from an inner attitude of hopelessness and futility that is transferred to outward circumstances. Old resentments, anxieties, and hatreds are easily magnified when one is no longer busy, when one is alone, and when one feels he is no longer needed.

"The past is ever with us." Sometimes in old age, when the past is at its maximum for an individual, there is a tendency for the past to dominate and to fill him with persistent feelings of resentment, anxiety, and insecurity. With confidence in himself so shaken that he may no longer feel competent economically, physically, socially, and personality-wise, the individual may become so severely maladjusted as to need institutional treatment for senility. Filled with despondency and dismay in the present, he also may fear the gradual approach of death, or he may long for death and even attempt to commit suicide in self-directed efforts to solve his problems.

Oftentimes older persons experiencing medical or mental health problems, such as those described above, are placed in nursing homes or mental hospitals. We do not wish to detract from the good services that are frequently found in these institutions, but it must also be acknowledged that in many instances the care received in these settings is poor. "Using mental hospitals as warehouses for the aged is detrimental both to the hospital and the aged. The hospital cannot function as intended because there are fewer beds available to those who really need psychiatric care."[58] Contributing to this is the fact that often staffs of both hospitals and nursing homes mistakenly label older persons as senile and not treatable.

---

58. George J. Alexander and Travis H. D. Lewin, *The Aged and the Need for Surrogate Management,* Syracuse University Press, 1972, p. 63.

Several recent developments that have come about primarily to meet the problem of older persons being treated in this manner are salient to clergy who frequently become involved in these matters. One of these is the independent living program wherein older persons stay in their own homes rather than go to nursing homes, mental hospitals, or other such settings.[59] This program is being developed as a parallel system, not as a replacement for institutional care. That is, independent living is not a substitute for institutional care, but is a second system of care that supplements it; many older persons would do better in this system, while others would prosper more in an institutional setting. This fact notwithstanding, many thousands of disabled older persons are remaining in their homes, and needed services are being brought to them. One result of this development is that ministers and other church leaders will most assuredly become more involved in helping to maintain older persons in their homes.

A second program illustrative of the many new developments that have implications for the clergy is reality therapy. This involves the use of calendars, clocks, newspapers, and other facts and techniques to assist the patients to overcome their confusion, apathy or depression.[60] The main objective of the program is to assist elderly patients on geriatric wards or in nursing homes in overcoming the process of confusion, disorientation, and memory loss which is so frequently found in those settings and which more often than not is labeled senility. Jack Hackley, Vice President for Professional and Consulting Services, Hillhaven Inc., Tacoma, Washington, reports that this program has been so successful that he plans to use it more extensively in the future. Commenting on the success his nursing home has had in using reality orientation rehabilitation with a disoriented female patient who had most of the symptoms of senility, he reports:

> Now, after six months of participation in our reality orientation program, this patient is engaging in many activities which were

59. For an extensive presentation of independent living see the special issue of *The Gerontologist* on "Rehabilitation to Independent Living," 15 (5, Part I), Oct. 1975.

60. Jack A. Hackley, "Reality Orientation Brings Patients Back From Confusion and Apathy," *Modern Nursing Home*, 31(3): 48-49, Sep. 1973.

impossible for her when she was admitted. She goes to music therapy, she enjoys playing Bingo, and she happily meets and visits with our other patients and her guests.[61]

Those involved in developing both the independent living and reality orientation programs are convinced that the success of these services depends upon the organization of a team approach wherein many persons play a prominent role in helping the older person to remain in his own home or to keep oriented to reality in an institutional setting. The role of the minister is obviously a most important one in both of these contexts, particularly because of his skills in counseling and providing spiritual and affective support. These same supports are invaluable in helping other elderly people adjust to circumstances which cause more serious adjustment problems for them than for other people. Thus, we must expect ministers and other church leaders frequently to join comprehensive team efforts to work with older persons in many different settings — a task over and above the individual pastoral counseling typically provided by the ministry in the past.

Many of the shocks suffered by the normal older person are crises greater than those that face most people at any other period of life. Death of the spouse, loss of a job and inability to secure a new one, the onset of incurable physical disorders, and the realization that one is old or is being treated as old may make an aging person forget that he has a future both before and after death. They may contribute to mental illnesses of varying degrees of severity and thus accentuate the various other problems he must face. In the emotional and mental problems of old age lies a distinct challenge for the church.

Contributing to the mental health problems of the aged is the fact that the American mental health establishment has tended to neglect the elderly. Robert Kahn, Associate Professor of Psychology at the University of Chicago, makes this charge in a paper which has received much attention from mental health workers. He points out there are many reasons why the aged have been neglected; foremost among these is the fact

61. *Ibid.*, p. 48. For a critical interpretation of reality therapy see Jaber F. Gubrium and Margret Ksander, "On Multiple Realities and Reality Orientation," *The Gerontologist,* 15(2): 142-145, April 1975.

that elderly persons have not sought psychiatric treatment and have been easily pushed around. Traditionally, they have been poorer and less educated than other people and as a result have gratefully taken whatever limited treatment society has provided for them. According to Kahn, all this is changing now as older persons have improved their financial positions and become better educated.[62]

These and other changes have resulted in older persons' becoming more sophisticated and demanding. Much of their attention is now being given to the quality of medical and mental health care which they receive in geriatric wards and nursing homes. According to Kahn, many of these treatment centers are primarily custodial and for a variety of reasons give little attention to rehabilitation. Negative attitudes lead to the accumulation of chronic patients who, once institutionalized at an early age, remain for the rest of their lives.

> Such persons thus constituted an aging resident population for whom custodialism had been a self-fulfilling prophecy, teaching them the "sick role," isolating them from families and from normal community activities, and making them incapable of living without extensive protective care.[63]

Kahn is voicing the growing concern that something more needs to be done to improve the medical and psychiatric care of elderly persons in this country. This concern is based not only upon the growing magnitude of the problem due to increased numbers of older persons needing medical and mental health care, but also because more and more senior citizens are demanding better medical care.

Of special import in the present instance is the increasing need for the clergy to be aware of this problem and the desirability of their keeping abreast of what is happening in this context. Similarly, clergy and other such persons would do well to become active participants in evolving community and medical programs that are now in operation or in the planning stages. More will be said about this in a later chapter; suffice it to say here that because of demands of older persons themselves, if for no other reason, we can expect major changes in

---

62. Robert T. Kahn, "The Mental Health System and the Future Aged," *The Gerontologist,* 15(1, Part II): 8-9, 24-31, Feb. 1975.
63. *Ibid.,* p. 27.

medical care for older persons in the future. The role of the clergy in this endeavor will depend to no little degree upon the initiative and strategy employed by them individually and collectively as they define their role with respect to this problem in the future.

SPIRITUAL PROBLEMS

There is a sense in which every problem of an individual is a spiritual problem, or at least has spiritual implications. Among the problems of older people, however, are some that are much more clearly of a spiritual and religious nature than others.

One of these is fear of the future, especially of death, which often torments the conscious or the subconscious mind of the person who cannot help but realize that he is nearing the grave. The comfort and hope imparted through religion can be a major source of alleviation of this dread.

When other problems interfere, it may be difficult to attend church in order to engage in public worship and in fellowship with others. In the winter in cold climates the heating and ventilation of church facilities may be poor and very uncomfortable for the older person. High steps at the church entrance, heavy and ominous doors that are difficult to open, and other physical obstacles discourage many older people from attending. The lack of suitable transportation facilities, the cost of paying membership dues or of contributing to voluntary offerings, poor eyesight, poor hearing, poor acoustics in the building, and careless enunciation and diction by the preacher and other speakers are among the difficulties in the church and within the older person which contribute to infrequent attendance and a low level of participation in the church by many older people.

Not only the religious group activities of the older person, but also many personal acts of devotion to God often suffer. Because of poor eyesight and small print, it becomes difficult for many to read their Bibles and devotional literature. Because of poor hearing, they may miss religious radio and television broadcasts that otherwise could impart spiritual help to them. The impairment of their senses may also limit the benefits received from visits of church groups and pastoral services provided by the clergy.

Many older persons carry a burden of guilt that sends them prematurely to the grave. They sometimes have a sense of failure and regret for not having attained goals set early in life. Some of them have violated the customs (folkways and mores) of society either privately or publicly, and others have engaged in activities definitely classified as sinful in both their religious and social circles. Their guilty consciences may result from truly despicable activities or from misconceived notions of moral and ethical standards. Regardless of the nature or the source of such guilt feelings, they create tensions and mental problems that are not easily resolved.

More directly than in the other anomalous conditions of the aged, the church has a significant task to perform in resolving spiritual problems and lifting spiritual burdens of older persons.

THE NEGLECT OF THE AGED

In spite of the numerous problems they face, widespread attention to older people and their needs has been long in coming to the United States. Fortunately, in many groups this situation has been rectified for several years as more and more attention has been given to the needs of the aged. The early tendency was neither to revere nor to reject old age, but to ignore it in the supposition that it is only a state of mind which can be eliminated if one keeps busy — that is, if one acts youthful.[64]

The neglect of the aged, especially in the past, has been seen among those who are concerned with the psychological well-being or mental health of our population,[65] among sociologists,[66] in the medical profession,[67] by the public in gen-

64. Havighurst, "Old Age—An American Problem," *op. cit.*, pp. 298-304.

65. George Lawton, "A Long-Range Research Program in the Psychology of Old Age and Aging," *Journal of Social Psychology*, 12: 101-114, Aug. 1940.

66. Belle Boone Beard's analysis of the tables of contents and indices of 20 sociology books on the family showed that 8 had no reference whatever to the aged, and only 2 treated the subject comprehensively. A total of 50 pages out of 10,697 were devoted to old people in these books. ("Are the Aged Ex-Family?" *Social Forces*, 27: 274-279, March 1949.) More recent

eral,[68] and even by the church and the clergy.[69] While the last few years have witnessed an upsurge in attention to the problems of older persons, their general neglect by almost all segments of society has continued into the seventies.

The neglect of the aged has been due partly to ignorance of their conditions and of the scope of the problem. We have suddenly realized that millions of aged in our own country are often economically dependent, physically impaired, mentally depressed, or socially isolated. Only as we have awakened to this realization have we begun to take action.

A second reason for the neglect of the aged has been the stereotyped disagreeableness of older persons. We often do find

---

books usually include data on the aged. See for example Bengtson, op. cit.; Blau, Old Age in a Changing Society, op. cit.; Herman B. Brotman, We Who Are the Aged: A Demographic View, Institute of Gerontology, Ann Arbor: The University of Michigan and Wayne State University, 1968; B. Neugarten, ed., Middle Age and Aging: A Reader in Social Psychology, University of Chicago Press, 1968; Rosow, Socialization to Old Age, op. cit.; Ethel Shanas and Gordon F. Streib, Social Structure and the Family, Prentice-Hall, 1965; R. H. Williams and Claudine G. Wirths, Lives Through the Years, Atherton Press, 1965.

67. Medical neglect of the specialty of geriatrics has been due in part to the lack of a spectacular element in that type of work, the fact that it is not as remunerative as some other branches of medicine, the fact that the physician's efforts ultimately must end in failure with the death of his patient, and the great demand for original observation and research by the specialist because so little has been written about it until recently. (This pattern has begun to change in recent years.) Cf. Malford W. Thewlis, The Care of the Aged (Geriatrics), 3rd ed., C. V. Mosby Co., 1941, pp. 25ff. See also Raymond Harris, "Breaking the Barriers to Better Health-Care Delivery for the Aged," The Geròntologist, 15: 52-56, Feb. 1975.

68. Although Edward J. Stieglitz wrote these words almost three decades ago, they still hold true to a great extent: "Society as a whole looks upon aging as either a catastrophe or a sin. Respect for mature years has been on the wane. This attitude creates a severe and at least partially unjustified handicap to the aging" (chap. 17 in Oscar J. Kaplan, ed., Mental Disorders in Later Life, Stanford University Press, 1945, p. 423).

69. See Paul B. Maves and J. Lennart Cedarleaf, Older People and the Church, Abingdon-Cokesbury Press, 1949, pp. 27-29. As recently as 1960 Henry Jacobson stated that the older person is beginning to receive the attention he deserves from government, industry, and everyone except the Christian Church ("The Problem of the Senior Citizen," Eternity, 11(10): 22-24, 39-40, Oct. 1960). Black churches also have been very apathetic about the plight of the 1,500,000 Blacks past age 65 ("Everybody's Aging: Interpretive Recommendations from the First Connectional Christian Education Conference and Institute on Aging and the Black Aged," African Methodist Episcopal Church, 1974, p. 9).

people who are repulsive and who fail to arouse our sympathy because of their peevishness, selfishness, offensive actions, disagreeable odors, and suspicious attitudes; but we tend to forget that there are countless others, perhaps a majority, who have very few if any of these unattractive characteristics.[70]

This neglect is also due to the psychological barriers that tend to become erected between the generations. Children may stand aloof from the parental generation, for their interests frequently are not the same as those of their parents. This tends to carry through either to a neglect of the older generation, or sometimes to a tendency to treat the elderly as they treated us when we were children. "After all, are not all aged people in their second childhood?" tends to be the reasoning that undergirds this practice. Some actually try to "get even" with their elders for abuses or imagined abuses suffered through them during the process of growing up.

A fourth source of neglect of older people is the fear many have of their own approaching later maturity. Some fear the time when they can expect to manifest characteristics of the aged and to suffer some of the abuses of old age. Whether one is a medical doctor, social worker, clergyman, other professional worker, or a citizen who has older friends, relatives, and acquaintances, a subconscious desire to avoid thinking about one's own later maturity can lead to avoiding association with them because of the painful reminders this association sends to the unconscious mind.

Mistaken ideas that people have about the aged and their needs constitute a fifth source of their neglect. There is a tendency to think that all they want is financial security and freedom from responsibility, when in reality they want a feeling of being useful, being wanted, being loved. Sometimes it is assumed that the economic distress many of them experience is a result of their own carelessness and improvidence. However, millions of older people in the United States have lived on a hand-to-mouth basis because of their position in the labor

---

70. See Malford W. Thewlis, *op. cit.*, p. 24, for a a discussion of some of these traits. The manner in which stereotypes are generated and sustained by the mass media is discussed in Beth B. Hess, "Stereotypes of the Aged," *Journal of Communication*, 24(4): 76-85, Autumn 1974.

force; we cannot condemn them for not saving that which they never received.

In an interesting project, older persons volunteered their services to help young mentally retarded children. They not only helped the children but also found love and the feeling of being useful. A summary of the findings is provided in a study report:

> This paper presents the results of an evaluation of a project which employed elderly people to act as foster grandparents to mentally retarded children. In addition to benefits accruing to the children from such individual care and training, the foster grandparents were found to have shown increments in life satisfaction and personal and social adjustment when compared with a similar group of elderly persons who were not employed on the project. This paper focuses on findings relating to the effects of the program on the elderly participants and supports the notion that meaningful, purposeful activities in addition to some financial remuneration are basic ingredients of good personal and social adjustment and increased life satisfaction in old age.[71]

As experiences of this and similar projects demonstrate, many older Americans will willingly give time and energy in return for love, attention, and the feeling of being wanted. The significance of the foregoing project is enhanced when it is considered that far more older persons volunteered for positions as Foster Grandparents than the program could employ, even though the pay was quite low.

By over-emphasis in our churches and other community organizations upon children and youth, we have cultivated the attitude that time spent with older people is wasted. The idea is expressed openly by some that if we spend time with the aged and help to meet their needs, we will soon have no congregations left. Others believe, mistakenly, that the aged cannot be changed; why spend time trying to convert them to Christianity or trying to develop Christian graces and wholesome personalities when it is impossible to do so? Other similar notions reflecting general ignorance about old people have stood in the way of improving their condition and have en-

---

71. Robert M. Gray and Josephine Kasteler, "An Evaluation of the Effectiveness of a Foster Grandparent Project," *Sociology and Social Research*, 54(2): 181, Jan. 1970.

couraged many people to avoid, neglect, or ignore them in our society.[72]

A sixth source, perhaps the most significant, of the neglect of the aged is the set of values that underlies life in America. Great emphasis is placed upon that which is new and upon those who are young in our relatively youthful and rapidly changing nation. We are encouraged to turn in last year's automobile or refrigerator for this year's model, and we are almost daily confronted with billboard and newspaper pictures, movies, radio and television programs, contests, and festivals that glorify youth and tend to identify all beauty with that which is new and young. This exaggerated premium on youth in American culture often has a calamitous effect on the mental health of the aging.[73]

Economic aggressiveness and the desire "to get ahead" tend to make Americans think that unless they are advancing economically and socially, climbing ever higher on the ladder of success, they are old and hence no longer useful. Whenever signs of diminishing economic competitive ability begin to appear in the individual, whenever he cannot fit in with the increasing efficiency, mass production, and automation of industry and business, and whenever he has lost the superficial signs of outward physical "beauty," he is relegated to the scrap heap of old age.[74]

A note of caution is merited at this point; it concerns the possibility that we have overstated the problems of older persons from the perspective of their own perceptions. For example, a national survey disclosed that many problems of senior

---

72. Even graduate students in a leading teachers college have been found to accept many stereotypes and misconceptions about older people. See Jacob Tuckman and Irving Lorge, "Attitudes Toward Old People," *Journal of Social Psychology*, 37: 249-260, May 1953. Cf. Seymour Axelrod and Carl Eisdorfer, "Attitudes Toward Old People: An Empirical Analysis of the Stimulus-Group Validity of the Tuckman-Lorge Questionnaire," *Journal of Gerontology*, 16: 75-80, Jan. 1961.

73. Maurice E. Linden, "Effects of Social Attitudes on the Mental Health of the Aging," *Geriatrics*, 12: 109-114, 1957. See also Blau, *Old Age in a Changing Society, op. cit.*

74. Cf. Eduard C. Lindeman, "The Sociological Challenge of the Aging Population," in *Proceedings of the Eastern States Health Education Conference, March 31-April 1, 1949: The Social and Biological Challenge of Our Aging Population*, Columbia University Press, 1950, pp. 171-183.

citizens were being overstated and that in truth these people felt much better off than is generally believed.[75] Taking this into account and recognizing that a majority of the elderly cope exceptionally well with their circumstances, we nevertheless maintain that the problems of hundreds of thousands of older persons are serious enough to merit increasing concern and action on both the national and local level.

CONCLUSION

Most authorities agree that disease and disability in old people are inextricably tied to their total life situation.[76] This important point was first presented by the President's Commission on the Health Needs of the Nation in its report to President Truman, which went on to say:

> Unfortunately, older persons today live in a society that is in many ways becoming uncongenial and unfavorable to them. Encountering adverse attitudes, older people tend to lose their dignity and their sense of worth. Their role in the family, if one remains to them, is not conducive to self-respect; opportunities for gainful employment are denied them on the basis of their calendar years; fewer and fewer opportunities for self-maintenance remain in a social order which still regards self-maintenance as the only respectable way to live; dependency, total or partial, is forced upon almost two-thirds of the older generations through no fault of their own.
>
> As the health and social needs of aging persons become more numerous, too often their own means to satisfying them either diminish or are entirely lacking. Dental treatment and dentures, hearing aids, eyeglasses, and other devices to help them to func-

75. National Council on the Aging and Louis Harris and Associates, *The Myth and Reality of Aging in America*, Washington, D.C.: NCOA, 1975. Erdman Palmore, "The Future Status of the Aged," *The Gerontologist*, 16(4): 297-302, Aug. 1976, has surveyed the status of the aged in the USA in comparison to other age groups in regard to their health, occupational status, income, and education. He concluded that their relative status is rising and probably will continue to rise for the rest of this century. This may result eventually in an "age-irrelevant society" from the perspective of socioeconomic status.

76. For an excellent account of the major medical barriers to health care delivery for older Americans see Raymond Harris, "Breaking the Barriers to Better Health-Care Delivery for the Aged," *op. cit.* Also see U.S. Public Health Service, *Health in the Later Years of Life*, U.S. Government Printing Office, Oct. 1971.

tion more effectively are hard to get; housing, which should be more adequate, tends to be much less so; leisure, of which they have previously had very little and of which they now have a super-abundance, easily becomes a source of boredom and may lead to withdrawal from life. This generalized description may appear exaggerated; certainly it does not apply to every older person.

The real point is that disease and disability in old people are inextricably bound up with their total situation — their social arrangements, their physical and mental fitness, their economic and occupational adequacy, their spiritual status. It is impossible to treat sick older people adequately without considering every area of their lives.[77]

It is because of these facts that aging can be considered a social problem. Old age in and of itself is not a social problem, for it is natural and inevitable. Old age is also a glorious occasion which is — and should be — looked upon as a significant accomplishment. Even so, many older persons do have problems that are at least in part due to their growing old. Sickness and physical disability, for example, are found in every age group, but more so among older persons. The natural concomitants of aging certainly contribute to the problem of the older person, but why should anyone set old people apart as a special age group and discriminate against them all? Instead, would it not be more consistent with democratic as well as Christian ideology to consider each older person as a *person* in the light of his own needs, interests, abilities, and surroundings? It is primarily the reactions of people toward aging and the conditions that surround the aged that create problems for them.[78]

These reactions of prejudice and discrimination against the older generation are now known as *ageism*. Ageism is a social disease as pernicious as racism and sexism, yet different in the sense that everybody who survives to the later years becomes its victim. It is perpetuated by a vicious cycle in which stereotypes, myths, discriminatory treatment, and nega-

---

77. President's Commission on the Health Needs of the Nation, *op. cit.*, Vol. II, p. 92.

78. Cf. George Lawton, *Aging Successfully*, Columbia University Press, 1946, pp. 167ff., and Edward B. Allen, "Psychological Factors That Have a Bearing on the Aging Process," in *Proceedings of the Eastern States Health Education Conference, op. cit.*, pp. 116f.

tive cultural expectations about aging become part of a self-fulfilling prophecy that leads older people themselves to internalize its predictions and, as a result, to experience many of its negative features as if they were natural and inevitable.[79]

Ageism is compounded and often reinforced by *gerontophobia*, a psychological tendency unconsciously and irrationally to fear one's own aging, hence to shun any reminder of it, such as that which would occur through contacts with aging people. Bunzel has estimated that one-fifth of the American population suffers from this phobia. It undoubtedly is a major source of the neglect of the aging in the church as well as in society at large.[80]

Confronted with all the problems which our society contributes to older people, the elderly often are more open to the message and ministries of the church than ever before. The remainder of this book is devoted to the contributions which religion, especially organized religion or the church, can and does make to them personally and to the prevention, alleviation, and solution of their problems. The negative influence of the church also receives due attention, for this is not a one-sided account attempting blindly to vindicate it as a social institution.

---

79. Erdman B. Palmore and Kenneth Manton, "Ageism Compared to Racism and Sexism," *Journal of Gerontology*, 28 (3): 363-369, July 1973; Butler and Lewis, *op. cit.*, pp. ix, 84, 127-130.

80. Joseph H. Bunzel, "Note on the History of a Concept—Gerontophobia," *The Gerontologist*, 12(2): 116, 203, Summer 1972; Bunzel, "Gerontophobia Pervades U.S. Life, Sociologist Says," *Geriatrics*, 27(3): 41-49, March 1972; Bunzel, "Concept, Meaning and Treatment of Gerontophobia," *Zeitschrift für Alternsforschung*, 25 (1): 15-19, 1971.

THREE

The Religion of Older People

Because of the numerous problems older people experience in our society, because of the gradual approach of death, because they have more time to think than they have had for decades previously, and for various other reasons, many people turn to religion in their old age with renewed fervor.

As psychologist George Lawton has indicated, the longer we live, the greater the number of past experiences we have had upon which to reflect, the greater our hunger to explain our lives to ourselves, and the greater our desire to seek justification for the world and for human nature as we have found them. The result is a declining interest in the material aspects of life. This takes place as a result of reduced ability to take part in them, but also as a result of the piling up of knowledge and experience. With declining interest in material things comes a growing concern in things spiritual.[1]

It is natural for older people to turn to the church. Usually it is more accessible than other agencies and institutions in the community. It is the only service agency known to many, and a large proportion grew up in the church and maintain various ties with it. As they grow older, many people find that religion means more to them than it did in the past; religious activities, therefore, do not decline as much with disabilities in old age as other activities do.[2] Research in two Kansas communities,

---

1. Lawton, *Aging Successfully*, Columbia University Press, 1946, pp. 167-168.
2. Paul B. Maves and J. Lennart Cedarleaf, *Older People and the Church*, Abingdon-Cokesbury Press, 1949, p. 31; and Frances C. Jeffers and Claude R. Nichols, "The Relationship of Activities and Attitudes to Physical Well-Being in Older People," *Journal of Gerontology*, 16:67-70, Jan. 1961.

for example, found church so important to older people that "regularity of attendance seemed to be an index of the measure of the man."[3] Self images are closely related to church membership and participation.

On the other hand, with the curtailed income typical during retirement, people who are sensitive to social conventions, such as not attending without contributing or wearing "Sunday best" clothing to church, are often reluctant to continue their church fellowship when they can make little or no financial contribution or when they are without what they consider to be suitable clothing. It takes great effort for many older persons to dress up and prepare for church, to say nothing of getting to the church building, up the flight of stairs that is a barrier to most of them, and into a pew where acoustics may be so poor that they can hear but little of the service because of their declining sense of hearing. Such influences might be expected to counteract the others and to encourage many older people to drop their church participation.

What do we know about the actual religious behavior and beliefs of the aging in the United States? Various surveys and studies give us some information from which we may be able to reach conclusions about the relative religiosity of older people and its effects.

THE RELIGIOUS ACTIVITIES OF OLDER PEOPLE

The late Professor Ernest W. Burgess of the University of Chicago summarized the findings of research to 1952 in one concise statement:

> Older citizens increase their religious activities and dependence upon religion. Frequency of church attendance drops in the 80s and 90s. Incapacity to go to church, however, is more than compensated for by listening to church services over the radio and by Bible reading.[4]

Subsequent research has not consistently supported that generalization. Careful examination of the findings helps to explain why.

---

3. Esther E. Twente, *Never Too Old,* Jossey-Bass, 1970, p. 24.
4. Burgess, "Family Living in the Later Decades," *Annals of the American Academy of Political and Social Science,* 279: 107, Jan. 1952.

Many studies have included reference to church membership. In nearly all communities in the U.S.A. more people are members of churches and other religious bodies than of any other type of voluntary social organization. There are variations in membership rates by ethnic identification, religious faith, social class, and type of community. Working class people tend to have few formal group activities besides those related to churches, while upper middle and upper class people have many, most of which are outside of religious groups. The middle class falls between the extremes. People in many rural areas participate proportionately more heavily in church groups than those in cities.[5] Mayo's study of older people in rural areas of Wake County, North Carolina, revealed that there were 149 memberships in religious organizations for every 100 older persons, but only 38 memberships in all other types of organizations.[6]

Poor people generally are not inclined to belong to organizations of any kind, but the national survey of Project FIND revealed that nearly 60% of the respondents named a church or synagogue as an organization to which they belonged. The next most frequent type of membership was fraternal societies, to which only 5% belonged.[7]

Membership is not the same as participation in church activities, however. Some members seldom or never participate, while some persons who are not members participate regularly in the activities of church congregations and parishes. Again, there are wide variations from one type of community and one religious faith or tradition to another. In both rural and urban areas of Kentucky, for example, nearly 9 out of every 10 persons aged 60 and older participated in church. The next highest participation level was 6% in "service and welfare organiza-

---

5. C.T. Pihlblad and Howard A. Rosencranz, *Social Adjustment of Older People in the Small Town*, vol. IV, no. 1, University of Missouri, 1969.

6. Selz C. Mayo, "Social Participation Among the Older Population in Rural Areas of Wake County, North Carolina," *Social Forces*, 30:53-59, Oct. 1951. A 1974 statewide survey in Michigan similarly found that aging citizens most commonly belong to church groups rather than others. Amanda A. Beck, *Michigan Aging Citizens*, Institute of Gerontology, University of Michigan and Wayne State University, Aug. 1975, p. 37.

7. Project FIND, *The Golden Years: A Tarnished Myth*, National Council on the Aging, 1970.

tions." In the urban area 94% of the women and 85% of the
men participated, compared to 93% and 73%, respectively, in
a rural county.[8] The higher levels of attendance and other participation by women than by men are characteristic of all age
groups.[9]

In another study aging men from the skid row, a low-
income area, and an upper-income census tract of New York
City all reported lower regular church attendance rates than
during middle age. Even though church attendance was the
most frequent, if not the only, form of voluntary affiliation,
"the older the metropolitan male becomes, the less likely he is
to turn to the church."[10] Unfortunately, no middle-class sample
was included in the research, nor was it a truly longitudinal
study.

In "Prairie City," a small midwestern city which University of Chicago researchers have studied over a period of years,
only 2% of the people past age 65 held such responsibilities as
church officers, committee members, and Sunday School teachers. An additional 61% reported frequent and active participation in religious activities with no responsibility, and 15%
more had passive interest, seldom attending church, though
perhaps listening to sermons on the radio. Only 18% had no
church affiliation and no attendance, and 4% rejected religion
and the church.[11]

There was no evidence of a large-scale "turning to religion"
in Prairie City as people grew older. Most of them continued
the religious habits of their middle years, although they cus-
tomarily dropped out of church leadership positions after the
age of 60. The older men dropped out more rapidly than
women, possibly because their activities were more apt to involve administrative and teaching positions which are passed on
to a younger generation, while women were more typically

8. E.G. Youmans, *Aging Patterns in a Rural and an Urban Area of Kentucky*, Univ. Ky., AES Bulletin 681, 1963, p. 45.

9. David O. Moberg, *The Church as a Social Institution*, Prentice-Hall,
1962, pp. 396-401.

10. Howard M. Bahr, "Aging and Religious Disaffiliation," *Social Forces*,
49(1): 59-71, Sep. 1970.

11. Robert J. Havighurst and Ruth Albrecht, *Older People*, Longmans,
Green, and Co., 1953, pp. 201-202.

involved in projects for which their services continued to be valuable and desired.[12]

The findings as to levels of participation in church by age are not entirely consistent. In four rural New York communities studied in 1947-48 the highest social participation in church among heads of households was found among men aged 75-79, followed closely by those aged 45-54. For homemakers the highest scores were found among women aged 70-74 and 75-79, with those aged 60-64 in third place and 45-54 fourth.[13] Among 597 institutionalized women living in Protestant homes for the aged, participation in religious activities increased with age.[14] The peak intensity of social participation, most of which was in churches, among older people in rural North Carolina, however, occurred at ages 55-59, with sharp drops at higher ages.[15] In a laboring area of Chicago one-third of the men past 65 attended church more and one-third attended less than they did earlier, but among women only one-fourth attended more and almost half attended less.[16]

Among Catholics in Fort Wayne, Indiana, increase in age was associated with decreasing church attendance, chiefly because of poor health.[17] In several other urban communities surveys of senior citizens have revealed a definite tendency to attend church less often than they did ten years earlier.[18] De-

---

12. *Ibid.*, p. 203, and Ruth Albrecht, "The Meaning of Religion to Older People — The Social Aspect," in Delton L. Scudder, ed., *Organized Religion and the Older Person*, University of Florida Press, 1958, pp. 53-70.

13. Philip Taietz and Olaf F. Larson, "Social Participation and Old Age," *Rural Sociology*, 21:229-238, Sep.-Dec. 1956.

14. J.S. Pan, "Institutional and Personal Adjustment in Old Age," *Journal of Genetic Psychology*, 85:155-158, 1954.

15. Mayo, *op. cit.*; see also Joel Smith, "The Narrowing Social World of the Aged," in Ida Harper and John McKinney, eds., *Social Aspects of Aging*, Duke University Press, 1966, p. 233.

16. Charles T. O'Reilly and Margaret M. Pembroke, *Older People in a Chicago Community*, Research Report of the School of Social Work, Loyola University, n.d. (c. 1957), pp. 30-38.

17. S.P. Theisen, *A Social Survey of Aged Catholics in the Deanery of Fort Wayne, Indiana.* Ph.D. thesis, University of Notre Dame, 1962.

18. W.W. Hunter and H. Maurice, *Older People Tell Their Story*, University of Michigan, 1953, pp. 62-63; C.W. McCann, *Long Beach Senior Citizens' Survey.* Community Welfare Council, Long Beach, CA, 1955, pp. 50-52; and D.O. Moberg, "The Integration of Older Members in the

clining attendance in the later years is related to problems of
physical mobility, financial costs of transportation, declining
health and hearing ability, and similar difficulties. The availability of transportation is important; its absence is related to
lower levels of participation. The greater the distance, the
greater is its impact.[19]

In a careful analysis of five probability samples with 6,911
adults in the Detroit metropolitan area, Orbach found that age
as such was not related to changes in church attendance, and
there was no indication of an increase in attendance in the
later years. He did find, however, that there is a polarizing
effect; people who are casual or cursory church goers tend to
shift into the category of either regular church attenders or
regular non-attenders. He was struck particularly by the con-
stancy of attendance in all age groups examined with the one
exception of significantly decreased attendance among those 75
and over.[20]

If the hindering factor of physical disability is accounted
for, it is probable that a larger proportion of the physically
capable elderly than of physically capable middle-aged adults
attend church services regularly. (The middle-aged have higher
attendance rates than young adults.) Older people are more
likely than others to have an image of themselves as being
religious and to say that they believe in life after death.[21]

A thorough survey of people aged 65 and over in one
section of Chicago found that 35.6% of the predominantly
Catholic sample reported monthly or more frequent church
attendance. Over half believed that religion had become more

Church Congregation," in A.M. Rose and W.A. Peterson, eds., Older People
and Their Social World, F.A. Davis, 1965, pp. 125-140.

19. Stephen J. Cutler, "The Effects of Transportation and Distance on
Voluntary Association Participation among the Aged," International Journal
of Aging and Human Development, 5 (1): 81-94, Winter 1974. See also
Frances M. Carp, "The Mobility of Retired People," in Edmund J. Cantilli
et al., eds., Transportation and Aging: Selected Issues, Administration on
Aging, U.S. Government Printing Office, 1971, pp. 23-41.

20. Harold L. Orbach, "Aging and Religion: Church Attendance in the
Detroit Metropolitan Area," Geriatrics, 16:530-540, Oct. 1961.

21. Milton L. Barron, "The Role of Religion and Religious Institutions in
Creating the Milieu of Older People," in Delton L. Scudder, op. cit., pp.
12-33. (Barron's conclusions are based on both nation-wide and New York
City surveys.)

helpful to them during the preceding ten years. Sixty per cent had not received a pastoral visit by a clergyman, but only 6% saw such visiting as a means by which the church could help them. Women were more active in church attendance and Catholic religious practices than men, but the men were more likely than the women to have increased their church attendance since the age of 65.[22]

Although church attendance rates generally tend to remain constant with increasing age in most groups of people, probably declining more often than increasing among those who have passed the age of 70 or 75, regular listening to church services and other religious broadcasts on radio and television, reading from the Bible at least weekly, prayer, meditation, and other personal and private devotional activities tend to increase steadily with age during the adult years.[23] Analysis of the findings of a cross-section of residents of the State of Washington interviewed by telephone in March 1974 led to the conclusion that age had a significant effect on increasing devotional practices, like Bible reading and private praying, but not on other dimensions of religiosity after the effects of education, income, sex, church membership, and marital status were controlled.[24] Older Lutherans also read the Bible and devotional literature more often, pray more, and take Communion more regularly than younger church members.[25]

Because most research represents findings on cross-sections of the population with comparisons of different people at the respective ages analyzed, there can be no assurance that the

22. O'Reilly and Pembroke, *op. cit.*, and Charles T. O'Reilly, "Religious Practice and Personal Adjustment," *Sociology and Social Research*, 42: 119-121, Nov.-Dec. 1958. Comparable findings are reported in Charles T. O'Reilly and Margaret M. Pembroke, *OAA Profile: The Old Age Assistance Client in Chicago*, Loyola University Press, 1961, pp. 67-75.

23. Paul B. Maves, "Aging, Religion and the Church," in *Handbook of Social Gerontology*, ed. by Clark Tibbitts, University of Chicago Press, 1960, pp. 698-749; David O. Moberg, "Religiosity in Old Age," *Gerontologist*, 5(2): 78-87, 111-112, June 1965; and Matilda White Riley and Anne Foner, *Aging and Society, Volume One: An Inventory of Research Findings*, chap. 20, Russell Sage Foundation, 1968.

24. John M. Finney and Gary R. Lee, "Religious Commitment and Age," paper read at Pacific Sociological Association, Victoria, B.C., April 1975.

25. Arthur L. Johnson *et al.*, "Age Differences and Dimensions of Religious Behavior," *Journal of Social Issues*, 30 (3): 43-67, 1974.

observed differences represent the results of aging rather than variations between age cohorts of the population. This means that we cannot be sure that the people aged 50 to 65 today will be similar fifteen years from now to those who are aged 65 to 80 today.

To summarize present knowledge about religious activities during the later years, the external practices which occur outside the home, such as church attendance, do tend to diminish during the later years when problems of health, mobility, and finances are felt. The internal and personal religious activities which do not depend upon health and mobility apparently increase among those persons who acknowledge having a religion. In addition to private devotional activities, religious beliefs and feelings also remain at a high level or even increase among those who are religious, possibly to some extent compensating for the declines in formal social participation.

RELIGIOUS BELIEFS AND EXPERIENCES OF OLDER PEOPLE

The highest proportion of people who believe in God, as well as the largest percentage who hold such belief with absolute certainty, occurs during the later years of life.[26] Over three-fourths of the national samples of the population who are aged 50 to 55 and over believe in life after death; younger age groups have smaller proportions.[27]

The belief that religion is important is held by a larger proportion of people past age 65 than by younger adults. A major national survey conducted by Louis Harris and Associates for the National Council on Aging revealed that the importance attached to religion increases steadily with age. Religion was "very important" to 71% of people past 65 but to only 49% of the other adults.[28] The feeling that religion has

26. Riley and Foner, op. cit., p. 492; see survey results in Catholic Digest, 17 (1): 4, Nov. 1952; (2): 5, Dec. 1952; (7): 80, May 1953; and 18(7): 24, May 1954.

27. David O. Moberg, Spiritual Well-Being: Background and Issues, Washington, D.C., White House Conference on Aging, 1971, p. 28; Gallup Opinion Index: Special Report on Religion, Princeton, N.J., American Institute of Public Opinion, 1969, p. 18.

28. Louis Harris and Associates, The Myth and Reality of Aging in America, National Council on the Aging, 1975.

become more helpful and of increasing meaning with advancing years is common among older people, including Southern Blacks and white welfare recipients.[29]

A study of 700 people who had passed the age of 100 revealed that over 90% said religion is "very important" to them. Large numbers were still actively involved in attending church, participating in sacramental rites, and even service activities on behalf of their churches and synagogues.[30]

There is a clear tendency for older people to feel that they are more religious than they were earlier in life, at least if they are religious at all. Unusual religious experiences and reporting a desire for personal experiences with the supernatural are more common among persons in the later years than among younger adults.[31]

Religious emotional supports for experiences of bereavement, illness, social deprivation, and other personal and social problems are sought by many older people. Increasing preoccupation with philosophic values and religious ideas has also been observed among them.[32] Orthodox or conservative religious beliefs about the deity of Jesus, miracles in the Bible, the devil, and other traditional Christian doctrines are held by more of the elderly than by middle-aged and young adults.[33]

In his study of Methodist and Baptist church members in 2 Indiana cities, Davidson found that knowledge of church history and church teachings was greatest among persons past age 60, next greatest among those aged 51 to 60, and lowest among

29. Tony E. McNevin and Howard A. Rosencranz, "Racial Differences in Life Satisfaction and Adjustment Between Welfare and Non-Welfare, Non-Institutionalized, Aged Males," in *Long Range Program and Research Needs in Aging and Related Fields.* Hearings before the Special Committee On Aging, Dec. 5-6, 1967, U.S. Government Printing Office.

30. Belle Boone Beard, "Religion at 100," *Modern Maturity,* 12(3): 1-4, 1969.

31. Wendell M. Swenson, "Approaches to the Study of Religion and Aging," in John E. Cantelon *et al., Religion and Aging,* Rossmoor-Cortese Institute for the Study of Retirement and Aging, University of Southern California, 1967, pp. 59-84.

32. Kurt Wolff, *The Biological, Sociological and Psychological Aspects of Aging,* Charles C Thomas, 1959.

33. Rodney Stark, "Age and Faith: A Changing Outlook or an Old Process?" *Sociological Analysis,* 29(1): 1-10, 1968; Yoshio Fukuyama, "The Major Dimensions of Church Membership," *Review of Religious Research,* 2 (4): 154-161, 1961.

younger adults. Members past 50 also revealed a marked decline in willingness to examine rationally, doubt, or question the teaching of their church. Although they had more religious knowledge than persons under 50, they were less disposed toward a rational-critical approach to religious issues.[34]

EFFECTS OF RELIGION ON OLDER PEOPLE

How do the religious activities and beliefs of the aged affect them personally? Psychologist George Lawton has listed trust in God or "health of the spirit" as second only to good health as a source of contentment in later life. After extensive counseling of older people, he saw fit to place it ahead of a cheerful state of mind, money, friends, gainful occupation, pleasant relationships with members of one's family, the satisfaction of doing things for others, and ordinary kindness and consideration from others.[35]

Similarly, sociologist Judson T. Landis found among a random sample of 450 people aged 65 and over that the happiest old people were those who visited with friends often and attended church regularly. He qualifies his finding with the reservation that it is probably not so much that church-going makes one better adjusted as that church attendance is an indication of a sociable nature: those who attend church also visit with friends often, belong to lodges and ladies' aids, and are active in other organizations in the community.[36]

Characteristics related to "success in old age" among 349 successful and 204 unhappy old people included church attendance and philosophy of life.[37] This correlation between church

34. James D. Davidson, "Religious Involvement and Middle Age," *Sociological Symposium*, 3:39, 1969.

35. Lawton, "Happiness in Old Age," *Mental Hygiene*, 27: 231-237, April 1943.

36. Landis, "Hobbies and Happiness in Old Age," *Recreation*, 35: 642, Jan. 1942. A careful analysis of national data from 1974 and 1975 surveys of the adult population found that life satisfaction and happiness were related to being a member of a church-affiliated group, but not to membership in any of 17 other types of voluntary associations. Stephen J. Cutler, "Membership in Different Types of Voluntary Associations and Psychological Well-Being," *The Gerontologist*, 16(4): 335-339, Aug. 1976.

37. S.L. Pressey and Elizabeth Simcoe, "Case Study Comparisons of Successful and Problem Old People," *Journal of Gerontology*, 5: 168-175, April

attendance, philosophy of life, and successful old age is an indication of a *possible* cause-and-effect relationship between religion and successful adjustment in late life. This possibility is also indicated by a series of studies that have used the Chicago Activities and Attitudes Inventory.[38] In the development of its two instruments and their use with 499 men and 759 women, social scientists found that the degree of participation and the attitude toward participation in social activities decreases with age after the sixtieth birthday. Nevertheless, satisfaction with religion and the derivation of a feeling of security from it increased with age. The percentage of both men and women with favorable attitudes toward religion was found to increase with age. Belief in a life after death, which was accepted by most people in their sixties, was universally accepted by all in their nineties.[39]

A study of patterns of poor adjustment of older people in Akron and in Kansas City listed 20 factors associated with poor adjustment in both men and women. Among these were a lack of or infrequent church attendance and less frequent church attendance in the present than in the past.[40]

Such items as church membership, regular reading of the Bible or prayer book, belief in an afterlife, religious faith or philosophy of life, listening regularly to broadcast religious services, and church attendance have been found related to good personal adjustment, happiness, morale, or life satisfac-

---

1950. Among persons successfully adjusted to retirement, 42% were church members, but only 17% of a contrasting group of unhappy, maladjusted retired persons were members (Paul F. Verden and Archer L. Michael, "A Comparison of Successfully and Unsuccessfully Retired Groups," *Geriatrics,* 14: 528-534, Aug. 1959). The "superiorly aging" persons studied at Lankenau Hospital in Philadelphia were influenced and supported by religion (Henry F. Page, "Health Maintenance and Rehabilitation of Older Persons," in *Papers Presented at the Seminar on the Aged,* The Bishop Edwin A. Penick Memorial Home, Southern Pines, N.C., Oct. 16-17, 1969, pp. 33-48).

38. E.W. Burgess, R.S. Cavan, and R.J. Havighurst, *Your Activities and Attitudes,* Science Research Associates, 1948.

39. Ruth S. Cavan, *et al., Personal Adjustment in Old Age,* Science Research Associates, 1949.

40. John F. Schmidt, *Patterns of Poor Adjustment in Persons of Later Maturity,* Ph.D. thesis, Department of Sociology, University of Chicago, 1950. See also "Patterns of Poor Adjustment in Old Age," *American Journal of Sociology,* 57: 33-42, July 1951.

tion among aging people in studies of retired school teachers,[41] retired YMCA secretaries,[42] residents of homes for the aged,[43] old age assistance recipients,[44] people in the "Back of the Yards" area of Chicago,[45] and nursing home residents and other persons past age 60 in Austin, Texas.[46]

Relationships between religion and personality problems have been observed and commented on by many behavioral scientists. The verbalized expressions of some mentally ill persons include many religious references, ideas, expressions, and experiences. This does not necessarily indicate, however, that religion in and of itself is the cause of their illness.[47]

During group therapy sessions with geriatric patients at a state hospital the preferred topic of discussion was religion. Religious beliefs and faith in God helped the disorganized members to overcome their grief when they were unhappy, lonesome, or despondent. They were eager to discuss a better life after death. The other members sensed the support that

---

41. Joseph H. Britton, *A Study of the Adjustment of Retired School Teachers*, Ph.D. Thesis, Committee on Human Development, University of Chicago, 1949. See also "A Study of the Adjustment of Retired School Teachers," *The American Psychologist*, 4: 308, July 1949.

42. Jean Oppenheimer Britton, *A Study of the Adjustment of Retired YMCA Secretaries*, Ph.D. Thesis, Committee on Human Development, University of Chicago, 1949.

43. Ju-Shu Pan, *A Study of the Personal and Social Adjustment of the Old People in the Homes for Aged*, M.A. Thesis, Department of Sociology, University of Chicago, 1947; and *A Comparison of Factors in the Personal Adjustment of Old People in the Protestant Church Homes for the Aged and the Old People Living Outside of Institutions*, Ph.D. Thesis, Department of Sociology, University of Chicago, 1950. See also Pan's "Factors in Personal Adjustment of Old People in Protestant Homes for the Aged," *American Sociological Review*, 16: 379-381, June 1951, and "Social Adjustment of Aged People," *Sociology and Social Research*, 33: 424-430, July-Aug. 1949.

44. Ethel Shanas, *The Personal Adjustment of Recipients of Old Age Assistance*, Ph.D. Thesis, Department of Sociology, University of Chicago, 1949.

45. O'Reilly and Pembroke, *op. cit.*, pp. 35-36.

46. Frances Gillespie Scott, "Factors in the Personal Adjustment of Institutionalized and Non-Institutionalized Aged," *American Sociological Review*, 20: 538-546, Oct. 1955.

47. See Wayne Oates, *Religious Factors in Mental Illness*, Association Press, 1955; and Victor D. Sanua, "Religion, Mental Health, and Personality: A Review of Empirical Studies," *American Journal of Psychiatry*, 125(9): 1203-1213, March 1969.

religion gave them because they themselves also received greater "ego strength" from religion. Delusions and hallucinations which involved religious symptoms, however, were not accepted by other group members as true and correct; when they were shared, the possibility of a mistake or incorrect interpretation was discussed.[48]

Elderly patients with ambivalent feelings toward life and death often wish to die, believing they have nothing left for which to live. Yet as they sense death is approaching, they may become insecure and disturbed, wanting others to be near them at all times, and even begin to fear the dark. They may attend church services more often than previously, confess their sins, and ask for forgiveness. Turning toward religion, they receive emotional support and relief from their fear that everything will soon end.[49]

The impact of religious faith is clearly evident in attitudes toward sickness and death. Patients who bring a Bible with them to the hospital and prominently display it sometimes make trouble for the nurses, doctor, and hospital staff. Their actions reflect insecurities which are absent in the stable, secure person who is active in civic and church life and who seldom brings a Bible to the hospital. Anxieties of patients are sometimes accentuated by the unexpected visit of a minister just before an operation or during illness, so medical doctors, recognizing the close relationship between the emotions and physical healing, are discouraged by the visits of certain clergymen. In addition, patients seldom speak with their medical doctor about religious matters. After 25 years of practice, the Director of Kirkpatrick Memorial Institute of Physical Medicine and Rehabilitation in Winter Park, Florida, stated, "I recall no person who called out to God or audibly prayed when he knew he was dying. Usually, these persons are exerting

---

48. Kurt Wolff, "Group Psychotherapy with Geriatric Patients in a State Hospital Setting: Results of a Three Year Study," *Group Psychotherapy*, 12, pp. 218-222, 1959.

49. Wolff, *The Biological, Sociological and Psychological Aspects of Aging*, *op. cit.* Margaret Clark and Barbara Anderson found that mentally ill older persons in San Francisco were more preoccupied with religion than the mentally healthy. *Culture and Aging*, Charles C Thomas, 1967, pp. 329, 342.

every bit of energy in a struggle to keep alive."[50] She observed however, that when patients regain consciousness after operations or a coma, they often give a spiritual significance to visions and thoughts similar to dreams.

The attitudes toward death of religious persons have been demonstrated by research to be significantly different from those of the non-religious. Although this may be due partly to traditional cultural definitions of death which include a religious interpretation, it "seems logical to infer that the eschatologically oriented person contemplates death in a positive manner," for there is a statistically significant relationship between religiosity and attitudes toward death. Persons who engage in little religious activity tend in general to have fearful attitudes about death.[51]

Among 260 community volunteers aged 60 and over in North Carolina, it was found that fear of death was significantly higher among those who did not believe in life after death and who read the Bible only infrequently.[52] Research on 58 adults from three Protestant congregations demonstrated that persons with greater religious participation had less fear of death. Older members were slightly more likely to report less fear of death.[53]

A psychological study of 210 Minnesota people aged 60 and over found a significant relationship between death attitudes and religiosity as indicated by both religious activity and scores on the MMPI religiosity scale, a measure of devotion to religion:

---

50. Nila Kirkpatrick Covalt, "The Meaning of Religion to Older People," *Geriatrics*, 15: 658-664, Sep. 1960.

51. Wendell M. Swenson, "Attitudes Toward Death in an Aged Population," *Journal of Gerontology*, 16: 49-52, Jan. 1961.

52. Frances C. Jeffers, Claude R. Nichols, and Carl Eisdorfer, "Attitudes of Older Persons Toward Death: A Preliminary Study," *Journal of Gerontology*, 16(1): 53-56, 1961.

53. David Martin and Lawrence S. Wrightsman, Jr., "The Relationship Between Religious Behavior and Concern about Death," *Journal of Social Psychology*, 65: 317-323, April 1965. A partial replication of this study by Richard D. Kahoe and Rebecca Fox Dunn, "The Fear of Death and Religious Attitudes and Behavior," *Journal for the Scientific Study of Religion*, 14(4): 379-382, Dec. 1975, confirms the positive contribution of religion to reduced fear of death and the negative correlation of intrinsic religious orientation with fear of death.

Persons with more fundamental religious convictions and habits look forward to death more than do those with less fundamental convictions and less activity. Fearful attitudes toward death tend to be found in those persons with little religious activity.... it seems logical to infer that the eschatologically oriented person contemplates death in a positive manner.[54]

As a result of her now-famous work with dying patients, Kübler-Ross has concluded that intensely religious people accept death more easily than others "if they are authentic and have internalized their faith." The significant variable, she believes, is not what one believes, but how truly and genuinely.[55]

Such findings support the conclusion that a sense of serenity and decreased fear of death accompany conservative religious beliefs. This does not necessarily prove that religious faith removes the fear of death, for it is conceivable that attitudes toward death among the religiously faithful differ from those of non-religious people because of such factors as variations in the degree of social integration.[56] In other words, religious people have a reference group that gives them support and security, and the non-religious are more likely to lack such social support. Swenson's finding that fear of death is related to solitude supports that hypothesis. Social isolation could be an intervening variable which explains the observed relationships.

This subject is complicated by traditional cultural definitions of death among people who have Christian convictions. Faithful believers are expected to "rest upon the promise" of salvation and thus to have no fear of death, expecting it to be the portal to immortality. The verbal statement that one does not fear the coming of death therefore could be an expression

54. Swenson, *op. cit.*, pp. 51-52. This finding is sustained in the psychological research of Roy E. Shearer, *Religious Belief and Attitudes toward Death*, Ph.D. dissertation, Fuller Theological Seminary, 1972.

55. Elisabeth Kübler-Ross, *Questions and Answers on Death and Dying*, Macmillan, 1974, pp. 161-162. K. G. Magni also found persons with intrinsic faith less fearful of death than those whose religion is extrinsic ("The Fear of Death" in L. B. Brown, ed., *Psychology and Religion*, Penguin Education, 1973, pp. 329-342).

56. Jean-René Treanon, "Comments, Symposium on Attitudes Toward Death in Older Persons," *Journal of Gerontology*, 16(1): 63, 1961. But most research on this is very weak; see David Martin and Lawrence S. Wrightsman, Jr., "Religion and Fears about Death," *Religious Education*, 59(2): 174-176, March-April 1964.

of a neurotic personality which disguises death and pretends that it is not a basic condition of all life.[57] Similarly, Feifel has hypothesized that "certain older persons perceive death as the beginning of a new existence for the purpose of controlling strong anxieties concerning death."[58] Should his hypothesis be verified through careful research, one of the social and psychological functions commonly attributed to religion by faithful believers when they seek comfort in Biblical teachings about the resurrection will have received scientific support.

SPIRITUAL WELL-BEING: NEEDS AND GOALS

One of the background and issues papers for the 1971 White House Conference on Aging dealt with Spiritual Well-Being.[59] This significant document defined "the spiritual" as pertaining to the inner resources, especially the ultimate concern or basic value around which all other values are focused, the central philosophy of life which guides a person's conduct, and the supernatural and non-material dimensions of life. As the source of life-enabling and life-sustaining values in society which provide the philosophical orientation to all life, the spiritual touches every aspect of human conduct. All people are "spiritual," even if they practice no personal pieties and have no use for religious institutions.

The study revealed many spiritual needs among the aging, needs which are not satisfied exclusively within the context of organized religious groups. Losses and deprivations during aging are accentuated by social and cultural values and practices. Discrimination against older people merely on the basis of their age makes them a new minority group in our culture, suffering problems similar to those of racial minorities and of the victims of sexism. The sense of being useless and rejected, the feeling of inner emptiness, boredom, loneliness, and the

---

57. Robert L. Fulton, "Comments, Symposium on Attitudes Toward Death in Older Persons," *Journal of Gerontology*, 16(1): 63-65, 1961.

58. Herman Feifel, "Older Persons Look at Death," *Geriatrics*, 11(3): 127-130, 1956. Fear of death may motivate some religious faith and activity (Kahoe and Dunn, *op. cit.*).

59. Moberg, *Spiritual Well-Being*, *op. cit.* See also Moberg, "Spiritual Well-Being in Late Life," chap. 12 in Jaber F. Gubrium, ed., *Late Life*, Charles C Thomas, 1974, pp. 256-279.

fear of time are among the consequences of socio-cultural forces that operate like a vicious cycle to the detriment of the social, material, and spiritual well-being of the aging. Other spiritual needs include the search for relief from anxieties and fears, the need to prepare for death, the problems related to integration of the personality, the search for personal dignity, and the central need for meaning that is satisfied only through developing a rewarding philosophy of life.

Many goals have been set forth for religious bodies and other groups in relationship to spiritual needs. Representative of the goals that have been proposed are the following:

1. Assistance in cultivating a satisfying philosophy of life.
2. Education — for life and for death.
3. Enrichment of living.
4. Therapeutic services to deal with the problems of people in a holistic manner whenever they arise.
5. The right to die in dignity.

Subsequent to the White House Conference on Aging, religious leaders organized the National Interfaith Coalition on Aging. NICA has conducted a major research project to identify the programs of religious bodies with and for the aging. It also has stimulated and sponsored various conferences and study groups, one of which produced this working definition of spiritual well-being:

> Spiritual Well-Being is the affirmation of life in a relationship with God, self, community and environment that nurtures and celebrates wholeness.[60]

This statement can be presented and used in any religious group. Each, however, will need to elaborate and explain it, using its own theology, concepts, traditions, and structures for application within its own frame of reference and context.

CONCLUSION

The studies reported in this chapter have agreed in the finding that religion is important to most older people and that it is significantly related to various indicators of their personal adjustment. Among those who have a religious orien-

---

60. For the accompanying commentary and other details see Appendix I.

tation and background, participation in out-of-the-home program activities of churches tends to decline when physical and economic problems begin to make their mark, but those religious activities which involve sedentary participation tend to increase. The degree to which people consider themselves to be religious, the holding of beliefs which are "orthodox" in their religion, and the level of satisfaction received from religion all tend to increase during the later years.[61] Their faith gives them happiness and comfort, contributing to their personal adjustment and life satisfaction, and it apparently reduces the fear of death.

Most studies leading to such conclusions, however, were not focused specifically upon the subject of religion. The following four chapters summarize studies that were made for the specific purpose of examining in detail the relationships between various aspects of religious beliefs and activities and personal adjustment in old age.

---

61. The contrast between "sedentary" and "program" participation in religious activities was noted by psychologist Kuhlen in his own research, as well as in his observations from the work of others (Raymond G. Kuhlen, "Religion and Human Needs," in John E. Cantelon et al., op. cit., pp. 15-26).

FOUR

Religion and Personal Adjustment in Old Age

This chapter begins with a study of 219 persons aged 65 and over who were residents of seven institutions in the Minneapolis-St. Paul metropolitan area.[1] Five of the institutions are homes for the aged, and two are publicly supported homes which include younger infirm and indigent persons. For each of the 219 subjects of the study a lengthy questionnaire was filled out by an interviewer. More detailed case studies were made of a portion of the total group. As we shall see toward the end of this chapter, subsequent studies have confirmed and extended the findings of this research.

The questionnaire included the Chicago Attitudes Inventory, which was used to measure personal adjustment in old age.[2] This inventory consists of eight scales which may be used either to produce a composite personal adjustment score or to measure adjustment in each of the specific areas of health, friends, work, economic security, religion, feeling of usefulness, happiness, and family. Personal adjustment is defined by this scale as satisfaction with activities and status, general happiness, and a feeling of usefulness.[3]

1. David O. Moberg, *Religion and Personal Adjustment in Old Age*, Ph.D. Thesis, University of Minnesota, Dec. 1951.

2. E.W. Burgess, R.S. Cavan, and R.J. Havighurst, *Your Activities and Attitudes,* Science Research Associates, 1948.

3. R.S. Cavan, *et al., Personal Adjustment in Old Age*, Science Research Associates, 1949, p. 111. For a sophisticated critique of concepts and measures of adjustment see Eugene A. Friedmann and Harold L. Orbach, "Adjustment to Retirement," chap. 30 in Silvano Arieti, ed., *American Handbook of Psychiatry, Vol. I, The Foundations of Psychiatry*, Basic Books, 2nd ed., 1974, pp. 609-645.

Other concepts that are used to indicate "successful aging" include morale, happiness, life satisfaction, social adjustment, and psychological well-being. Some people assume that the use of a term like "personal adjustment" implies complete complicity with the status quo when, they feel, it would be more desirable to change it or, at least, not merely to adjust. Our use of that term in no way implies that we believe no changes are needed in society and its institutions in order to meet the needs of people more effectively. Quite the contrary, as is indicated in many passages throughout this book and particularly in chapters 8 and 10, we feel that numerous changes should be made in order that institutions may more truly become the servants of people rather than their masters.

The aging individual can participate in political and other activities to change social structures. Such changes only come slowly, however. In the meantime, each individual must adapt his or her life and activities to present realities of the sociocultural and physical environment. To do so in a manner that produces personal satisfaction, happiness, and a feeling of usefulness is to attain good personal adjustment.

Four major types of religious experience which were thought possibly to be related to personal adjustment in old age were analyzed in the research reported here. These were church membership, past and present religious activities, positions of leadership in the church or in church-related organizations, and orthodox Christian beliefs. In each case two groups of older persons were compared. One had been exposed to the type of religious experience under consideration; the other had not. Individuals in the two groups were paired with one another on the basis of similarity of selected background characteristics so that the two groups were as much alike as possible except for the difference in the phase of religion that was the topic of the specific study.[4]

4. This type of analysis is technically known as an *ex post facto experimental design*. It makes possible an approximation to a controlled experiment through indirect "mental" control by the experimenter rather than by direct manipulation of the individuals involved in the study. For discussions of its theoretical and logical bases and illustrations of other applications of this research methodology, see F. Stuart Chapin, *Experimental Designs in Sociological Research*, rev. ed., Harper and Brothers, 1955; and Ernest Greenwood, *Experimental Sociology*, King's Crown Press, 1945.

CHURCH MEMBERSHIP AND PERSONAL
ADJUSTMENT IN OLD AGE[5]

Of the 219 subjects of this research, 132 were church members and 87, at the time of the interview, were not. The church members had an average[6] personal adjustment score of 28.4 and the non-members 23.3 on the attitudes inventory. (The higher the score, the better the personal adjustment.) The better personal adjustment of the church members at the time of interviewing was statistically significant;[7] so great a difference normally could not result from chance variations alone.

The church members of seven denominational groupings (Baptist, Catholic, Christian Science, Episcopal, Lutheran, Methodist, and "all others") were compared with non-members who preferred the same denomination. In every case the members had higher personal adjustment scores. The superior adjustment of church members was also evident when the data were analyzed by sex, age, nativity, place of residence, years of schooling, marital and family status, self-rating of health, participation in social organizations, and self-rating of happiness. When each of these was held constant, the church members had higher adjustment scores. The hypothesis that church membership is related to good personal adjustment in old age seemed by this evidence to be corroborated strongly.

Fifty-three pairs of church members and non-members were then matched on the basis of sex, present employment or its absence, past and present club participation, marital status, number of living children, education, and self-rating of health. The average personal adjustment score of the church members was 26.8 and that of the non-members 24.9 — not a statistically significant difference.

Because the differences in adjustment of the two groups had decreased as a result of careful matching, the members and non-members were compared on an even more rigorous basis. As a result of imposing two additional matching controls, nativity and place of residence at the time of interviewing,

5. David O. Moberg, "Church Membership and Personal Adjustment in Old Age," *Journal of Gerontology*, 8: 207-211, April 1953.
6. "Average" in this chapter refers to the arithmetic mean.
7. Statistical significance is generally at the .01 level of confidence in this chapter, and never less than the .05 level, whenever it is reported.

only nine pairs of persons remained. This increased the similarity of the backgrounds and reduced the personal adjustment scores of both groups, the church members' average score being 24.1 and the matched non-members' 24.2.

The lack of association between church membership and personal adjustment for these matched groups of individuals may reflect both the "quality" of church membership and the influence of the church on non-members. It is probable that many people join a church without any personal convictions and only as a result of family influences and other social pressures. This can be true of adult as well as childhood church joiners. Others may enter the church for various ulterior motives rather than because of a truly religious commitment. If such church members could be distinguished from those who have come into the church as a result of genuine, personal, meaningful religious experiences and convictions, important differences might be found between the two groups, including differences in personal adjustment in old age.

We know that churches in America exert a definite influence on persons who are not members.[8] Many attend services regularly and take part in other church activities without ever becoming full members. In addition, the churches' influence often operates through persons who are church members to affect many secular activities both directly and indirectly, especially when moral and ethical standards are involved. Even non-members who have had nothing to do directly with the church may thus be influenced by it throughout their lives. Furthermore, because of the role of religion in the historical development of our nation, the influence of the church is diffused throughout all areas of social life. The indirect influence of the church may therefore be a partial source of the lack of significant differences in personal adjustment between the older church members and non-members who are the subjects of this study.

Some persons drop their church memberships in later life. Clifton's study of a random sample of old age assistance recipients in Minnesota indicated that many older people had dropped out of their churches, although churches held their

---

8. John F. Cuber, "Marginal Church Participants," *Sociology and Social Research*, 25: 57-62, Sep.-Oct. 1940.

members better than other organizations.[9] Such people have been under the church's direct influence in the past. Even if they are no longer members, they may have the same types of personal adjustment as those who still are, if church membership is related to personal adjustment in old age.

Analysis of the subjects of our study tended to support this conclusion. The 23 non-members who did not indicate ever having been church members had an average personal adjustment score of 21.5, while the 64 non-members who had previously been church members had a score of 24.0. In the latter category, the 32 who had been members during part or most of their adult years had an average score of 25.5.

Individual matching of the non-members who did not indicate ever having been church members with those who had once been members resulted in eleven pairs when seven control characteristics were used in the matching procedure (sex, education, marital status, number of living children, similar club activities in the past and present, self-rating of health, and present lack of employment). The church members had an average of 25.5, and the non-members 21.5, but this difference was not statistically significant because of the small numbers involved.

The evidence from this study suggests the probability that the frequently observed relationship between church affiliation and good adjustment in old age is spurious or false. It is not church membership in and of itself that contributes to good personal adjustment in old age, at least in our nation, where it is so easy to become a church member. The observed relationship must be due to other factors related to or accompanying religious affiliation.

RELIGIOUS ACTIVITIES AND PERSONAL ADJUSTMENT IN OLD AGE[10]

A logical time to look for any relationship between reli-

9. C. Stanley Clifton, *A Study of the Leisure Time Interests and Activities of Old Age Assistance Recipients in Commercial Rest Homes in Minnesota*, Ph.D. Thesis, University of Minnesota, 1951.

10. David O. Moberg, "Religious Activities and Personal Adjustment in Old Age," *Journal of Social Psychology*, 43: 261-267, May 1956.

gious activities and adjustment is in old age. If there is a relationship, we can expect it to be most evident after prolonged operation of the influence of religious activities. In chapter 3 we noted that several studies found certain religious activities to be related to good personal adjustment in old age. These findings, we observed, were only fragmentary side-lights and subsidiary findings of the investigations of which they were a part.

To study this subject specifically, each of our 219 respondents was given a "religious activities score." This score could range from 0 for a person who indicated no activity in any of the eleven areas included to 23 for one who indicated much activity in every one of them. The areas summarized by this score are church membership, present attendance at religious services, present attendance at religious services compared to attendance when about age 55, attendance at religious services when about age 12, positions and offices held in the church, frequency of listening to religious programs over the radio, reading from the Bible, reading other religious books, private prayer, saying grace at meals during most of the adult life, and family prayers or some form of family worship during most of the adult life.

The religious activities score tended to discriminate against non-church members in two ways: Church membership was itself one of the areas included, and the holding of offices is usually limited by most churches to members. It also discriminated against the infirm who were unable to attend, the hard-of-hearing who could not hear religious radio services, those with eyesight too poor to read the Bible, and the like.

Good personal adjustment and a high religious activities score were found to be significantly correlated. A relationship of this type, however, could result if persons who are well-adjusted for other reasons than religious activities are the ones who are religiously active, and vice versa. For instance, if all persons who have a good education, good health, and living children are religiously active, while all those who have a poor education, poor health, and no living children are religiously inactive, then the relationship observed between personal adjustment and religious activities could be due entirely to these other factors and not to religion at all.

To hold constant some of the possible biasing characteristics related to personal adjustment in old age, persons with high religious activities scores (15 or higher) were matched with persons who had low scores (8 or less).

The 86 persons with high religious activities scores had an average personal adjustment score of 31.1, and the 41 with low scores had an average score of 18.3. Members of the religiously "active" group (high scores) were paired with the "inactive" group (low scores) by the use of seven matching controls (sex, marital status, number of living children, education, present employment status, club activities, and self-rating of health). In addition, certain "secondary-control factors"[11] were used to increase the comparability of the two groups whenever there was a choice of which persons to retain in the matching process.

The average personal adjustment scores of the paired individuals were 28.7 for the 19 persons in the "active" group and 16.3 for those in the "inactive" group. This difference was not only statistically significant, but it was also found to prevail within each of the eight sub-areas that make up the personal adjustment attitudes inventory.

We may conclude, therefore, that either those who are well-adjusted engage in many religious activities, or that engaging in many religious activities contributes to good personal adjustment in old age, or that both processes occur together.

CHURCH LEADERSHIP AND PERSONAL ADJUSTMENT IN OLD AGE[12]

In her study of 100 persons over the age of 65, Albrecht found that active social participation during the younger years seemed to contribute to good adjustment in old age. She also discovered that well-adjusted old people tended to withdraw into a more relaxed kind of participation instead of continuing to compete for status positions of high office or responsibility.[13]

---

11. See David O. Moberg, "Two Problems of Experimental Designs," *The Midwest Sociologist*, 16(1): 10-12, Winter 1954.

12. David O. Moberg, "Leadership in the Church and Personal Adjustment in Old Age," *Sociology and Social Research*, 37: 312-316, May-June 1953.

13. Ruth Albrecht, "The Social Roles of Old People," *Journal of Gerontology*, 6: 144, April 1951.

Her findings suggest two things: (1) Older persons who have held positions of leadership in the church in the past, a form of active social participation, may be better adjusted in old age than those who have not held such positions, and (2) older people who cling to positions of leadership in the church may be less well-adjusted than those who no longer hold such positions. (Purely honorary positions, such as elders or deacons in certain churches, might be an exception.)

On the other hand, Burgess has suggested the hypothesis that "downward vertical social mobility in old age is correlated with problems of adjustment in the later decades."[14] This suggests the possibility that the older person who has once held a position of leadership in the church and then has been forced to relinquish it by ill health, declining physical vigor, social pressures, or other influences may be poorly adjusted in his old age.

Thirty-three of the 132 church members in our study were either Roman Catholic or Greek or Russian Orthodox. None of them still held a formal position of leadership in the church; four had held positions in the past, and two more had held such minor positions as choir member and janitor. Of the 99 Protestant church members, five still held one or more positions of leadership, 35 had held such positions only in the past, and four had held only minor positions.

The 35 Protestant church members who had held positions only in the past had an average personal adjustment score of 31.6, compared to a score of 27.2 for the 55 who did not indicate ever having held positions of church leadership. Eight control characteristics, in addition to Protestant church membership, were used to match comparable pairs in the two groups. These were sex, marital status, education, present employment status, number of living children, club activity, self-rating of health, and age within five years of each other. The 22 former church leaders had an average personal adjustment score of 31.5, and the matched non-leaders had a score of 27.0, a statistically significant difference. (The five who still held positions of leadership in the church had a score of 30.6.)

It appears from these findings that taking an active part

---

14. Ruth S. Cavan *et al.*, *op. cit.*, p. 145.

in church activities by assuming positions of leadership contributes to good personal adjustment in old age, even after
these positions have been lost to the individual except in
memory. Perhaps this is because the older persons who were
leaders in the past are still permitted or encouraged to give
their advice and guidance to church activities through informal
channels. If this is so, they may not feel they have lost social
prestige and status within their group with the loss of office.
Many of them may retain their prestige within the group by
virtue of past services and accomplishments. It is possible that
the tendency of many to desire to drop out of positions of
leadership in old age and their accompanying voluntary withdrawal from them, together with the policy of many churches
and church organizations to change leadership at regular intervals, also helps to prevent a lowering of personal adjustment
when leadership positions are lost.

On the other hand, it is also possible that the personal
adjustment of former leaders in the church was so good in the
past that, even with substantial reduction of its level from the
loss of leadership, they have adjustment scores that are superior
to the rank and file of church membership.

The higher adjustment scores of former church leaders
therefore may reflect a causal relationship between personal
adjustment in old age and the past holding of leadership positions in the church. It is also possible that some third factor or
configuration of related factors may be the cause of both good
personal adjustment and being accepted as church leaders.

CHRISTIAN BELIEFS AND PERSONAL
ADJUSTMENT IN OLD AGE[15]

Five items in the questionnaire dealt with prayer, sin, the
future, the Bible, and Jesus. The answers to these were com-
bined to form a single "religious belief score." The scoring,
done by simple addition of weights representing various kinds
of answers, made possible a highest score of 10 and a lowest
score of 0. A score of 10 indicates a person who, at the time of

15. David O. Moberg, "Christian Beliefs and Personal Adjustment in Old
Age," *Journal of the American Scientific Affiliation*, 10(1): 8-12, March 1958.

interviewing, said he believed in heaven or a future life, believed in a prayer-answering God, believed that there is sin
and that his own sins were forgiven, believed in the Bible as
the perfect Word of God, and believed in Jesus Christ as the
Savior who died a vicarious death. A score of 0 designates a
person who indicated no hope for the future, did not pray, did
not believe in sin and its forgiveness, believed the Bible is in-
spired only like other great pieces of literature, and believed
Jesus was merely a great man.

For purposes of analysis, persons with high religious belief
scores (7 through 10) were called "believers," and persons with
low scores (0 through 4) were called "non-believers." Some
would classify "believers" thus defined as conservative, fundamental, evangelical, or orthodox Christians, while the "non-
believers" are more like non-Christians or, if they are members
of Christian groups, liberal or "modernistic" Christians.

A serious limitation of this portion of the study was the
tendency of many respondents to think to themselves, "What
ought I to believe about this?" Sometimes this was outwardly
expressed in the words, "What *should* I say?" or "What is the
right answer?" When and if there were differences between
the individual's personal beliefs and the conventional beliefs
adhered to by his church, it is possible that conventional answers tended to predominate; some persons seemed to be
striving for consistency with their religious groups.

Religious beliefs were closely associated with religious activities. There was a high correlation between the religious
activities scores and the religious belief scores. This may be in
part because prayer was an aspect of both scores, but it also
reflects the probability that those who believe in the Bible as
God's perfect Word are the most apt to read it reverently and
consistently, and those who believe in Jesus as a vicarious
Savior are the most likely to engage in the religious activities
associated with Christian worship and praise.

Personal adjustment scores were also highly correlated with
the religious belief scores, "believers" having higher adjustment
scores than "non-believers." However, "believers" in the highest belief score category who were not church members had
higher personal adjustment scores than church members in the
same category. Church members with low belief scores also

tended to have lower personal adjustment scores than non-members with similar belief scores. This suggests that deviant church members may have guilty consciences because of the inconsistencies between their personal beliefs and the profession of faith they implicitly make by being church members.

The 155 "believers" had an average personal adjustment score of 28.0, and the 35 "non-believers" had a score of 19.9. The matching of individuals from the two groups by the use of seven controls (sex, self-rating of health, marital status, number of living children, education, present employment status, and similar past and present club activities) left 22 comparable persons in each group. The "believers" had an average personal adjustment score of 27.2 and the matched "non-believers" 19.9, a statistically significant difference.

Why should "believers" have better personal adjustment in old age? The "non-believer" who realizes death is approaching may be disturbed, at least subconsciously, at the thought of dying and at his lack of assurance of a life beyond the grave, as we saw in chapter 3. One may be bothered by feelings of guilt in not being certain one's own sins have been forgiven, even while saying he or she does not believe in sin. One person interviewed, for example, denied the existence of sin and then strongly affirmed that her own sins had been forgiven!

The "believer" probably feels, conversely, a greater sense of usefulness than the "non-believer." Because of the belief that God hears and answers prayers, there is faith that one can help others by interceding for them even when physically unable to offer any personal tangible or material assistance to those who are in need. Even though he or she recognizes personal sinfulness and lack of perfection, the "believer" may rejoice in the faith that confession of sins to God brings forgiveness because of the vicarious sacrifice of Jesus Christ. Such a person may be well-adjusted, even in the midst of suffering from physical infirmities and afflictions, because of the assurance that there is a purpose in everything that comes into his or her life. Even if only God knows that purpose, there is faith that God will make all things work together for good. The adaptability and adjustability of the individual may be increased by faith in Biblical promises to the faithful, such as those expressed in Romans 8:28, Philippians 4:19, I Thessalonians 4:13-18, Hebrews 13:8, and I Peter 5:10.

On the other hand, the subjects of this study were reared in an era when the position of those we have called "believers" perhaps was more prevalent than it is among the present generation. It is possible that the religious beliefs imparted in one's childhood and youth give the greatest comfort and make for the best personal adjustment in old age. If so, children and youth reared in our current religious climate may experience the best personal adjustment in their future old age when they adhere to the type of religion into which they have been indoctrinated during their own early decades of life.

RELATED RESEARCH

Subsequent studies have resulted in similar findings with but minor exceptions. The same general pattern of relationships between religious variables and adjustment has been observed in research on 37 institutionalized older persons[16] and a sample of 55 persons aged 65 and over who lived independently in a middle-class urban community,[17] even though the overall pattern of the personal adjustment scores was higher.

Secondary analysis of data also used the Chicago Attitudes Inventory to measure adjustment in a study of over 5,000 persons aged 60 and over who were interviewed in five surveys in four midwestern states. It revealed that the adjustment scores of church leaders (officers and committee members), other church members, and non-members were significantly different, with the leaders consistently highest and non-members lowest. Cross-tabulations of the data for 1,340 urban respondents in one of those states demonstrated that these differences remained statistically significant at the .001 level when they were analyzed within categories of sex, age, education, marital status, home ownership and type of residence, participation in civic, social,

16. Annette Burgess, Karin Jessup, and Carolyn Tenove, "The Relationship Between Religion and Personal Adjustment in Old Age," unpublished ms., Bethel College, May 1960.

17. Kathleen Renfrew, et al., "Religion and Personal Adjustment in Old Age," unpublished paper, June 1, 1961.

and professional organizations, organizational activity levels compared to those during the respondents' fifties, self-rating of health, and self-identification of age. Only in the area of employment were the differences non-significant, but even these were in the anticipated direction. The hypothesis that church participation is related to good personal adjustment in old age was overwhelmingly supported by the evidence.[18]

Adjustment also was found related to religious adherence among Orthodox Jews aged 65 and over. No non-religious persons were in the well-adjusted category; all of the latter were intensely or fairly religious. Three-fourths of the fairly-adjusted group were either intensely or fairly religious, but only 35% of the poorly- and very-poorly-adjusted groups were.[19]

Lepkowski's study of institutionalized and non-institutionalized Catholics past age 60, using the same basic measure of adjustment as our study, found no significant differences in personal or social adjustment between his samples.[20] This supports the possibility that findings on non-institutionalized people are in the same direction as those of institutionalized people.

Barron's research on 496 persons in New York City, 325 of whom were Jewish, found that only 39% mentioned religion and the church as the source of the most satisfaction and comfort in their lives. Being home with the family, keeping house, "doing things I like to do by myself at home," having relatives visit, and spending time with close friends were sources of satisfaction for larger numbers of respondents. Worry about getting older was less among those who found religion comforting only in the 40-45 age group; 37% of those who derived comfort from religion worried about aging, compared to 41% of those who did not find religion comforting.[21] While

18. David O. Moberg and Marvin J. Taves, "Church Participation and Adjustment in Old Age," in Arnold M. Rose and Warren A. Peterson, eds., *Older People and Their Social World*, F. A. Davis Co., 1965, pp. 113-124.

19. E.S. Oles, *Religion and Old Age, A Study of the Possible Influence of Religious Adherence on Adjustment*, Thesis, Bucknell University, 1949. Reviewed in *Journal of Gerontology*, 5: 187, 1950.

20. Richard Lepkowski, "The Attitudes and Adjustments of Institutionalized and Non-institutionalized Catholic Aged," *Journal of Gerontology*, 11: 185-191, April 1956.

21. Milton L. Barron, *The Aging Americans*, Thomas Y. Crowell Co., 1961.

these measures of religiosity are very limited, Barron's finding suggests the need for further research about the impact of religion upon personal adjustment. The social sources of support mentioned by his subjects of research may be important intervening variables, but they may also reflect a relatively greater emphasis upon family and social relationships among Jewish than among Christian people.

Robb has suggested that there is reason to believe that persons reared in a psychologically secure family may find religious orthodoxy compatible, while those whose life experiences lead toward deviation find religious orthodoxy less compatible.[22] If he is correct, good personal adjustment is more a cause of conventional religious beliefs and activities than a result of them. This is not to imply, however, that old age is viewed by the elderly as the most satisfying period of their life. On the contrary, most view it as the least happy period, with the one exception of finding it the most satisfactory for their religious activity and orientation.[23]

Happiness was not related to level of church attendance in Graney's study of 44 elderly women living independently and interviewed as a panel a second time after a four-year gap. Activity increases generally were associated with happiness and decreases with unhappiness, but this relationship did not hold for the most elderly respondents with respect to attending religious services. Although there was a decline in their church attendance, the change in level of activity did not affect their happiness.[24]

Religion is associated with purpose in life, at least among retired professors.[25] This relationship may be a part of the reason why religious orientations and behavior are associated with good morale and happiness during the later years.

The complexity of the relationships between religion and

---

22. Thomas Bradley Robb, *The Bonus Years: Foundations for Ministry with Older Persons,* Judson Press, 1968, p. 103.

23. D.B. Bromley, *The Psychology of Human Aging,* Penguin Books, 1966, p. 87.

24. Marshall J. Graney, "Happiness and Social Participation in Old Age," paper presented to the 26th Annual Meeting of the Gerontological Society, Miami Beach, Florida, Nov. 9, 1973.

25. Gene Acuff and Donald Allen, "Hiatus in 'Meaning': Disengagement for Retired Professors," *Journal of Gerontology,* 25(2): 126-128, 1970.

adjustment is evident also in Ferguson's study of senior citizens on the mailing list of a large Southern California church. He found that there was no correlation between the frequency of participation in organized religious activities and life-satisfaction scores, and those who were church members did not have higher scores than non-members. Yet people who participated in a larger number of organized religious activities had significantly higher life-satisfaction scores than those participated in few.[26]

The religious items in the Chicago Attitudes Inventory apparently measure a different kind of adjustment dimension than the other parts of the attitude scale. The Duke University longitudinal study of aging, which has periodically reexamined a panel of 272 volunteers who were aged 60 to 94 at their first interview (between 1955 and 1959), has found almost no correlation between religious attitude scores and the total attitude score at any point in time.[27] This may be part of the reason for the unexpected lack of relationship between church-related activities and adjustment among many of the oldest cohorts of people which have been studied. Among the 178 Duke study members who had died from nonaccidental natural causes by December 1974, there had been declines in religious activities but no declines in religious attitudes. Most participants maintained stable levels of satisfaction despite the declines of aging and approaching death.[28]

Longitudinal measures in the Duke study indicate that religious activities tend to decline gradually in late old age, but religious attitudes and satisfactions tend neither to increase nor to decrease substantially. Religion tends to become an increasingly important factor in the adjustment of older persons as they age, in spite of the decline in such activities as church attendance. Their religious behavior nevertheless correlates

26. Larry Neil Ferguson, *Life-Satisfaction among the Elderly as a Function of Participation in Organized Religious Activities*, Ph.D. dissertation (Psychology), Fuller Theological Seminary, 1975.

27. Erdman B. Palmore, "The Effects of Aging on Activities and Attitudes," chap. 7 in Virginia M. Brantl and Sister Marie Raymond Brown, eds., *Readings in Gerontology*, C.V. Mosby Co., 1973, pp. 61-69.

28. Erdman Palmore and William Cleveland, "Aging, Terminal Decline, and Terminal Drop," *Journal of Gerontology*, 31(1): 76-81, Jan. 1976.

more strongly with various measures of adjustment than their religious attitudes.[29]

It is possible that increased religious orientations are in part a compensation for declining activities in older areas of life. Similarly, the persons who are the most highly religious during the later years may have been so throughout the other stages of the life cycle. It goes without saying that additional research is necessary to determine whether the observed relationships between religion and personal adjustment in old age are characteristic of all groups of older people or only of some, as well as to determine the degree to which they reflect cause-and-effect relationships or only coincidental, spurious correlations between the variables studied. Some evidence, for example, suggests that morale or life satisfaction is influenced by the surroundings in which people live. For this reason and because the aging are so diverse, whatever produces good adjustment for one group in one type of setting may not do so in a different setting or for another group.[30]

Perceived health also is a very important intervening variable between activity levels and life satisfaction.[31] It can have a significant impact upon the extent to which people engage in social activities, whether these involve attending church, participating in church-related organizations and groups, or sharing activities entirely outside the scope of institutionalized religion. Numerous studies have shown that those who perceive their health as poor tend generally to have lower levels of morale, life satisfaction, and personal adjustment than those who consider their health to be good. They also tend to have lower levels of social participation, so observed correlations which fail to control the health factor (as was

29. Dan B. Blazer and Erdman Palmore, "Religion and Aging in a Longitudinal Panel," *The Gerontologist*, 16(1, Part 1): 82-85, Feb. 1976.

30. Ruth Bennett, "Recent Developments—Social," paper presented at the Eighth International Congress on Gerontology, Washington, D.C., Aug. 1969, pp. 7-9. See also Gordon L. Bultena, "Structural Effects on the Morale of the Aged: A Comparison of Age-Segregated and Age-Integrated Communities," chap. 2 in Jaber F. Gubrium, ed., *Late Life*, Charles C Thomas, 1974, pp. 18-31.

31. Stephen Wolk and Sharon Telleen, "Psychological and Social Correlates of Life Satisfaction as a Function of Residential Constraint," *Journal of Gerontology*, 31(1): 89-98, Jan. 1976.

done by using self-ratings of health in the matching process for the study reported earlier in this chapter) may be spurious.

CONCLUSION

Our survey of relationships between religion and the reality which lies behind and beneath that which is variously called adjustment, morale, life satisfaction, happiness, mental health, and well-being has revealed that the association often observed between church membership and good personal adjustment does not result from the membership in and of itself. Rather, certain activities and attitudes which do contribute to good adjustment are more likely to prevail among church members than among non-members.

Religious behavior and beliefs apparently are causal factors which contribute to life satisfaction among older people. When infirmities force a decline in such behavior outside the home as church attendance and participation in church-related groups, a personal devotional orientation, a faith commitment, and religious attitudes are retained which bring comfort, assurance, hope, and life satisfaction, thus contributing to good personal adjustment and morale among "religious" people.[32] It is likely that spiritual well-being is a key to the other dimensions of satisfaction and adjustment, serving reciprocally as both cause and consequence of numerous other observed factors in personal adjustment.

The findings of interviews and case studies which are reported in the next three chapters help to clarify some of the dynamics involved in the impact of the church and religion upon personal and social adjustment.

---

32. Variations in degree are undoubtedly found, and many individuals deviate from the general pattern. An important clinical problem is how to determine what they personally would be like if they lacked their religious activities, beliefs, and attitudes.

FIVE

Personal Adjustment of the Older Person Within the Church

Older persons in the United States are confronted with many social conditions which make it difficult for them to adjust to modern society, as we have seen in chapter 2. As a result, a sizable proportion of them have serious emotional and personal problems. Supporting this point are the observations of Erdman Palmore, one of the directors of the notable Duke University Longitudinal Study of Aging:

> While mental illness is not "normal" in the sense of "healthy," some degree of mental or emotional difficulty is fairly common among the aged. Both hospitalization rates and community surveys show that the older age groups have substantially more mental illness than younger groups.[1]

The literature abounds with case histories and results of community surveys documenting Palmore's summary, so we will not restate this literature here other than to specify that, whatever the magnitude of the mental health problem, it promises to become vastly larger in the future unless much more is done to alleviate its causes and to provide additional treatment facilities. Fortunately, great strides are being taken throughout the country in this regard, particularly with respect to the development of community health centers and allied facilities to deliver services for all persons needing them. The goal of these centers is to help people with mental health problems stay in their homes rather than becoming patients in mental hospitals, except in those cases where necessary treatment is available only in the hospital.

---

1. Erdman Palmore, ed., *Normal Aging*, Duke University Press, 1970, p. 75.

This objective is to be accomplished by providing outpatient treatment at a nearby community health center and providing other services through cooperation with agencies such as mental counseling, finding employment, etc.[2]

A nationwide complex of community mental health centers has become this country's main program for the prevention and treatment of mental health problems for older persons as well as for other people. The success of these centers both collectively and singularly has depended in the main upon coordinating community resources into a united program oriented toward preventing and treating mental health problems on the local level. That the church and religion have a role here is obvious, even though they have lagged behind the other community resources and agencies which have entered the community health center program. Accentuating the potential role of the church both in this respect and concerning its relationship with community mental health programs is the well-accepted fact that a sizable proportion of the population turn to the church when they have personal problems.

Butler and Lewis provide an insightful explanation as to why many older persons turn to the church in old age:

Old people are led to see themselves as "beginning to fail" as they age, a phrase that refers as much to self worth as it does to physical strength. Religion has been the traditional solace by promising another world wherein the self again springs to life, never to be further threatened by loss of its own integrity.[3]

Clergymen therefore have an important role to fill both in terms of providing individual counselling and cooperating in community mental health programs.[4] There is an abundant literature available concerning pastoral counselling, and chapter 10 gives further perspectives on this subject.

Our purpose here is to discuss how the church in general can be mobilized to assist older persons in adjusting to the problems of the later years. In doing this we will report briefly

---

2. Robert M. Gray, "What About the Future?" in Robert Kane *et al.*, eds., *The Health Gap: Medical Services and the Poor*, Springer Publishing Co., 1976, p. 226.

3. Robert N. Butler and Myrna I. Lewis, *Aging and Mental Health: Positive Psychosocial Approaches*, C. V. Mosby Co., 1973, p. 17.

4. David O. Moberg, "Needs Felt by the Clergy for Ministries to the Aging," *The Gerontologist*, 15(2): 170-175, April 1975.

on a study by one of the authors designed specifically to determine the influence of the church experience on the personal adjustment of older persons.[5]

The persons studied were from two large churches in separate denominational groups in the Chicago area. Both are included among the religious bodies with over 1,000,000 members in our nation. This investigation was directed first toward determining if there is any difference in the personal adjustment of older (age 60 and over) and younger (age 50 to 59) aging church members and second toward finding out if church members who are closely related to the church have better personal adjustment than members who are not so close to the church. Third, the study sought to discover if church members increasingly turn to the church in old age when they confront the problem of making the transition to the later years. Finally, the investigation tried to locate those circumstances in the church experience that contribute to or hinder personal adjustment in old age. The results of this investigation relative to the first three problems stated above are presented in this chapter. Findings concerning the older persons' experiences in the church are presented in the following two chapters.

In briefest terms the study analyses disclosed the fact that there were no major differences in personal adjustment between the older and younger aging members studied in either church congregation. As a group, the persons aged 60 and over as well as the younger members between 50 and 59 were enjoying good personal adjustment. This is not necessarily the case with other older persons in this country, as we know from various scientific studies.

CLOSENESS TO THE CHURCH
AND PERSONAL ADJUSTMENT

The opportunities furnished by organized religion for satisfying the needs of older persons are manifold and extend

---

5. Robert M. Gray, *A Study of the Personal Adjustment of the Older Person in the Church,* unpublished Ph.D. dissertation, University of Chicago, 1953. See also Robert M. Gray, "The Personal Adjustment of the Older Person in the Church," *Sociology and Social Research,* 41: 175-180, Jan.-Feb. 1957.

into many areas of life. Even though the church has shared to some extent the prevailing attitudes of our times toward older people, it can safely be said that the church is vitally interested in the older person and has a place for him; the gospel makes no age distinctions between children of God. This is not necessarily the situation in other social institutions where changes in capacity which accompany old age are of prime importance in determining attitudes toward and positions of older persons.

There are other reasons why church membership possibly may be of importance to adjustment in later maturity. One is that the person who has enjoyed an active role in the church program may well have experienced life-long personality development in it. If he has, he will be in a much more favorable position to adjust in old age than the non-member. A further important function of church experience which may benefit personal adjustment in old age is that the individual in the church develops friendships and ties that do not end at retirement but continue to flourish and provide satisfaction. This is an obvious contribution toward the adjustment and happiness of the older church member.

In addition to these factors, there are other phenomena with regard to the church that may be presumed to aid adjustment in old age. It is generally agreed by physicians, psychiatrists, and social scientists that many illnesses, much unhappiness, and thwarted personalities are a result of negative emotions, such as anxiety, worry, apprehension, and fear. These emotions cause spasms of a muscular, nervous, or glandular nature which, when and if continued for any extended length of time, sometimes result in psychosomatic illnesses, frustrations, irritations, and maladjustments. It is further agreed that one of the best ways to overcome these conditions is to replace negative emotions with more positive ones, such as joy, contentment, satisfaction, security, and so on. One way that the church may contribute to this process and at the same time aid in personal adjustment is to provide compensations and satisfactions to release the tensions and anxieties resulting in other areas of life. Finally, the church provides a wholesome environment which is conducive to the development of the

positive emotional tone so necessary to happiness and adjustment in any period of a person's life.

The foregoing observations in conjunction with other findings reported in this book set forth a number of factors common to contemporary church groups which would seem to
indicate the importance of church membership to personal
adjustment in old age. It is possible, however, to project this
study further and to develop information which gives even
more valuable data in our quest to develop information concerning whether or not church membership is important to
adjustment in old age. The adjustment of persons who are
closely affiliated with the church can be compared with that of
members who are not so close to the church.

Our analysis has indicated the importance of church membership to older persons, but we have not developed specific
information concerning the relationship between the degree
or intensity of church membership and personal adjustment.
If it is true, as studies reported in chapters 3 and 4 suggest,
that church membership and associated religious characteristics
tend to aid a person's adjustment during the later years, then
this positive influence should be commensurate with the degree
of integration into the church fellowship or the closeness of
church membership. Obviously it would not be expected that
a person who maintains only loose ties with the church would
receive the same benefits as the member who is close to the
church. A test of this assumption was made by comparing the
personal adjustment of closely affiliated and non-close church
members of the two church groups.

Analysis of the relevant study data disclosed that persons
who were close to the church had, as a group, better personal
adjustment than comparable members not so closely affiliated.
This is added evidence that the church does contribute to good
personal adjustment in old age. Another significant finding
was that only five out of the 296 older church members were
found to have poor personal adjustment.

In sum, we may safely state that our analysis has revealed
that the church plays a positive role in personal adjustment
in old age. An overwhelmingly large majority of our church
membership had "average or better" adjustment, and closely

affiliated members had slightly better personal adjustment than non-close members.

THE OLDER PERSON'S ACTIVITY IN AND ATTITUDE TOWARD THE CHURCH

A final statistical analysis of the study data was carried out to determine if church members increasingly turn to the church in old age when meeting the problem of making the transition to their later years. Because of the many factors that influence a person's behavior with respect to participating in a church, it is difficult to obtain conclusive answers as to whether or not people turn to the church in old age. Therefore the findings concerning this question should be considered circumstantial evidence rather than a firmly demonstrated conclusion.

The data relative to the two church groups disclosed approximately the same findings for both males and females. There were no differences between the younger and older aging men in either church group with respect to church activities and attitude toward religion. The women in both study groups, except for two items, did not differ significantly. Older women tended to read their Bibles and listen to church radio services more frequently than younger female members.

The conclusion, though tentative in nature, is that older persons who are already church members fit right in and have their basic needs met without increasing their activities in and dependence on the church. The findings suggest that it is better for a person to become active in the church in his early years than to turn to the church and religion only upon meeting the problems of old age.

SIX

Contributions of the Church to Adjustment

The relation of the church to successful aging involves a number of factors, both negative and positive.[1] In this chapter and the next attention is turned to a description of some of these factors, together with circumstances which have been found to be of particular relevance specifically with respect to the personal adjustment of older church members.

The analysis is based upon personal observations, a systematic search of the literature, and concrete case materials obtained in personal interviews with 48 persons.[2] They were carefully selected from aging members of the church groups discussed in the previous chapter to represent categories of age, sex, and closeness of church affiliation. The interviews were conducted with as little direction as possible by the interviewer; the average duration of each was about two and one-half hours. Notes were taken during the interview, and a more thorough transcript was made immediately following it.

These interviews are presented in order to convey to the reader more vividly the feelings and attitudes of the older persons' experiences in the church, particularly as they affect

---

1. For an insightful account of the mental health of older persons in this country including a discussion of the role of religion and the church, see Robert N. Butler and Myrna I. Lewis, *Aging and Mental Health: Positive Psychosocial Approaches*, C. V. Mosby Co., 1973.

2. Robert M. Gray, *A Study of the Personal Adjustment of the Older Person in the Church*, unpublished Ph.D. dissertation, University of Chicago, 1953. See also Robert M. Gray, "The Personal Adjustment of the Older Person in the Church," *Sociology and Social Research*, 41: 175-180, Jan.-Feb. 1957.

their personal adjustment.[3] They supplement the statistical materials of the previous chapter and concern specific areas suggested by the conceptual scheme of the Social Science Research Council's Committee on Old Age.[4] Our task here is to present further insights concerning data that have already been objectively reported. We do not intend to evolve an exhaustive classification of the areas in which the church contributes to adjustment or maladjustment; we do intend to signify, by selection and emphasis, those which have been of obvious importance to the adjustment of the persons whose experiences are reported.

These data portray older persons' views of their experiences in the church. They represent personal illustrations of and explanations for the findings previously reported. The values of the church for adjustment are summarized in this chapter, and difficulties which contribute to maladjustment are summarized in chapter 7.

"The opportunities furnished by organized religion for satisfying needs of older people are manifold and extend from the sphere of religion proper to other areas."[5] The following sections demonstrate this truth. They include cases and quotations representative of the study's findings concerning adjustment values of experiences in the church. They indicate that the church indeed can satisfy needs beyond the sphere of religion proper. For the subjects of this study it alleviated anxieties concerning death, provided companionship and an environment for continuing friendships, gave opportunities for participation in a social group in which the older person was welcome, assisted adjustment to the death of loved ones, furnished comfort in times of discouragement and crisis, met spiritual needs by coming to the person no longer able to come to church, and satisfied basic social and psychological needs.

---

3. Further documenting the value of studying and describing the role of the church in maintaining good personal adjustment in later maturity are estimates of the American Psychological Association made in 1971 that at least 3 million (15%) of the older persons in this country have serious mental health problems (Butler and Lewis, *op. cit.*, p. 46).

4. Otto Pollak, *Social Adjustment in Old Age: A Research Report*, Social Science Research Council, 1948, p. 162.

5. *Ibid.*

THE CHURCH ALLEVIATES THE FEAR OF DEATH

By providing comfort and reassurance the church alleviates the individual's anxiety concerning approaching death.[6] The anxiety concerning the approach of death appears to be related to several motives. First of all, the desire to live and to continue living is apparent in most individuals, regardless of age.[7] Although many have a general fear of the death process or of death itself, belief in the hereafter tends to mitigate these fears.[8] It is also true that religious teachings concerning punishments and rewards after death may create a considerable amount of anxiety concerning the after-life. Finally, there may be concern over the fate of dependents who would be left without support. These factors and how the church experience affects them are illustrated in the following excerpts from interview records.

A retired man who was living in his own home described his attitude toward approaching death as follows:

> I'm 76 years of age and realize that I can't live forever. Why I might be gone tomorrow. I hope that when I do go the Lord will be good to me and let death come quickly. I have faith that this will be the case with me. After death I don't know exactly what will happen but I know my soul will go to heaven if I don't do anything wrong between now and then. I've lived a good life and set a good example for my children.

A woman living in a private home expressed her attitude toward death in the following manner:

> While I'm not positive about the resurrection of the body I am certain there is an after-life. As far as hell and damnation are concerned, my conception of God is that he would never con-

---

6. See Butler and Lewis, *op. cit.*, pp. 35-45, for an excellent coverage of the responses of older persons to death and dying as well as a description of common emotional reactions expressed in old age.

7. Pollak, *op. cit.*, p. 161. It is also true, however, that persons beyond 75 years of age are less worried about dying than about becoming a burden to relatives or society through illness, disability or poverty. John E. Anderson, "Placing the Adult Years in Proper Perspective in Development Through the Life Span," in *The Middle Years*, Proceedings of the Sixth Annual Iowa Conference on Gerontology, Iowa City, 1957, p. 6.

8. Dr. Melvin J. Krant, professor at Tufts University Medical School and director of a cancer unit, provides many insights that could be used by clergymen in helping a person die with dignity. "The Organized Care of the Dying Patient," *Hospital Practice*, 7: 101-108, 1972.

demn us — we condemn ourselves and I'm sure that I have not done this as I have tried to live a good Christian life. I like life very well but will not and do not fear death.

A man 80 years of age, who had been retired for quite a few years, was supporting his wife by running a mail-order business. He said he had planned on this job years earlier because "I knew if I didn't work I'd dry up and die." His feelings toward death were expressed as follows:

> I'm not worried about death because I don't expect to die for years to come. I'm in good physical condition. How old do you think I am, young man? Well, I'm 80 and have taken good care of myself all of my life and it's been the church teachings which have aided me to do these things.
>
> I've got a brother in the hospital who has lived the kind of life that I admire, honest, married, church member and kind — but he is dying at only 68. He got to eating a lot and got stout and this worked on his heart and it has gone back on him and he is in an oxygen tent now.
>
> I believe in God and everlasting life but how it will be no one knows. But I do know that I will see my brother again.

A concern for those left behind, even though sure of meeting again in the hereafter, was expressed by a married man as follows:

> Am I worried about death? Certainly not. I don't want to die if that is what you mean, but I am not worried about it other than leaving the wife not well cared for. You see we haven't always had it so good and for about three years there we had a lot of sickness and now we are paying for it, and I wouldn't want to die now and leave all these bills for my wife. Yes, I believe I will meet my wife in the hereafter. If I didn't believe in the hereafter, I wouldn't be going to church. This is my only worry about death; other than that there is nothing to fear, only I hope to live a long time yet.

An elderly man who was quite ill at the time of the interview, and had been so for a long time, explained why he tried to get to church on Sunday:

> The church means everything to me and I am very particular about getting there each Sunday if I can make it. I am ancient and it seems impossible that I am this old. Going to church is the most important thing in my life. With regards to how I feel about death and the hereafter, I would like to live longer but I have no fear of death. I just take it for granted what I've been taught all of my life and what I understand is true and do not

fear when my turn comes. It's hard to say definitely just what will happen — I don't really know, as no one definitely knows, about the hereafter. All we can do is live a good clean life and depend on the Lord and he will take care of you. It's a consolation to me to know this.

The following remarks were made by a woman whose husband had been crippled by arthritis. Like other members in similar circumstances, she indicated how important church membership had been in alleviating fear of impending death:

I have always been active in the church and would have been lost without my church membership. It has many times been all that my husband and I have had to fall back on and that's the way it is now. I have no worry about death. I feel this way as I have been taught all my life that this life is a prelude before death which leads to a new and wonderful life. I hope that I am an over-comer. If not I will not make as much a grade as I want. But I love the Lord and am grateful to him for the sacrifice he made for me and for others whereby all can be saved if they accept him as their Savior.

The explanation of this woman is typical of nearly all persons interviewed in that they expressed a concern for rewards and punishments in the after-life. Apparently she, like the others, finds solace and comfort in her faith in the Savior and in having lived a good Christian life, which traditionally has been regarded by many church members as the way to salvation.

A woman referred to her anxiety concerning the pain and suffering which sometimes accompany death.

I don't worry about death because it will come to all of us sometime and there is a beautiful life after this one. Only thing I don't want to be sick for a long time or suffer or be a nuisance to anyone. These are the only things that bother me because I'm sure of the others.

This woman's fear of experiencing pain and suffering prior to death was mentioned by many others and indicates one area in which the church does not mitigate anxieties related to death to any great extent, at least not for many older people.

An elderly man aged 80 expressed the thought that death will be a beautiful thing for him because he will once again be united with his loved ones who have all previously passed away.

I have no fear of death; it can come any day to me. It's only a change over death to life. I know I am worthy to be resurrected. Christ was the first of all the children of God to be brought up and someday I will do likewise. I thank you, God! I am the last of the family and am looking forward to meeting all my loved ones again. I know we will all be together again.

A similar instance of not fearing death because it would be a time of reunion with loved ones and friends was depicted by a woman who had never married and lived alone with her aged father in a small apartment behind the store she managed.

I don't worry about death. When I die I am going to look for mother and my dear sisters. I am going to see how they feel and act. They were just as good as I, and we are anxious to meet them.

This woman was not able to go to church because of the necessity of keeping her store open on Sundays. She indicated the value of the church in alleviating anxieties regarding death and the hereafter in persons unable to participate in church activities.

I never get to go to church because I have to keep open on Sundays or I would soon be out of business. Although I can't go to church, the church leaders come here to visit me very often and they nearly always give me a lesson. Besides, I learned all about the church before and I still have my church books and prayer. I'm still close to the church and know I will live again after this life.

These cases could be supplemented by others which demonstrate the value of the church in alleviating anxiety concerning death through provision of comfort and reassurance. The illustrative material reveals that the church members' fear of death was diminished through belief in an after-life which they had acquired through the church.

THE CHURCH PROVIDES COMPANIONSHIP AND FRIENDSHIPS

One of many factors which contribute to good personal adjustment is having a number of enduring, intimate, and personal friends. The church offers the individual an opportunity to participate in an atmosphere conducive to finding companionship which will not end at an arbitrary age, as in so many other spheres of life. The church member has many friendships which endure over a period of many years and has the opportunity to continue making new friends.

One of the special benefits of the church in this context is that it generally continues to be a permanent fixture in deteriorating neighborhoods even though most members move away, leaving the older persons behind. The church usually remains behind, becoming ever more important in the lives of the older persons who stay on in their private houses and apartments. The church serves a similar purpose in the high mobility neighborhoods which are becoming more common as millions of Americans move about, keeping pace with technological innovations and subsequent social change.

Laury underscores the plight of the older person left behind in rapidly changing neighborhoods:

> In the United States the problems facing the elderly are compounded by the high mobility of the general population. The older person who stays in a fast changing district finds one day that he has become a stranger in his own neighborhood. He feels lonely, and alienated.[9]

The church provides a special service to these older persons who remain in disrupted neighborhoods as well as for other aging people by providing a permanent anchorage or setting for the continuation of friendship ties with others experiencing much the same type of isolation in modern society. The materials presented here pertain to these friendships and the value of the church in providing a setting for companionship.

The first case is that of a married man 80 years of age who had been retired from his job five years.

> I have belonged to my church since 1900 when I was a young man and moved here from the west side of Chicago. What I like about the church best is the associations. I meet more honest and better people in the church than outside. All of my friends are in the church.

His remarks exemplify an attitude manifested by nearly all of the subjects interviewed. This was an appreciation of the many friendships to be found within the church. A widow remarked:

---

9. G. V. Laury, "Some Reflections on Aging in the United States," *Geriatrics*, 28: 178, May 1, 1973.

The church is wonderful. The thing that helps me is the many friendships which I have developed since I became a member some 30 years ago. I belong to many of the church organizations and have many friends. I haven't been too well because I worked too hard helping my husband before he died, and because of this I don't take a too active part anymore. I still go over and visit my friends as often as possible. This is one thing that is worthwhile for older persons and that is to belong to a church and other organizations where you can meet and enjoy friends.

Maintaining friendships was one of the primary functions of the church for this woman; it was the first thing she mentioned when asked the value of church membership to her.

Another woman who expressed an appreciation for the many fine friends that she had in the church stated that one of the most important functions of the church is to provide a place where a person can go and find good wholesome companionship regardless of how old or young one is. She said:

We have a wonderful group of people at our church and it makes you so happy to go out and meet them during the week. I believe that this association is the most important function of the church in that it provides activities and friendships for everyone, and there are so many lonely oldsters. I wish we could bring them all to church; I know they would be much happier.

Finding help through friendships in the church was the theme of a woman who commented as follows:

I needed help at one time in my life and I did not know what to do. I was given a spiritual vision that God was my Father and that He is ever with me. This gave me much comfort when my husband was so sick in the hospital. When I went over to the church everyone was so nice to me they just welcomed me into all of their activities. I thought at first they were just being kind because my husband was sick but later found that they were so to everyone. I appreciate more than I can say the friendship that I found in the church.

This experience of going to the church in time of trouble and finding there a rich source of friendship was also expressed by another woman.

I would have been lost without my church membership. I have always been active in the church. In fact I was once a missionary. We haven't been to church lately; my husband is too ill. The women are wonderful and I love every one of them. I went there a stranger but they accepted me right away and they invited me into a circle. They all love my husband and I thought it was because of him, but it was because they love me. This made me so happy that I went home and cried for a long time. I am never lonely because I go to all the association meetings and meet all the wonderful women.

A school teacher offered an explanation of the value of the church which is typical of many others:

The best thing in life is to have friends. I don't care who you are or what you do; unless you have many friends and have the opportunity to get out and mix with other people you will never be entirely happy. That is the main reason why so many of your older persons are so unhappy today . . . they don't have any place to go and they do not have anything to do with their spare time. Idleness is the devil's workshop and most of the people spend too much time without doing anything. I think the church is the answer to this problem. I go there and enjoy the friendship of numerous persons who I know live good and appreciate me. We all feel the same way at church. It's too bad that the rest of the people don't have the same experience. I have taught school for years right here in this city and I know that this would be good for the young people as well as the older ones. You've got to have good friends to be happy and you also have to have something to do with your spare time.

A married woman mentioned the value of the many friends that she had in the church. This woman, who had become a member 41 years earlier, stated that any church is a good place to find friends.

The church has been an incentive for me to get ahead. Those who don't belong to a church never seem to get ahead. I think you will have better companions and associates in the church, and from the way conditions are today this is the only place where you ought to meet your friends. Of course there are many fine people who are not church members but by and large people who go to church are generally good people. The friends that I have at church are an essential part of my life and I would not like to be without them.

This statement expresses a common attitude among church members; they desire to cultivate wholesome friendships in a healthy environment and believe that the church is a good place to do this.

An elderly man who had spent 25 or more years working with young boys in the church said he thought that working with the Boy Scouts and cultivating the many friendships had done more than anything else to make his life happy.

The church has brought peace of mind to me and I have learned that there is a God and this has helped me over many of the problems that I have had to meet in life. The thing in the church that has meant most to me is working with the boys and meeting the many wonderful people that it has been my privilege to associate with all of these years. I don't know how my life would have been without this but I do know that I have been ever so happy, and I am certain that my relationships with the boys and the many fine people that I have met while I have been a member of the church have meant more to me than anything that I can think of.

An elderly lady stated that the only people who were ever nice to her any more were her friends in the church.

I don't have any relatives because they have all died and I am alone except for my friends in the church. I love the church and the people there. Most of them are real nice to me. They are the only people that I know who try to be nice to me. Even my landlord does not try to be nice to me and I try to be nice to her. Over at church I meet lots of people. If you don't feel welcome there, it's your own fault. If you smile, others will smile back at you. If you come with a long face, they will act that way back to you and pass you by. I shake hands with everyone, and I won't let them pass me by. It makes us all happy and they won't pass me by. If you belong to a lodge, people are friendly there I suppose, but when you get old, people are not nice to you except in church where we are brothers and sisters.

These illustrative materials are assembled to depict the role of the church in providing a setting for friendships and a place where a person can find companionship in a wholesome environment. These few cases do not encompass all of the instances wherein the 48 church members expressed the value of the church experience in providing friendships, but they are sufficient to illustrate this function of the church.

A related support that is provided by the church is the assurance that a person always has a friend in the Lord. Thus, for thousands of older persons, and particularly those who are lonely, the church provides the comfort of being reassured that someone cares and is always present. Of interest here are the views of Deeken, who believes that when one turns to the church, being lonely oftentimes can be a blessing rather than the serious problem it is for many persons:

... the experience of aloneness need not be a negative experience. On the contrary, the emptiness of feeling alone can open man's heart and make him more perceptive of the presence of God, who likes to speak in silence. Loneliness can be a blessing. The experience of being alone can strip man of his masks and force him to confront his real self. It can deepen his faith and inspire him to seek a more personal relationship with God.

The best way to face the loneliness of old age consists in a more conscious sharing in the exchange of life and love between the three persons of the Blessed Trinity.[10]

In sum, the church most assuredly provides a setting where people can find companionship with friends and with their God; as a result, one needs never be alone.

THE CHURCH WELCOMES OLDER PERSONS INTO ITS ACTIVITIES

Another important function of the church which assuredly contributes to good adjustment is that it provides many types of activities. These give members an opportunity to take part in one or more programs, depending upon personal interests and desires. Furthermore, these activities do not end upon reaching a certain age but continue as long as the person is able and desires to participate. The church makes no unkind distinction between age groups. In it the older person finds an opportunity to work and to be part of a social environment in which he is welcome, as is not necessarily the case in other social institutions.[11] The following excerpts from interviews illustrate the salutary influences of this service of the church.

A married man living with his wife indicated that his church activities took up all of his spare time, for which he was very grateful.

The church has always meant a great deal to me and my family. I was brought up with a strict religious background and I have never fell off from that. I have never placed denomination first; as we raised our family, the children and my wife and I would attend the church closest to our home. I have spent my whole life working in the church, and even now when I am not able

10. Alfons Deeken, "Growing Old—And How to Cope With It," *America*, 124: 317, March 27, 1971.

11. Psychotherapists have long recoognized the importance for self-esteem of the human need to belong and to have recognition and status, which are best provided by primary groups such as those found in the church. See Abraham Maslow, *Motivation and Personality*, Harper and Row, 1970.

to get around too good, I am still active. I've been active as a trustee and ruling elder for some eight years. I don't take a real active part any more like teaching in the Sunday school. I am chairman of benevolences and past president of the Men's Club and am active in the organization of the Men's Council. Throughout my life the church has taken nearly all of my spare time and I know that this has made my life better because so many persons spend their time being idle or doing bad things. I am happy I joined the church because it has given me something to do even now when I am old and can't do much of anything else.

One man said he went to church because he enjoyed the many activities and associations that he found there.

I feel very welcome over at the church and more so than any place that I know of. I get much happiness in going and meeting with all my friends and associates there. Sunday without church would be meaningless. There is a material as well as a spiritual satisfaction in going to the church. We get to take part in many activities and I know of many older persons who don't have any other social life but what they get at the church. I know that I will always enjoy my friends and the activities at the church, and I don't care much what happens on the outside because the church takes very good care of its members. In fact all of our social needs are satisfied by the church and its activity.

A well-to-do woman, devoted to her husband and children, had few outside activities except those which she enjoyed in the church.

I don't get to participate in many social activities in the community, and the reason I don't go too often is that my family takes up all of my time. When I am through caring for them I don't have time for anything else. I do participate in some church activities, and I belong to an association and a church circle which I try to attend regularly. This is the extent of my social life.

A retired man of 76, living only with his wife, expressed his appreciation in being able to go to church for recreation and for something to do with his spare time.

I am hard of hearing and for this reason I have not been a leader over at the church, but I have worked on many church activities. I always go out on Christmas and Thanksgiving to visit the poor people and go over to the old folks club parties all the time. That sure is a good idea giving us something to do. I really appreciate their efforts and am so much more happy there than I would be in a tavern.

A woman expressed deep satisfaction that the church offered such a wide range of activities for young and old alike.

> All of our needs are satisfied in the church, such as friendships, social and mental security. Our daughter was raised in a rough high school and yet all of her friends are church members, and this has given my husband and me so much comfort. We all try to participate in all the church activities and in this way hope to keep our family together and happy.

A man who had been a church member for all of his 75 years mentioned how he felt welcome at church and liked to take part in its activities.

> I go to church every Sunday and every chance I get on other days. They make me feel welcome at church and I make them feel welcome. I like to meet the strangers and to make them feel right at home because I know how much it means to someone to be made felt welcome. . . . In my day I have done a lot of work at the church. I have never been lonesome at the church because I make it my business to talk to people. I'm a good one to mingle with people, but I don't force myself. But I do love to meet people. About the only place I know of to do this is over at the church.

A man who regularly attended church expressed a common feeling among many older members:

> I feel very welcome at the church. There are so many new faces and most are young members. I've always been one to want to meet people at church. I love to participate in the church because I know that I am loved by my brothers and sisters as I love them because we are one big happy family. It's truly wonderful.

A woman who had lived in relative poverty mentioned that she and her husband found satisfaction participating in the church activities where it did not make any difference how rich a person was:

> I don't have anything, and that is why I have to lean so much on the Lord. My church is my staff. We haven't had it so good and my husband has worked hard but never made much and I have had to work much of my life. When we go to church we feel quite comfortable even though neither my husband nor myself are the active type. They work hard to make it nice for us. We enjoy all of the activities and know we are just as welcome as are those members who have done much better. This is just about the only recreation and social life that we get.

These characterizations represent common experiences of

church members who find in the church an opportunity to participate in activities according to their interests, to do worthwhile church work, and to feel that they are loved and wanted by the other members.

THE CHURCH HELPS ONE ADJUST TO BEREAVEMENT

Another important function of the church is to help people adjust to the death of their loved ones. One of the finest books available concerning the art of providing practical ministry and care at this time is edited by Dr. Austin Kutscher and his wife Lillian, who write in their foreword:

> From ministers of many faiths to the bereaved of many faiths come these messages of solace and words of reassurance for support in accepting inevitable facts in life and unchangeable events. There is at the core of every Western religion, whether or not the concept of immortality is espoused, an ineffable spiritual strength that can be transmitted by thoughts inspired by the tenets of a faith. What is so very striking is the fact that each man, while speaking from the altar of his own faith, can offer words of comfort that transcend the boundaries of parochial dogma or ritual.[12]

As the various contributors to the Kutscher text so clearly illustrate, the church provides many services for those who have lost loved ones through death.

A man and wife usually become so thoroughly wedded that they work out a single life pattern during their married life. As a result, a severe crisis oftentimes results when one must adjust to the loss of the other. Havighurst often heard older persons in his research say,

> "I hope when my wife (husband) dies I can go too. Life won't be worthwhile after that." This expresses the fear that a man or woman has, after living 40 or 50 years with a marital partner, of having to face life without the partner.[13]

This is an important problem of old age and one to which the church makes noteworthy contributions. Foremost among

---

12. Austin H. and Lillian G. Kutscher, eds., *Religion and Bereavement,* Health Sciences Publishing Corporation, 1972, p. vii.
13. Robert J. Havighurst, "Old Age—An American Problem," *Journal of Gerontology,* 4: 298-304, Oct. 1949.

these is the love and comfort given to the bereaved church member by church leaders and other members. In addition to this, a certain alleviation of anguish and sadness is experienced by the church member who believes in an after-life; he realizes that death is not the end and has faith that he will be united in the hereafter with his mate. These and other beliefs and feelings tend to make the adjustment to the death of one's spouse easier for the church member. The following materials were selected to emphasize those items which were of obvious importance with respect to the problem of adjusting to the death of one's spouse.

A widow living with her daughter in a two-room apartment described how the church had aided her at the time of her husband's death.

> I have been living with my daughter for the past ten years, ever since my husband passed away. Although I had never been very active in the church, it was such a comfort to me at the time of my loss of my husband. There were several times when I just didn't know if I could stand it all by myself. Without the support of my religious beliefs and the church, I don't think that I would have made it.

Religious experience is valuable in alleviating the sorrow of losing one's mate and is enhanced by the church which has provided lifelong support and encouragement for most members. The church is always there. The older individual naturally turns to it in time of trouble, having done so on many previous occasions. A woman who had become maladjusted at the death of her husband, and who apparently had not yet made a proper adjustment, told how the church had aided her in meeting this problem.

> I tell you I hate to pass on my feelings about how I felt when my husband died because when I think or talk about it I get all broken up inside. My husband was so kind and good with such high morals I find it hard to understand why the Lord took him away from me. [At this point she started to cry and put her face in her hands and kept it there for ten minutes or more. When she finished she went over and picked up a photograph of her husband and started to talk about him and to cry once more. Finally, she gained control of herself, and the interview continued.] I lost control over myself when my husband died, and this is my stumbling block. All through it all it was wonderful to belong to the church. There is no way to measure the loss

but I know the only things that keep me going are my two granddaughters and the hope that I will see my husband again in the hereafter.

A widow declared her appreciation for all the fine men and women in the church who came to her aid when her husband died.

> The church has meant everything to me, and it helps me over everything. It gave so much comfort to me, and I know that the church is the biggest part of our lives. When my boys died, they came over and stayed with me and this helped me a great deal. When my husband died, they came over and stayed all night. It makes me feel good when these men of the Lord come to the house. They don't come too often for me.

These few cases illustrate the value of the church to the member in meeting the problem of loss of spouse. The most frequently mentioned factors generally are the following. First, the church furnishes comfort and reassures the member that death is not the end. Next, comfort and service are given by the members of the church. Especially noteworthy here is appreciation for the visits and reassurance given by church leaders who, in some instances, come in pairs and spend the night after the husband or wife passed away. Nearly all subjects mentioned how much the nearness of their church leader or pastor meant to them at this time and how they appreciated his service. Much emphasis is also given to the comfort and love that always comes from the other members who are in fact brothers and sisters in time of need. Third, the church furnishes them with something constructive to do with time which was previously taken up with the deceased husband or wife. There are other areas in which the church aids the person to meet the problem of the loss of a spouse, but these are the ones most frequently mentioned.

THE CHURCH OFFERS SUPPORT DURING DISCOURAGEMENT AND CRISES

Throughout the ages the church has furnished comfort and reassurance to its members in days of discouragement and at times of crisis. The illustrative materials which follow depict a few of the important ways the church performs this function.

A man who holds a doctor's degree mentioned how prayer often helped him to meet the problems of life.

> The church has helped me many times when I have had no other place to turn. There is always prayer when you are in trouble. I have several times asked them over at the church to pray for me to attain some goal or office, or to help me in time of need. This has helped me so many times, and they especially make an effort to reach out and try to help you as much as they can. I am just as sure of it as I am alive that the church and the teachings have helped me meet obstacles and serious problems during my life.

A married man, afflicted with a severe case of arthritis, disclosed how the church and its teachings had come to his aid and helped him meet his problem.

> I don't know what I would have done without this only comfort. There was the satisfaction of opening my heart to God in prayer. When a person is real sick and suffering so much that he cannot endure it and is in tears because of the pain, the suffering becomes light and others around you feel it more than you do. When the burden is lifted, it is beyond description how wonderful it is to know that God has done this for you.

A business man mentioned that his church connections had helped him meet a financial crisis that nearly ruined him:

> During the depression I lost everything that I had, which amounted to a financial loss of about $40,000. I was completely ruined, and it was only through the comfort that I received from the church that I was able to regain any sense of balance.

Another man told how the Lord had blessed him many times and similarly had been helped over the dark days of the depression:

> Whenever I have been in a bad fix, the Lord has always come to my aid. When I was in such financial trouble during the depression, I asked the Lord to help me and He did. The man who had my mortgage said to me that because I was a good Christian he was going to make it easy for me. I owed $12,000 or more and it was past due, but he called me in and said that he was going to cut down the payments and the interest almost one-half. The Lord had blessed me because I tried to be a good church member and kept close to Him at all times.

A married woman living with her husband in a private home said the church had aided her on many occasions.

> We have always turned to the church in time of trouble and

crisis in our family, and it has never failed to help when all other means have seemed in vain. I'd hate to think what we would do without the church, as there would be a void in our lives without it. I have been healed many times by the Lord and know of many persons who have also been healed and comforted by the Spirit of the Lord. It has helped us through business undertakings and problems of all types. We always meet our difficulties with prayer and always receive an answer.

A married man who had been a member for 40 years indicated that the church helps one over the rough times in life and alleviates tension by preserving hope:

Naturally, a person going to church will meet his problems and crises better than will the non-church person. The member will have a better outlook on life in general. I imagine it would be terrible to be without religion. It gives you peace of mind because it answers a hope for the future. This is America's only hope in this time of crisis — to turn back to faith and religion. Unless we do, we are doomed. It has answered a lot of questions many people fret and stew about because it gives you a hope for a brighter tomorrow.

A single woman, living alone in a small apartment with her father, described her life as one crisis after another with the church being her only source of comfort.

It has not been easy for me to bear the troubles that have been mine since I came to America from Germany so many years ago. I have had to support both my father and myself. My life has been one problem after another, and sometimes I get so blue and unhappy I don't feel like living any more, and then I remember the church and its teachings. Everything that I am and what I am doing is because of the church. I pray as I have been taught in the morning and at night and know that the Lord does watch over me and my father. The church has meant so much in everything.

An elderly lady who had never married and was living alone in a small apartment told how church members always cheered her up when she was in trouble or felt bad.

All I have to do is go there and they cheer me up, and this is so nice since mother is gone and can't aid me. Whenever I have any problems, the brethren from the church come right over and take care of them for me. I'm so thankful to the Lord for the church because it has helped me so many times in my life.

In this case, as in many others, the value of the church stems directly from the aid and comfort that comes from other members, contrary to the frequently reported reliance on church teachings and doctrines alone, in meeting a given problem.

One last case similarly illustrates how the church experience can be a comfort in time of family crisis.

> When my daughter had a ruptured appendix and when my grandchild had pneumonia, we all got down in family prayer to ask the Lord's blessings during our time of trouble. Our prayers were sure answered. The doctor said he had done all he could do for us and to go home and pray because we were in God's hands. It's a wonderful thing that He's blessing us and taking care of us. It has helped us to meet all our troubles. We have had so many troubles I can't remember all of them, but the Lord has helped us in every case.

Such quotations indicate that the church does offer support and encouragement in dark days and during times of crisis. We have found evidence of this in crises such as those resulting from death of loved ones, economic ruin, broken homes, sickness, chronic disability, and in the discouraging days of life when specific problems are too numerous to mention.

THE CHURCH GOES TO MEMBERS IN THEIR TIME OF NEED

A valuable contribution of the church with respect to alleviating the problems of old age is the fact that the minister or church leader and his co-workers will continue to be interested in and come to the aid of the aged person in times of need even though his relatives, friends, and other associates sometimes will not. Though older people generally are victims of neglect in society, the church has a long tradition of ministering to the aged as well as to other members. When a member is unable to go to the church, the church goes to the individual, a process which contributes to the well-being of the older person.

The first case illustrating this concerns a man who is unable to go to church very often because of a physical condition:

> I don't know what I would have done without the church, which has been my only comfort during these days. I used to go often but not of late for obvious reasons. We appreciate it when the church people come here to visit us, and we also get beautiful sermons on the radio which make up somewhat for our not being in church.

A lady who served as a church visitor had this to say:

> The church tries to visit all of the members and especially those who are unable to come out to services. Everyone likes to feel that he is somebody and that he is an interest to someone. We try not to neglect anyone.

A disabled woman disclosed how much she appreciated the visits from these church workers.

> The church visitors come here very regularly. I don't get to go often, and they come to see me. I had a stroke and it was so wonderful to have the members come to visit me. No one came to see me except the church people. I don't care whether they come to see me any more or not, but I do want the church people to come. They are the only ones who really care about me.

An elderly man who didn't get to church every Sunday reported that he found satisfaction in having church members come and visit him. He said:

> I used to go visit the older members when I was younger, and so I know something of what it means to go visiting. I enjoy having them come and teach to me, because no matter how old we get, we can still learn something.

A man, physically unable to get about well, expressed what must be a common feeling among many older persons in the church when he said:

> I have been sick all year and am just now feeling better. I haven't been out of the house since last September. I haven't had many visitors except one or two neighbors and a friend. The church people come regular, and this has meant an awful lot to me. I haven't lived up to the Gospel like I know it, but I appreciate how wonderful the church has been since I became ill.

These cases point out a unique function of the church: it continues to serve even when the member is unable to continue in the church activities. Members appreciate this and are made happier by it.

THE CHURCH SATISFIES
SOCIO-PSYCHOLOGICAL NEEDS

Church activities and the religious experience tend to satisfy such basic social and psychological needs of members as the need to belong, to be valued, and to be understood. The opportunities furnished by organized religion for satisfying needs of older people are manifold and cover a wide area. The church may give the older person a sense of usefulness which has been lost in other spheres of life and thus help him to retain a feeling of self-respect. The church experience, in addition, may alleviate the feelings of loneliness and being unwanted which are so prevalent among older persons. The following excerpts from interviews and those in earlier sections of this chapter illustrate these behavior patterns as they occurred to members in the study group.

A man found in the church an opportunity to serve his less fortunate fellowmen. This gave him much personal satisfaction:

> My greatest happiness comes from going down to skid row and working for the church. We go down and put on non-denominational services for those fellows. After a night there we come away uplifted knowing that we have done good for somebody.

A widow described the importance of her job in the church, which was to visit members who were unable to attend services. She said:

> I am not able to do much of anything anymore because I have lost the sight in one eye, and the vision in the other is not too good. About all I have time for nowadays are my home duties and, of course, visits to the semi-invalids who are on my list who I go to visit often. This is my job, and because I'm old like they are, they love to have me come and visit with them. It's better to have a person your own age come to visit you, and that's why I have so much to do, because I'm about the only older person able to make these visits.

A married woman described her usefulness to the church in the following manner:

> I feel sometimes that I am really useful to the church. I know that I try very hard anyway. I have a class with the children in Primary and have had this job for three years, so I am performing a good service there, don't you believe? Whenever they have a dinner or anything, they always come to me, so I suppose that they appreciate me and that I am of some use to the church.

A man who had been a member all his life told how he found satisfaction for all his needs in the church.

> I have tried to live a good clean life and know that the Lord has blessed me way beyond my worth. I love the church and can testify to you that it is the most important thing in this life.

It satisfies every need, and many times when I could not turn to my friends or even to my immediate family I have found love and kindness in the church. It has made me what I am today. I have worked with the boys for years and this has influenced my life so much. No, I could never be lonely with all my friends in the church and with all the boys who come to see me all the time. You see, if you do something good for a person he never forgets it, and these boys all remember me.

These materials illustrate some of the ways church experience helps to satisfy the need to belong, the need to be valued, and the need for a sense of usefulness which many times has been lost in other domains of life. It also tends to overcome feelings of loneliness which are prevalent among older persons.

Although more will be said in a later chapter about the ways the church can be of service to older persons, it is worthy of mention here that many of the foregoing and other contributions are now being accelerated by new programs to train older persons so that they can assist other persons in the church and community. Because of these programs, older church members are more frequently coming out of retirement to work in a multitude of services, such as senior volunteers, educators, and home visitors. This trend and the opportunity for the church to support it is described by Hougland as follows:

Hundreds of other oldsters would like to serve but do not know how because they have not been prepared. The church, however, is in a position to provide both opportunities of preparing people for ministry as elders and the support structure for this ministry. Indeed this might well be the focus of the church's program of adult education, especially with regards to adults whose children have grown up and left home.[14]

We can expect that this trend will continue to grow in the future so that hundreds of thousands of elderly church members, both on a voluntary and paid basis, will be engaged in personally satisfying activities of helping their neighbors adjust to the difficulties of modern society.

SUMMARY

The interview data presented in this chapter show that the

---

14. Kenneth Hougland, "Liberation From Age-ism: The Ministry of Elders," *The Christian Century,* 91(12): 342, March 27, 1974.

church performs a valuable function in alleviating problems
of old age and contributes to good personal adjustment. They
demonstrate that church experience plays an important role in
the alleviation of anxiety and fear concerning death through
the provision of comfort, reassurance, and belief in an after-
life, which is fostered by the church's teachings.

The church offers the individual an opportunity to participate in an atmosphere that is conducive to finding companionship and to continuing friendships even when such contacts are ended in other spheres. A significant finding is that
the church provides its members with activities and opportunities to participate in a social environment in which the older
person is welcome, which is not necessarily the case in other
community institutions.

These cases also illustrate how the church helps a person
in making an adjustment to the death of one's spouse and to
other crises of life. An aged person's relationship continues in
the church after the time of retirement, physical disability, or
old age, even though associations with friends, co-workers, and
relatives sometimes do not. When he no longer is able to go to
church, the church comes to him. Church experiences help to
satisfy some of the basic social and psychological needs of
members, such as the need to be loved, to belong, and to be
useful. Finally, they also tend to minimize the feelings of
loneliness which are so common among older persons.

The significant conclusion of this chapter is that the
church does perform a valuable function in alleviating problems of the older member. In doing so it contributes to good
personal adjustment in old age.

SEVEN

Problems of the Older Person in the Church

Various writers have described the many problems faced by older persons as they attempt to adjust to circumstances of the later years of life in American society.[1] This adjustment process has contributed to both positive and negative attitudes on the part of both younger and older citizens. Because they so frequently are deep-rooted, it would be expected that many of these attitudes would be carried over into the church. Therefore, even in the church which holds the aged in high esteem, we very likely might find serious differences in attitudes between younger and older members, such as how they differ with respect to their conceptions of the older persons' role in the church. Furthermore, it may be anticipated that the older person would bring with him into the church tensions and anxieties experienced in other spheres of life and would direct some of his hostility toward fellow church members.

One source of possible dissatisfaction is a tendency for the aged person to feel that he is being pushed aside by younger members and that he is no longer wanted in the church. Another source of conflict that may arise is that the older person may conceive of himself as the backbone and strength of the church and feel that the younger member who is pushing

1. R. C. Atchley, *The Social Forces in Later Life: An Introduction to Social Gerontology*, Wadsworth, 1972; Z. S. Blau, *Old Age in a Changing Society*, New Viewpoints, Division of Franklin Watts, 1973; V. Brantl and M. R. Brown, eds., *Readings in Gerontology*, C. V. Mosby Co., 1973; Herman J. Loether, *Problems of Aging*, 2nd ed., Dickenson Publishing Co., 1975, and Bernice L. Neugarten, ed., *Middle Age and Aging*, University of Chicago Press, 1968.

him aside lacks the maturity necessary to provide proper and adequate leadership.

Additional problems may lessen the value of the church experience to the older person. Some may stay away from church, or feel ill at ease if they do come, because they are unable to dress properly. Some may not attend because they are unable to contribute to the church as they have in the past due to the reduced income which is typical of old age.

Others may be dissatisfied with changes that have taken place in the church framework and desire the old ways. Conflict may arise if the younger members feel that the aged are old-fashioned, set in their ways, and as such are blocking progress and change to newer and better things. The elderly may sense and resent these attitudes of the younger members, find it difficult to cooperate with them and consequently stay away from church. Finally, older members may feel that they are being squeezed out of positions in the church by younger members and may not, as a result, feel as secure and close to the church as they would if this were not the case.

In summary, church experience may negatively affect successful aging by a number of conditions. Attention is now turned to case study descriptions of these and of circumstances which have brought them about.

SOME OLDER PERSONS FEEL THEY ARE PUSHED ASIDE BY YOUNGER MEMBERS

The first problem to be considered is the feeling of many older members that they are being pushed aside by younger members in the church. The first example concerns a woman who was trying her best to do well at her church job because they would not, as she said, squeeze her out as long as she was efficient.

> I sometimes feel that I am excess baggage over at the church and know of other older persons who feel the same way. I am surprised how many older people get squeezed out of their positions in the church, and it bothers me to no end. They won't squeeze us out if we are efficient, and I work very hard so that they won't feel that I can't do my job any more.

A male church member points out that this problem is present in his church and the image of the church suffers for it.

> This problem of older persons being pushed out of their jobs in the church is a critical area and much more extensive than is generally believed. A well-run church has a program for both the young and old members. We have this problem in our church where they are so interested in the younger people that they are always pushing us older members aside. Just recently they made us move into the auditorium to make more room for the younger members. I know that this made quite a few of the old timers quite upset. Sometimes the church does not encourage us to come, and the church is even cold and cruel at times.

An elderly man stated that he knew many older persons had been eliminated from jobs in the church and stayed home on that account.

> I know many older persons who have been pushed off their jobs and then have been squeezed out of their positions in the church on account of their age. Not me though, because they treat me nice, and young fellows treat me nice, too. No one has ever made me feel unwanted.

These remarks suggest that some persons either imagine or actually experience the phenomenon of being ejected from their position in the church. Perhaps those who express such experiences are unduly sensitive because of frustrations and rebuffs encountered in other spheres and are projecting their afflictions to the church.

A lady member told how one of her friends had been deeply hurt when he was forced out of his job in the church because of his age:

> This problem of older members getting pushed out of their jobs in the church is one of the problems we have at our church. They are continually saying that we ought to put in the young blood and to get rid of the old. They don't realize that they need old blood in there running things. The elders, for instance, should be the most mature Christians. Some of our people are not mature, and yet they take over the jobs. We should be able to look up at an elder when we need help and get the benefit of his years of experience in the church. A dear friend of mine was hurt because of the way they put him out of his church job, which incidentally was about the only thing he had to take up his time during the day. They changed the by-laws to state that you could not serve more than two years. They make exceptions for the young members but not for the old ones. They were put

out just because they are old. One of them was told that he was an old fogy and this made him feel so bad he resigned.

Other subjects mentioned that the reason this by-law concerning the time of service for elders was changed was not to push the elderly out of their church jobs but to give more persons an opportunity to serve on church councils. These interviews were made just after this by-law had taken effect. It was obvious that the church was not appreciated by many older members who had been in office for many years.

An elderly man who had been a member of the church for 50 years claimed that some members were being neglected at the church and were staying home because of this.

> I am getting older and I have been a member of the church for a long, long time. There have been quite a lot of our older members leave the church on account of they are dissatisfied. They have left the church and will never come again except on Christmas and Easter. The two most important reasons for this trouble is that we get put out of office and because [the pastor] passes up the older ones and mingles with the younger. One man and his wife in my pew don't come because they feel they are neglected. He shakes hands with us older people but we are not respected. All we do is go and listen to the sermons.

This man also remarked that he had contributed financially to that church for years, that it was as much his as anyone else's, and that he could not see why he was not wanted.

A woman told of how her father was affected when he was put out of his church job after having served, according to her, 50 years.

> It's a terrible mistake to squeeze the older persons out of their church jobs. They don't seem to realize how much those jobs mean to them when they get older and can't do much of anything else. My father was an elder since I was two. Just last year they put him out. It just about crushed my father. Though he isn't as active as he used to be, they at least should have given him a less active job. It aged my father quicker and took his last interest. He was retired and his only interest was the church, and when they took that, he had no further interest.

A man told how he had been slighted at the church. He said some of the older members stayed away rather than be treated that way.

> There is more conflict in the church than there used to be. It used to be that the younger people were more obedient and

ready to be led. Today they want to take over and lead the older people. They do this in the church. It shouldn't be so, but I know this is the case. Still they don't stop to think about the older person. They feel that a man of 50 is not capable of holding up his end of it, and I think he is better because he has had experience and is holding firm. You can't stop being a human being when you go to church, and it's that way on the outside. Nature will take its course because people don't stop to think. Sure, some of the older persons are staying home because they feel they have been slighted and don't like the way certain churches are being governed and their little say-so doesn't matter much. They stay away rather than be embarrassed because of the way they have been treated.

A summary description of how some older persons feel when they think the younger members believe them to be "old fogies" and are pushing them aside is taken from the remarks of an elderly woman who concluded:

One thing I would like to say is that no matter what anybody says or does, they ought to remember that the older a person is, the more religion they have in them. I know an old lady who died of a broken heart and no one cared for her. The church doesn't care for its old people like they used to. We need a home here. They do cater an awful lot to the young to keep them in the church, but they look on us as old fogies who are useless. The old persons are pushed aside, as they have lived their lives and are no longer useful. They keep after the young because they have money, and they don't want them to mix with the other denominations. I think old people will keep coming out as long as they are able to, no matter what they do at the church. It's to be expected that older people are better and more religious. Younger people need more life. They just ignore the old people and cater to the young people. They know we won't leave the church, so they give all the attention to the younger members.

This lady had lived her whole life in the church and now felt that she was being treated discourteously to make room for younger members.

From the foregoing statements it is evident that many older persons in the church either are being neglected in favor of the younger members or imagine that they are. Others report being dismissed from jobs, which apparently has an unhealthy effect on older members, causes embarrassment, and "crushes" the individual. Whatever the causes, real or fanciful, it is evident that some aging members have these experiences, and it appears that the condition is not favorable to good adjustment in old age.

SOME OLDER MEMBERS STAY AWAY BECAUSE THEY ARE UNABLE TO CONTRIBUTE FINANCIALLY

Another factor that may tend to keep the aged from attending and feeling secure in church is their inability to continue to contribute to it financially. A large proportion of older people have had to adjust to reduced incomes; many cannot afford to contribute as freely as was once possible.

A lady related that she would make every sacrifice to contribute to her church and that if she were unable to do this, she would not attend:

> Yes, if I was not able to contribute to the church, it would bother me so that I wouldn't feel right if I went to attend. Although I don't account according to Hoyle, I have no use for members who don't contribute to the church. I'd do it if I had to cut my leg off or go without everything to pay it.

This member, in addition to pointing out that she would not attend if she were unable to contribute financially, reveals an attitude toward persons who are unable to contribute that may well be a source of difficulty. It is very likely that such views are shared by others and felt keenly by those unable to pay.

A man who said that even though he wouldn't stay away from church if he couldn't contribute, he knew the importance of money in the church commented:

> I wouldn't stay away from church under any circumstances, including not being able to pay my pledge. I do know that they value the attendance of the old people by the amount of money they donate. I've been around long enough to know that they do ease the poor ones out.

Another lady said that she knew some old people who stayed away because they didn't have funds to give to the church.

> No, I wouldn't stay away, I've given so much all my life, but I would be embarrassed if I couldn't. There are a lot of people who stay away, even though they shouldn't, for this reason. They use this as an excuse to stay away.

It is significant to note that even though this lady believed it wrong to stay home because of lack of funds, she would be embarrassed if she were not able to give to the church.

A retired man said that he would stay home and gave a typical reason why he would do so.

> You know I gave my first $25 to the church, but I would stay home if I couldn't pay up now. I would because they don't pay any attention to those who don't pay.

A widow 65 years of age told how she had stopped going to church because of money matters.

> Money shouldn't matter in the church, but it does. I stayed home because I was offended because they preached on how stingy we were with God. They don't know if we are or not. We might be starving, and they would never know. I give all I can, which is different than when my husband was alive. Inflation or not, I don't give any more. I just felt so bad when I couldn't give that I felt I ought not to go so much until I was able to pay again.

Another statement came from a married woman:

> I've seen certain people forgotten and overlooked in the church. It's like politics — those with money get attention and those without do not. In church people are just like they are any place else; there are always those who think they are better because they have more money. We get $43 each week after taxes and have to work hard for that. We can't do much with that. We can't contribute to buildings and all the other things. It makes us feel real bad, but we won't quit the church because the Lord knows our circumstances, and He knows our situation and is our judge. But you must realize by now that your prestige in the church depends on how much money you have. I've got letters in my house right now asking me to contribute to the church. I just am not able to do this and don't know what to do about it. I don't believe in that stuff, but it doesn't change my mind about the Gospel.

These statements indicate that being unable to contribute sometimes causes older persons to stay away from the church. In other cases the members continue to participate but experience dissatisfactions with the church because of their own financial condition. The effects of their problem are thus compounded; older persons already have a difficult time adjusting to a reduced income in other areas of life.

We may conclude that lack of funds sometimes does cause persons to stay away from the church, even though the gospel through the ages has made no distinction between the rich and the poor.

SOME OLDER MEMBERS STAY AWAY BECAUSE THEY ARE UNABLE TO DRESS WELL

Coincidental with the many other problem areas of old age is the inability of many older persons to dress as well as they did when they were younger. Many times this is the result of reduced income; other times it may be due to physical inability, general indifference, or other reasons. Regardless of the cause, it is possible that this inability to dress well plays an important role in keeping older people away from the church. This is illustrated by the following cases.

A married man who was well dressed when interviewed charged that some churches are to blame for the problem:

> Some churches don't encourage us to come if we are not dressed well. If we do come, we won't be welcome. It isn't like it should be or like it used to be. I remember out in Kansas when the old Civil War veterans with long beards were welcomed and they slept out in the open and came to church plenty dirty. I am against relegating old persons to oblivion. A poorly dressed person is given the cold shoulder at church by the members. It's a human tendency, and it's bad but very widespread.

From these remarks we gather that this situation may not be uncommon, for this man, having been a professional organist, had spent a lifetime visiting various churches. It is significant that he stated that the poorly dressed person is given the cold shoulder by other members. Another older member stated directly that he himself had no use for those who did not dress well:

> Put this down for me. Some have means to do it but are in a savings rut and tight. If they would appear more tidy, the reaction wouldn't be to have them stay home. We leave them alone, and they are overlooked if they are sloppy and dirty at church, and they ought to be.

One man said this about some of his friends:

> Do older people ever stay home from church because they can't dress as well as they did when they were younger? Yes, I know that they do because I know of some people in this church who stay at home because they can't dress so well.

A woman stated that she thought the younger generation put too much stress on clothes and sometimes hurt the older ones who were not able to dress as well.

It's terrible how the younger generation only think of clothes. And when the older person forgets and begins to slip all over, it shows in his dress first of all. The young people just think of clothes and hurt many of these older persons by just snubbing them. It's a real shame, too.

These few remarks selected from the interview materials illustrate the idea that some older persons stay away from church because they do not dress as well as they did when they were younger.

SOME OF THE AGING STAY AWAY FOR OTHER REASONS

In addition to the foregoing factors were other items which accounted for older persons' staying away from church. The illustrations presented in this section were secured in answer to a question asking why besides the reasons already given older people tend to stay away from the church.

(1) *Some feel neglected or slighted for reasons besides those mentioned earlier.* The first case is that of an older man who disclosed that some stay away because they believe that they are not appreciated.

I know of some older members who are sensitive and think they are not noticed and appreciated. Because of this, they are not satisfied today. I know how this is, because I've been this way all of my life, but it isn't good enough. These people think they are doing as well as they can but are not appreciated, so they stay home.

A similar statement came from a married woman. She said:

For one thing, older persons stay away because they have lost vision and interest. Also they feel neglected. They are not really, but they feel that they are neglected, and because of this some stay away.

A final statement comes from a woman member who says that many oldsters stay away because they have been disregarded.

Many stay home because they have been slighted and don't like the way certain churches are being governed, and their little say-so doesn't matter much, and they stay away rather than be embarrassed because of the way they have been treated.

These few cases might be supplemented by others from interview records. They are sufficient to make it clear that at least some older persons stay away from the church because they feel they have been neglected or slighted.

(2) *Many older people are kept away from church because of transportation problems.* The following excerpts from the case materials illustrate this factor. A widower living with his sister related the following reason why he felt some oldsters were staying home from church.

> I suppose it is quite a chore for a lot of older people to get ready and to come to church. Most of them live a long ways away from the church and can't get transportation. I know several that way. It's a hard job to get to the church.

A similar instance of staying away because of lack of transportation is depicted by a woman member.

> One of the most important reasons why old persons stay away from church and other activities is because they do not have adequate transportation. They usually do not drive their own automobiles and are seldom able to ride the street cars and buses.

These cases point out that the lack of transportation does contribute to keeping the aging away from church in many instances.

It was indicated earlier that inability to contribute financially to the church because of reduced income kept many older persons from attending. A closely related item is that many older persons are unable to pay the transportation charges without disrupting their budgets. While this may appear trivial to the average person who has not experienced the loss of income, it nevertheless is a real problem for numerous older persons, as the following materials demonstrate. A widow living alone related the following:

> Many older people stop going to church because it is hard to get there and especially when the weather is bad and rough. Another reason is that it costs 30 cents, and I have to figure these 30 cents, and I stay home on account of this many times. Because of this I am going to change to a church which is on the corner.

Other persons reported comparable experiences. An elderly woman living just a short distance from the church said:

> Both my husband and myself have a hard time getting out to church because of difficulty in getting there. Although we seldom miss, we find that it is quite expensive in making the round trip. We appreciate it when we get a ride with other members.

A final case is that of an elderly member who spoke of the expense involved in getting to church.

> One does everything he can to go to church if he is close, but 34 cents is too much for going on the car. When it was five cents it wasn't so bad, but it costs too much now. I've tried to walk it, but I get so tired that I just can't do that very often.

Here was a man of 80 years trying to walk ten blocks or more to church because he did not have 34 cents to pay his way on the streetcar. This case, which most likely is typical of many, exemplifies the pitiful condition wherein reduced incomes affect church attendance in old age.[2]

(3) *An increase in the extent and severity of physical illnesses is a common experience in later life. It is another reason why older persons stay away from the church.* A man living with his sister spoke as follows:

> I used to go often but not of late for various reasons, the most important reason being my physical condition. We get our sermons mostly from the radio.

A woman told how the bad weather affected her so that she could not attend regularly.

> It is hard for me to go when it is cold or when I get my feet wet, so I have to stay home on many occasions.

An ardent member told how his poor health often kept him from going to church:

> I love to go to church, but sometimes I just can't make it because

---

2. That lack of transportation is a major problem for older persons in this country has been soundly documented in the literature. For example, see N. Ashford and F. Holloway, "Transportation Patterns of Older People in Six Urban Centers," *Gerontologist*, 12: 43-47, 1972; W. G. Bell and W. T. Olsen, *Public Transportation and the Elderly in Florida*, Research Report I, Florida State Univ., 1971; F. M. Carp, "Mobility Among Members of an Established Retirement Community," *Gerontologist*, 12: 48-56, 1972; J. Markovitz, "Transportation Needs of the Elderly," *Traffic Quarterly*, 25: 237-253, 1971; L. S. Pignataro and E. J. Cantilli, "Transportation and the Aging," *Traffic Engineering*, 41: 42-46, 1971.

of my poor health. When I am able I never miss, but sometimes I can't help myself and have to miss.

A woman member said:

I get sick if I go out too much and I stay home because of this quite often. There must be many old ones who just can't come out physically.

These few remarks illustrate clearly that poor health and physical conditions keep many older members from attending church regularly, as would be expected.

The illustrative interview materials in this section have uncovered several factors besides those previously discussed which account for many older members' staying away from the church. First, it was disclosed that many stay away from the church because they feel neglected or slighted by the other members when they do come. Further, it was found that lack of transportation plays an important role in keeping many elderly people from church. Another item closely related to the lack of transportation is the high cost of transportation which many are unable to pay because of reduced income. Finally, it was disclosed that chronic conditions of disability and infirmity play a major role in keeping many older members from attending regularly.

MANY OLDER MEMBERS ARE DISSATISFIED WITH CHANGES IN THE CHURCH

An important adjustment problem of many older people observed by specialists is an inability to adjust to changed conditions. In agreement with these observations, it was found that many older persons were discontent with changes that had taken place in the church and that they longed for the old ways, which they believed were better. The first case is an elderly man who spoke as follows:

Frankly, the church is not as good as it used to be. There are too many people with new ideas that are not good for the church.

A married woman said:

I have a hard time slipping into the women's activities because they have odd ideas. Although my interests have always been in the choir and Sunday school, it isn't the same anymore. The choir is best, but the other organizations are trying to change too fast. It is very different than when my dad was alive. People don't realize what they are doing, or else they don't pay attention.

Another woman expressed a common feeling among many older persons in the following statement:

I don't mind the new ideas they bring into the church if they are good, but for the most part they are not and they only lead to confusion for all concerned. The old methods are objective, and there is no sense in changing.

One man declared that he stayed home because things are not like they used to be in the church.

The younger people are too smart for one thing. They know it all. If you can't make them change their minds, they run wild with new ideas. The kids in church don't have sense to speak to you. They ruin our church. We never allowed all this when I was younger. That is a house of God, and it ought to be like it used to be a long time ago. Many of us stay home now because it isn't.

Whether or not this member actually experiences such behavior or is merely projecting his own shortcomings to the church is not discernible. However, this exemplifies an inability to adjust to change and manifests itself in his being so disturbed that he would rather stay at home.

Another lady stated that the church was getting too complex:

The church is getting too complicated today. I'd like to go back to the old ways. The Gospel and the church are okay, but there are too many complications today.

One older lady summed it all up:

The old way is the best way.

From these cases we see that many of the elderly are displeased with changes that have taken place in the church. This has resulted in negative attitudes on the part of older persons, which range from general dissatisfactions to discontinued attendance. It is evident that some of the aging lack the ability to adjust to changed conditions in the church and, as a result, are quite dissatisfied with present conditions.

CONFLICT OFTEN EXISTS REGARDING THE ROLE
OF THE OLDER PERSON IN THE CHURCH

The final factor which was found to influence attitudes of the older members who were interviewed was a conflict which exists between the younger and older members regarding the role of the older person in the church. The following cases, in addition to those in the first section, illustrate this behavior.

An elderly lady did not voice her opinions on vital matters at the church because she felt younger members did not care for her opinions.

> I often keep quiet when they discuss things over at the church because the younger ones don't have much respect for we older ones' opinions. They think we are old fogies and has-beens.

Another woman voiced somewhat the same view when she said:

> They call us old crabs whenever we try to say anything about the way things ought to be at the church.

Still another woman spoke as follows:

> Yes, some are put out just because they are old. One of the things they told them was that they were old fogies and they railroaded the young ones in office. Because they said the old ones were old fogies, this made them feel bad so they resigned.

These remarks reveal something concerning the attitude of older members with respect to their relations with younger members in the church. Here we see some older members refusing to participate in church activities while others quit the church altogether because of the attitudes of younger members.

Generally the older members feel that there is a definite place for them in the church, as is expressed by an older man:

> I think old people can do much work in the church. There is a place for them. Some firms employ older persons and get along well with them, and these persons are good for years. For instance, Toscanini is 82 and his conducting is superb. He is a master of music and has the most beautiful interpretation possible. This idea that younger people should replace older ones is all wrong.

Other older members stated that they believed that younger members were important in the church but that they should always be under the supervision and direction of older members who have more experience and knowledge and are in essence the backbone and strength of the church. A simple pertinent statement came from a lady member when she said:

> We oldsters ought to be present to watch over the discussion of the younger members who lack wisdom and experience.

Another woman believed some of the younger people would like to take over, but the older people were more qualified for most positions in the church.

> Older men have more power and respect in the church and any place else, but the younger men are always trying to push them aside. The younger people push too much and try to dominate everything. Old ones are not too anxious like the younger people. They take the bull by the horns and push on. People want young people and young ideas, but older ones are better in nearly all positions in the church.

A man who believed the younger members could neither do a good job nor were living as they should spoke as follows:

> They are not older people. I'm one, and we are still young. I don't go to shows on Sunday and other things like that. We used to study our Bible on Sunday afternoons. We were never allowed to go to dances and shows on Sunday. My dad always said this was a day set by the Lord, and we observed it. We were good humble people in those days. That's what's wrong with people today. They don't care about the church, but they want to take over and push us good Christians aside, and they couldn't do a good job if they did take over.

This man brought out one significant difference between the younger and older members which probably is responsible for their conflict as much as anything else: young people today have been brought up in a much different society from that in which the older members lived in their youth. Along with the shift from a rural to an urban type of living has come a similar shift from sacred to secular patterns of life. Younger people today generally do not experience the same need for Sunday observance, respecting the Sabbath, and church-going as did their elders, who went to church as a family and seldom missed. This, of course, could be elaborated upon, but it suffices here to suggest that this is one source of the conflict between the younger and older members.

A final statement, given by a woman, reflects the feeling common among the elderly that there is a place for the younger person as long as the leadership is supplied mainly by older members.

> The young ones should do many jobs in the church. Older people can do things well, but young ones bring in new ideas. Lots of times I thought, why do they give the older people jobs when the younger people could do it? They shouldn't take over altogether because the old have more wisdom and knowledge. Ever since I was in the church the older persons have held all the important jobs, and that is the best way.

These statements indicate the older members in the church sometimes experience dissatisfaction because they sense that younger members believe them to be "old fogies" or "has-beens" and are trying to take over their jobs. The aged members not only resent this intrusion of young people into what they believe is their special sphere, but they also believe that they are capable of furnishing the basic leadership in the church. They believe that, because they are mature and have experience and knowledge, it is only right that they should supply the leadership necessary to conduct the affairs of the church. The quotations have shown that these older persons are very sensitive about this and have in some instances become so dissatisfied with the attitudes of younger members toward them that they have kept out of church activities and sometimes quit the church altogether. This is another important area in which older people experience dissatisfaction in the church.

SUMMARY OF PROBLEMS IN CHURCH

The cases presented have shown that the circumstances which contribute to the dissatisfaction often experienced by older persons in the church are exceedingly varied. They have shown that older persons often experience dissatisfactions in many areas in the church and that this, together with certain other factors incidental to old age, is responsible for their not being regular church attenders.

We have seen that many of the aged feel that they are being neglected in favor of the younger members. Some feel pushed out of church jobs because of their age. Others report dissatisfactions and embarrassment because they are unable to contribute financially to the church as a result of reduced incomes typical in old age. Some older persons are discontented and stay away from the church because they cannot afford to dress properly. Others say they stay away from the church, reflecting general feelings of unhappiness, because no matter how hard they try, they are not appreciated by the younger members. Another reason given for staying home is the lack of suitable transportation. Most find it too cumbersome to ride on public conveyances and either do not own an automobile or do not drive. Some, in addition, cannot afford to pay the fare when they do choose to use public transportation. Even 30 cents each way puts a serious crimp in budgets already skimpy due to inflation. Some also miss going to church because of physical illness. According to the interview materials, many old people are dissatisfied with changes that have taken place in the church and are unhappy with things as they are at the present time. Finally, older persons sometimes experience dissatisfactions because they believe younger members imagine them to be "old fogies" and "has-beens" who are trying to take over their jobs in the church. The aged not only resent this, but many feel that they, because of their wisdom and experience, should supply the leadership for the church. This conflict has been so severe that, in at least a few cases, members have quit participating in certain church activities, and others stopped attending church entirely.

The significant conclusion which develops is that many aging members are not getting all they possibly could from the church because they experience dissatisfactions in their relationships with the younger members and because of other factors stemming from old age.

While it was not a major concern of the study reported here, it should be pointed out that the church experience in general and religion specifically sometimes contribute to the anxieties and worries of people in such ways as placing emphasis on the sinfulness of man and on other human weaknesses. Nelson documents this point when he says: "It is easy to see how a soul damaged by sin can be subject to mental breakdown and disease."[3] Leming, in pursuing this issue by surveying

---

3. Marion Nelson, *Why Christians Crack Up,* Moody Press, 1967.

the social-psychological literature dealing with death,[4] found three studies that demonstrated a significant relationship between religiosity and death-fear.[5] On the other hand, he found ten other studies which indicate that such factors as religious commitment, religious orthodoxy, religious devotionalism, and belief in an after-life were significantly related to the reduction of fear and anxiety concerning death.[6] The study reported in this chapter, along with numerous others in the literature, soundly documents the fact that the religious experience can have negative as well as positive influences on both younger and older persons. The interview data presented above are illustrative of some of these pervasive influences.

CONCLUSION

The data summarized in chapters 5, 6, and 7 are based primarily upon experiences of older members in two large, city churches. The conclusions are not limited to them, however, for many of those interviewed told about friends' experiences in other churches. In addition, every American church shares some characteristics with others. The discussion dealt

---

4. Michael R. Leming, *The Relationship Between Religiosity and the Fear of Death,* unpublished Ph.D. dissertation, University of Utah, 1975.

5. See Herman Feifel, "Older Persons Look at Death," *Geriatrics,* 11: 127-130, 1956; Marcelle Chenard, "Traditional Christian Beliefs and Attitudes Toward Death and Dying," *Dissertation Abstracts,* 33 (2-A): 8160, 1972; and W. A. Faunce and R. L. Fulton, "The Sociology of Death: A Neglected Area of Research," *Social Forces,* 36: 205-209, 1958.

6. A. Berman and J. Mays, "Relationship Between Death Anxiety, Belief in Afterlife, and Focus of Control," *Journal of Consulting Psychology,* 41: 318, 1973; Thornton Hooper and Bernard Spilka, "Some Meanings and Correlates òf Future Time and Death Among College Students," *Omega,* 1: 49-56, 1970; D. Martin and L. S. Wrightsman, Jr., "Religion and Fears About Death: A Critical Review of Research," *Religious Education,* 59: 174-6, 1964; Arlene B. Burros, "Fear of Death and Attitudes Toward Death as a Function of Religion," *Dissertation Abstracts,* 32 (6-B): 3630, 1972; D. Templer, "Death Anxiety in Religiously Very Involved Persons," *Psychological Reports,* 31: 361-362, 1972; David Lester, "Religious Behavior and the Fear of Death," *Omega,* 1: 181-188, 1970; Michael Osarchuk and Sherman J. Tatz, "Effect of Induced Fear of Death on Belief in Afterlife," *Journal of Personality and Social Psychology,* 27: 256-260, 1973; Herman Feifel and A. B. Branscom, "Who's Afraid of Death," *Journal of Abnormal Psychology,* 81: 282-288, 1973; and Ijaz Haider, "Attitudes Toward Death of Psychiatric Patients," *International Journal of Neuropsychiatry,* 3: 10-14, 1967.

only with certain selected topics. Numerous additional adjust-ment values were suggested, and more problem experiences were intimated in the interviews but are not emphasized in this report because they were not systematically analyzed in the research project upon which it is based. As a sociological study, emphasis was placed upon inter-personal relationships and socio-psychological problems and their impact upon the per-sonal and social adjustment of the older person. Theological doctrine was not stressed in the analysis.

Among additional experiences in the church which pro-mote personal adjustment are the assistance the church often gives in the midst of personal problems of health, disability, economic difficulties, and social needs. The welcoming of all people into the church often helps to integrate older and younger persons into a common fellowship like that of an extended family which includes people of all ages. When the aging are treated as individuals who are a part of this larger fellowship, and not categorically as *old* people, the morale of older members is greatly built up. Since the church is known to be a source of help in time of trouble and has been used that way in earlier crisis experiences of life, it often is called upon when emergencies arise in old age. This may be labeled by the skeptic as "ambulance service," but ambulances indeed are needed for people who are suffering from wounds inflicted by a world filled with problems. Churches that have programs of the kinds referred to in the next chapter to meet specific needs of the aged do a great deal to promote the adjustment of members and others who come under their influence.

Peripheral findings from this and the other studies re-ported in this book indicate that older persons have many additional problems in their relations with the church. Al-though these studies were not theologically oriented, it is apparent from their findings that theological beliefs often fall short of the ideal held for them by the church. Uncertainty about the resurrection, nagging doubts about the nature of the future life, the belief that heaven is solely a reward for doing good, living a clean life, or "making a grade," misquotations of the Bible which distort its teachings, equating financial contributions and church attendance with godliness, and the idea that belief in an after-life or a lack of fear of death is equivalent to faith in God and assures salvation seem to be implicit in certain of the interviews.

The problems of adjusting in the church to the changing ideas of right and wrong as society changes and to social and cultural modifications which are a basis for generational conflict were not explored as thoroughly as they could be in future studies. The way in which physical health is related to life-habits, such as over-eating, has implications for the church and the practical ethics it teaches. The preference of a social club over the church because of different attitudes of members toward clothing, as well as unmet problems of transportation and other material needs, were evident in some cases. A major problem implied for church leadership is how to keep the older members interested in the church with a continuing vision of their place of service and fellowship in it.

If the problems of older people in the church, the adjustment values they do experience, and those that could be provided in church for them are kept clearly in mind by church leaders, the church will be able to do far more for them than if it simply continues its traditional program with no special thought given to the peculiar needs of the various sub-groups represented within the congregation and the community. The suggestions in the following three chapters are not related item by item to the problems and adjustment values which have been indicated by these case studies. Their overall message is that the church and the clergy should use that which is wholesome to best advantage and at the same time they should try to overcome the problems often met by older people in the church. This implies simultaneous use of older persons in the church program, with the result, among others, that their personal adjustment will be enhanced as they are accepted by others and by themselves. Equally important is that everyone must learn that older persons have a useful role to play in the work of God through His church.

EIGHT

What the Church Can Do for Older People

Of all the voluntary institutions in the typical American community, the church is the one in which older people are most apt to participate and to hold membership. They are not expected to retire from it in the later years.

Today the church ministers to the physical, social, and economic as well as the spiritual needs of people because it recognizes that all areas of life are intimately interrelated and religious concerns cannot be isolated from other concerns. One would expect the church's ministry to emphasize primarily spiritual needs of senior citizens, yet most official publications of major Protestant denominations reflect the church's stress on social, economic, health, and mental hygiene needs. A "social-service orientation" is more pronounced than the "personal religious-experience orientation" if the amount of attention given a topic in published materials is an adequate index of the emphasis placed on that topic in actual affairs.[1] Regardless of the chief focus of its attention, however, the church increasingly shoulders a specific responsibility of serving the aging population.

The Judeo-Christian theological orientation that views all of life as sacred makes a church ministry to educational, housing, social service, mental health, and other needs a "spiritual" service whenever sacred attitudes and motivations are stressed and a conscious attempt is made to keep goals properly directed. In other words, we believe that transforming a church

---

1. Leonard Z. Breen and Carol Trumpe, "Religious Groups and Conceptions of Aging," Abstract of Paper at the 14th Annual Meeting of the Gerontological Society, *Journal of Gerontology*, 16:400, Oct. 1961.

into a social agency would constitute a form of goal displacement by which its secondary or derivative functions displace its primary task. The consequences of faith commitments and means for putting them into practice must not become the exclusive ends of the church.

As we consider the role of the church in relation to older people, we must realize, of course, that every church is unique. No two churches are identical in their membership composition by age, race, social class, occupation, and other characteristics. They differ in social and cultural traditions, environmental settings, and administrative organization as it actually functions in details of their work. Some churches are in the country, others in the city, and still others in suburban areas; some are large while others are very small; some have a large number of well-educated lay leaders while others have none; some have many older people in the church and the surrounding community, while others have very few. Because of these and other variations, the suggestions that follow do not apply to all churches with equal force. What would work well in one church might be a complete failure in another. Hence there is a need for careful study of proposed programs by those who will lead, take part in, or be affected by them.

The suggestions in this chapter are examples of activities by the church on behalf of older people, and chapter 9 suggests things older people can do in and for the church. The overlap between these will be obvious to the careful reader; in actual practice in the local church no sharp distinction can be drawn between what the church can do for older people and what older people can do for the church. As the church helps older people, e.g., in a social or a recreational program, it will at the same time need help from older people for leadership as well as for carrying out the routine functions that are necessary.

Not all of the suggestions given come directly out of empirical studies; many are the products of personal observations of church programs and systematic study of current literature, of which only examples can be mentioned in the footnotes.[2] The suggestions are prudent, practical, and con-

2. Valuable "how to do it" pamphlets to help churches and church groups face the problems and needs of older people have been produced by agencies

sistent with current social science knowledge, but no finality is intended by this listing. Rather, as we indicate in Appendix II, some need additional testing and evaluation, and new means for meeting needs inevitably will emerge from human creativity in the future.

THE PROGRAM PLANNING PROCESS

The general principles of planning church programs with and for older adults are basically the same as for other ministries. Basic to all is a clear understanding of the mission of the church, including its basic purpose and goals. In many churches this foundation for activities and programs is implicit rather than one that has been developed explicitly and rationally. It is very easy to get side-tracked into lengthy theological and philosophical discussions of the goals for mission, exhausting energy and time without ever providing any services, so it it is not always wise to make this topic a primary focus of direct attention.

Although program planning can be done by an individual alone, it usually is far better to have a committee or task force, including older persons, to aid in the planning process. A survey to identify needs of older persons in the congregation and community is basic. Leaders in community social service agencies can be very helpful, and even more helpful will be the older persons themselves. What are their needs? What do *they* think the church ought to do for them, their friends, and their neighbors? What resources (people, facilities, financial support, materials, leadership, etc.) are available or can be obtained? How can older persons themselves help to meet the need? Do other groups within the congregation desire or need a service project? What community programs and resources are already helping to meet the need or could be available tools in the development of the church's own program?[3]

---

of most major denominational bodies. References in footnotes below and especially in Appendix III will also be helpful.

3. For a more detailed description of where to find such resources, see David O. Moberg, "Discovering and Using Secondary Sources for Effective Program Planning and Prioritizing," *Program Bulletin,* No. 3, National Interfaith Coalition on Aging, May 5, 1975 (available for 10¢ plus stamped return envelope from NICA, 298 S. Hull St., Athens, Georgia 30601).

Having made an analysis of the need and resources available, a specific program may then be planned and implemented, always with flexibility to change its details as a result of experience. Orientation and training of volunteer workers may be a necessary part of the preparation, as is publicity to inform people of the availability of the services and to relate them appropriately to other community resources.

By having clear goals and anticipated outcomes of the new programs, it will be possible to evaluate whether or not it is effective. Evaluation provides feedback to leaders on the basis of which they can review and assess the consequences and adapt the program to be more effective in the future.[4]

THE CHURCH CAN MEET SPIRITUAL NEEDS

A primary task of the church is to help satisfy people's spiritual needs. Some of these needs relate clearly to social and cultural forces which aggravate the problems of aging persons, as noted particularly in chapter 2 above. The church's spiritual ministries should help to overcome the ageism and gerontophobia which are so widespread in our society. The spiritual ills of feeling useless, lonely, and rejected, experiencing inner emptiness and boredom, and fearing the passage of time are aggravated among older people.[5] As a result, they suffer a heavy toll of "spiritual fatigue."[6] Spiritual problems are at the

4. This section is based in part on chapter 2, "How Does A Congregation Begin A Ministry with the Aging?" in Donald F. Clingan, *Aging Persons in the Community of Faith,* Institute on Religion and Aging, 1100 W. 42nd St., Indianapolis, Indiana 46208, Sep. 1975 ($1.00), and Synagogue Council of America Project on Aging, *That Thy Days May Be Long in the Good Land: A Guide to Aging Programs for Synagogues,* Institute for Jewish Policy Planning and Research, 1776 Massachusetts Ave., N.W., Washington, D.C. 20036 ($1.50). Many helpful suggestions for the planning process, including the Christian theological basis for social involvement and a summary of evaluation procedures, can be found in David O. Moberg, *Inasmuch: Christian Social Responsibility in the Twentieth Century,* Wm. B. Eerdmans Publishing Co., 1965 ($2.45).

5. Abraham J. Heschel, "The Older Person and the Family in the Perspective of Jewish Tradition," paper presented at White House Conference on Aging, Washington, D.C., 1961.

6. A. Köberle, "Seelische Anfechtungen im Alter als Aufgabe der Seelsorge," *Zeitschrift für Gerontologie,* 2(1): 58-60, 1969.

center of many of the personal burdens, as well as the societal rejection and ageism, which plague the elderly.

It is evident from the interview excerpts in chapters 6 and 7 and findings of other studies reported in this book that many older people have inadequate interpretations of the doctrines of their church. To whatever extent sound doctrine promotes personal adjustment, they lack the full benefit of the church's potential contribution to their lives. Some of them may never have been in study groups to systematically learn theology and its implications for living. Others have been exposed only to incompetent teaching which has led them to pick up a hodgepodge of erroneous interpretations or a jumble of unintegrated ideas. If a basic task of the church is to teach spiritual lessons, there is good reason to believe that it has failed in this task for many members. Religious education needs improvement so that the doctrines held by church members will not have to be unlearned and corrected when they become elderly. In its emphasis upon meeting the needs of people in this life, the church must neither forget the part it ought to play in preparing people for life beyond the grave nor think that its sole task is to promote adjustment to temporal conditions.

Many older people have a sense of insecurity, a feeling of insignificance, a fear of death, or a sense of regret for past mistakes or failures. To these the church brings comfort and assurance. It offers opportunities for service that can restore a feeling of importance and worth to the individual, opportunities for worship that can impart a sense of security in a world of uncertainties, opportunities for confession and forgiveness that can take away the sting of regret, and opportunities for the exercise of faith in the promise of God that He will never leave nor forsake the one who is trusting in Him. "Death education" to provide a balanced and wholesome view of death is one task of the church.[7]

---

7. Betty R. Green and Donald P. Irish, eds., *Death Education: Preparation for Living,* Schenkman Publishing Co., 1971; Joseph R. Sizoo, "The Answers of Christian Faith," in Janet H. Baird, ed., *These Harvest Years,* Doubleday and Co., 1951, pp. 247-263; and H. Lee Jacobs, "Spiritual Resources for the Aged in Facing the Problem of Death," *Adding Life to Years,* 6(3): 3-8, Mar. 1959.

To those who are frustrated in the failure to make sense of life as they have experienced it, the church offers a basic attitude toward life that will develop a sense of serenity and feelings of security; to those who feel unwanted, it offers the assurance of God's continuing love; to those who are lonely, it offers both fellowship in the church and assurance of the omnipresence of God; to those who are self-centered, it offers a perspective that includes all humanity through time and eternity.[8]

The church's "care of souls" is oriented in part to coping with anxieties and fears, providing comfort, hope, forgiveness, assurance, love, sympathy, and other forms of spiritual support. The need to prepare realistically for death, to construct one's life story and thus explain many mysteries of life while producing a wholesome integration of the personality, to promote personal dignity, and to develop an overall philosophy of life are included among human spiritual needs which the church can help to meet better than any other organization or institution in society.[9]

An interfaith consultation on spiritual well-being in February 1975 arrived at a working definition it felt could be used in all faith groups, whether Protestant, Catholic, Jewish, Orthodox, Eastern religions or others. The definition was later adopted by the National Interfaith Coalition on Aging as a definition of spiritual health to be studied by religious body members. It states that *Spiritual Well-Being is the affirmation of life in a relationship with God, self, community and environment that nurtures and celebrates wholeness.*[10] Each religious body can develop and interpret this statement in light of its own language, traditions, theology, and ministries. As a church meets spiritual needs and cultivates spiritual well-being, it promotes individual growth, remedies many personal ills, alleviates social problems, and motivates people to serve others.

---

8. Federal Security Agency, *Man and His Years: An Account of the First National Conference on Aging,* Health Publications Institute, 1931, pp. 206-210.

9. David O. Moberg, *Spiritual Well-Being: Background and Issues,* White House Conference on Aging, 1971, pp. 5-15.

10. NICA INFORM, No. 1, p. 4, Aug. 24, 1975 (italics added). See Appendix I for elaborating statements of the complete report.

There are various ways in which the church imparts these spiritual benefits to its older constituents. Not only can it use its regular channels of worship and prayer services, but it can also work through effective programs of pastoral counselling and care of the aged and infirm. The spiritual message can be conveyed through tape-recorded services played back to shut-ins during the week, perhaps under sponsorship of a youth group or other organization, and through special services such as "gospel team" meetings for shut-ins and the residents of retirement and nursing homes. Special classes in the church school can encourage them to share in the study of the Bible and to learn the application of Scriptural principles to their own specific needs. Transportation can be provided to aid those no longer able to attend church services without help. Publications of the local church as well as of denominational and interdenominational bodies can contribute to spiritual edification. Serving Communion to shut-ins and various other activities of the church and its pastor can help promote the spiritual life of older members.

A conscientious attempt should be made to meet the spiritual needs of all persons, not only those who come regularly to the worship services and other activities of churches. Those who have the greatest spiritual need frequently are the social isolates and other persons entirely outside of churches and community associations. A strong case can be made for the position that

> ... our one claim to service for our elderly in institutional ministry, or in our parishes ... must lie in our ability to aid persons in maintaining communication with God. The spiritual needs of each, whether felt or unrecognized, expressed or instinctively sought, must be met by us.... Our faith in God as a personal friend who has created us all for a purpose directs us to seek that purpose together with our elderly friends.[11]

THE CHURCH CAN EDUCATE

The educational program of the church can help older

---

11. Robert W. McKewin, "Seminar Summary," in *Papers Presented at the Seminar on the Aged,* The Bishop Edwin A. Penick Memorial Home, Southern Pines, N.C., Oct. 16-17, 1969, p. 64. (See also Thomas E. Bollinger, "The Spiritual Needs of the Ageing," *ibid.,* pp. 49-60.)

adults to become better persons by preparing them to cope effectively with present and future problems and by developing their spiritual wisdom and social maturity. The church also can help younger people prepare for their later years, thus preventing many of the problems that accrue in late life or alleviating their severity. It can eradicate common errors about old age and the elderly from the minds of older persons as well as younger people. In other words,

> Old age education must be directed to all ages: to little children, to adolescents, to adults, and to those who are old. It must have a two-fold purpose: to prepare one's self for the coming of age, and to help others to deal wisely with those who are old.[12]

In its education for children and youth the church can cultivate wholesome attitudes toward aging and older people. These will improve the lot of the present older generation, and they also will help children and youth to prepare more realistically for their own aging process. The church can help them develop wholesome interests and social relationships which can be perpetuated into the later years of life, and it can help mature adults prepare for retirement from work in such manner that they will not only retire from but also will retire *to* something. It can stimulate the adjustability and adaptability which seem so intimately related to good personal adjustment at any age. It can help develop spiritual maturity that will assist the person facing a crisis to realize and to practice dependence upon God in the faith that comes through complete consecration to Him. The traditional adult Bible class is not sufficient to meet all these needs.[13]

The church also can help older persons directly through its formal program of education. It can make them realize that there still is a future ahead of them — a future in this life as

---

12. Irene K. Ogawa, "Old Age Education: An Approach to Dealing with Aging and Retirement," *Religious Education*, 49: 607, Sep.-Oct. 1974. See also David A. Peterson, "Life-Span Education and Gerontology," *The Gerontologist*, 15(5): 436-441, Oct. 1975, which indicates broader needs for educational experiences throughout life, and Jean Beaven Abernethy, *Old Is Not a Four-Letter Word*, Abingdon Press, 1975, which is written to challenge and overcome the downgrading of the aging process and older people.

13. Mrs. Geneva Mathiasen, "Preparation for Retirement," *Social Action,* 26(5): 7-15, Jan. 1960.

well as in the life to come. This recognition will give them new sense of importance, a feeling of belonging, a sense of direction, and a share in creative activity. The church helps older people face the complexities of living in our modern age through its sponsorship of church libraries, special lectures, discussion groups, extension membership in the church school, and similar activities. Education of older people as to the reasons for changes in society, the backgrounds of current customs and practices, the advantages and disadvantages of alternative ways of meeting practical problems, the cooperative arrangements by which older people can help one another, and various other subjects will help them cultivate the social, psychological, and spiritual virtues that will enable them to live more wholesome lives.

The church also can be an indirect but important and wholesome educator by its influence on the community as a whole. It can rightfully fulfill its place as the conscience of society, setting a healthy example in its own dealings with and about the aging people in its midst; it must serve as "the light of the world" with regard to moral and ethical problems, indicating to persons what they ought and ought not to do. One of the ten commandments is that people should honor their fathers and mothers. Showing such respect toward members of the older generation, according to most Jewish and Christian interpretations, is not limited only to children and adolescents.

Contents of the churches' educational programs can be as diverse as the needs of the children, youth, adults, and older persons who are in them. In this as in other matters, cooperation with other community agencies is especially appropriate with reference to subjects like consumer education, arts and crafts, basic education, retirement preparation, job training, and programs to cope with such special problems as dying and bereavement.[14]

The church, through its educational program, must make a conscientious effort to dispel and eliminate numerous mistaken notions about old age, the aging process, and older

14. Roger DeCrow, *New Learning for Older Americans: An Overview of National Effort,* Adult Education Association, Washington, D.C., 1975. DeCrow's inventory revealed that a large number of the community-oriented adult education opportunities are located in churches.

people.[15] One of these is the idea that the elderly are all the same. That they are *old* often makes us forget that they are *people*.[16] They have pronounced individual differences, often to the most accentuated degree, for they have had a longer time to develop differing personalities than young people. Some older people are conservative, but others are very liberal and progressive; some are physically infirm, but others are vigorous and agile; no two are alike in every way. Since each is different from all the others, wise church leaders recognize the differences and purposively educate people to treat each one as an individual in his or her own right. The church can teach that each older person should be given the right to make his own decisions, except in cases of extreme senility, and each ought to be respected as a person, instead of being treated as a child along with all others who are supposedly in their second childhood.

A second error the church can help eradicate is the idea that the aged are no longer able to grow, to learn, or to adjust to new circumstances. There are so many problems during senescence that everyone must adjust and change. In urbanized, industrialized civilization people have become accustomed to change to a much greater extent than in rural pastoral cultures of certain other lands and of earlier days. As a result, they are probably more adjustable in old age than the others. Yet many people even in American cities have immigrated from rural societies where change has taken place only very slowly. Such persons have had less practice adjusting than the majority; therefore, there are great variations among older people in this regard.

The older person who has been learning all his life, who has adjusted frequently to new circumstances, and who has been growing and developing mentally can continue to do so during old age. The notion that "you can't teach an old dog

---

15. Cf. Paul B. Maves and J. Lennart Cedarleaf, *Older People and the Church,* Abingdon-Cokesbury Press, 1949, pp. 50-58.

16. See George Lawton, "Old Age, First Person Singular," in George Lawton, ed., *New Goals for Old Age,* Columbia University Press, 1943, p. 169; and Francis Gerty, "Importance of Individualization of Treatment in the Aging Period," *Geriatrics,* 12: 123-129, 1957.

new tricks" may apply to dogs, but it definitely does not apply
to people!

A third mistaken idea the church can help correct is that
old age is an unimportant period of life when the individual
can no longer be active and can no longer contribute. This
idea prevents many older people from trying to contribute and
makes many of them feel they are now on the scrapheap with
nothing to live for except the anticipation of death.[17] The
older person who is a Christian can continue to lead a fruitful
life. While consciousness remains, she or he can contribute to
the needs of others. Even if in no other way, "mountains" can
be moved through intercessory prayer.

Older people need to feel useful in order to be well-
adjusted, happy individuals. Their creative ability can be
great, and they will have much to live for, if life remains
meaningful to them and if constructive interests are kept alive.
Many older people can continue in active employment far
beyond age 65. Department of Labor studies have indicated
that older workers do not lack physical steadiness of body,
arm, and hand; they have better attendance records at work
than young people; they have fewer disabling injuries; and
they are more dependable and efficient.[18]

Fourth, the church can help eliminate the false idea that
older people are devoid of sexual interest and drive, an error
which is sometimes reflected in calling them "the third sex."
Studies of sexual behavior indicate that many married persons
continue to have active sexual relationships into their 80s and
90s. If they think that this is abnormal or that it is sinful to
retain the sexual interests, serious mental — and hence spiritual
— problems may result.[19]

A fifth fallacy which the church's educational program can

---

17. For a discussion of this see Geza Revesz, "Age and Achievement,"
Hibbert Journal, 53: 273-279, April 1955.

18. James P. Mitchell, "What About Older Workers?" *The American
Weekly,* Sep. 4, 1955, p. 2. See articles in the journal *Industrial Gerontology.*

19. Public Affairs Committee, *Sex after Sixty-Five,* Public Affairs Com-
mittee, 1975, and Eric Pfeiffer, "Sexual Behavior in Old Age," in Ewald
W. Busse and Eric Pfeiffer, eds., *Behavior and Adaptation in Late Life,*
Little, Brown & Co., 1969, pp. 151-162. A helpful monograph by ten authors
is Irene Mortenson Burnside, ed., *Sexuality and Aging,* Ethel Percy Andrus
Gerontology Center, University of Southern California, 1975.

help correct is the idea that older people wish to be relieved of responsibility. Many of them do wish to be relieved of *some* responsibility and to carry a lighter load than previously, but to force them to retire suddenly and completely from all responsibility is often the equivalent of forcing them prematurely into the grave. Overprotection and overindulgence make them feel depreciated, incapable, incompetent, and inferior. Inestimable injury to self-respect and the inner sense of worthiness results from such policies, as we saw in chapter 7.

Many people mistakenly believe a sixth fallacy, that it is old age in and of itself that constitutes a social problem. The church has an excellent opportunity to teach that old age is natural and inevitable, but conditions that surround the aged and attitudes of other people toward them create the problems.[20] There is a need to recognize that many problems of old age arise from the failure to understand either the true handicaps of some aged people in our society or the personal assets they all possess, or both.

Closely related is a seventh fallacy — the myth that most older persons are physically incapacitated or mentally senile. This, in turn, contributes to the perspective of many churches that they have fulfilled their responsibility by establishing a retirement home or sponsoring pastoral care in a nursing home. Actually, only about 5% of all persons past the age of 65 in the U.S.A. are in institutions like hospitals, retirement homes, and convalescent facilities. Any church group that orients all its ministries to that group will tend to ignore the other 95%. Modern medicine, prosthetic devices like pacemakers, and other means of controlling chronic physical ailments make it possible for nearly all older people to live rather normal lives. Like people at other ages, they vary widely in their physical abilities and emotional health. The majority are alert and interested in public affairs and civic life. While aging tends to slow down some of the mental and physical processes, the vast majority of older people continue to be active physically and mentally.[21]

---

20. Thomas B. Robb, *The Bonus Years: Foundations for Ministry with Older Persons,* Judson Press, 1968, p. 18.

21. Clingan, *op. cit.,* pp. 1-5.

An eighth fallacy the church can correct overlaps with several others. It is the mistaken idea of many churchmen that it is no use to work with the aged: they are too old to change, too old to be converted, too old to contribute to the church; if one gives any of his time as a church leader to older people, the youth work will suffer and before long nothing will be left of the congregation. Such ideas are more widespread than most church leaders care or dare to admit.

Because the aging are so often neglected or are even rebuffed by conventional churches, in their spiritual striving and seeking, they may turn to enticing sects and cults that are eager to receive them. The spiritual benefits offered through the church are not intended only for youth, although all too often its publicity and programs of evangelism seem to indicate that. There perhaps are only two periods of life when people are more open to receive the gospel than in old age. One of these is early adolescence and the other the period of child-bearing, especially during infancy of the first child.[22]

The church can do its part to dispel the gloom that results from these and similar mistaken ideas held by many older people as well as by youth. It can do so directly through its educational program, indirectly through pastors who break down these stereotyped ideas in their sermons instead of reaffirming them, and through leaders who help older people work in the church in such a way that they are living examples refuting the false ideas. By helping to "educate away" mistaken notions about old age and older people, the church helps people of all ages.

The educational influence of the church is evident also in the tuition-free programs provided by several church-related colleges for persons aged 65 and over.[23] One of the best examples is the Senior Learners program of Seattle Pacific College

22. This is a topic on which research is needed. In groups emphasizing the need for a conversion experience, most conversions to Christianity occur during late childhood or adolescence in our culture. This may be a result of the selective process of "weeding out" persons most prone to conversion at this early age. Does the same pattern prevail elsewhere and with all types of evangelistic outreach?

23. Most higher education institutions offering special courses or services for older people are public community colleges ("500 Colleges Offer Courses for Elderly," *AARP News Bulletin,* 17(1): 8, Jan. 1976).

which allows senior citizens to take tuition-free courses and even to work toward degrees on a tuition-free basis in classes which have open places following regular registration each quarter. The Life Enrichment Center and Adventures in Learning of the Shepherd's Center in Kansas City, the extensive continuing education curriculum of St. Luke's United Methodist Church in Oklahoma City, and the La Farge Institute for Life-long Learning in Milwaukee are among the pace-setting educational programs for older people.

The church teaches by its example as much as, if not more than, by its pronouncements. If its demand for youthful pastors continues to cause premature retirement of the clergy,[24] if its lack of adequate pension plans for employees causes them to suffer economic need in old age, if its acceptance of compulsory retirement at a fixed age in many areas of society encourages wasting the resources of physically and mentally capable persons, if its over-emphasis upon youth operates to the detriment of mature older adults in the church and community, then it not only implies that such practices are ethically and spiritually proper, but it also encourages the rest of society to follow in its steps.

If materialistic standards prevail in the church to such an extent that property, money, prestige, and power are placed ahead of the welfare of people, can it expect the rest of society to be any different? The church teaches by what it does even more than by what it says.

THE CHURCH CAN CONTRIBUTE TO PERSONALITY DEVELOPMENT

Even though our society has not institutionalized them by establishing clear rites of transition and roles, there are developmental tasks for older persons, just as there are for children, adolescents, young adults, and the middle aged. These tasks include adjusting to changes in one's physical, mental,

24. See John Irving Daniel, "Premium on Youth," *Christian Century*, 65: 478-480, May 19, 1948. This problem is less severe since the clergy of most denominations have been covered by Social Security. Cf. S. Waldman, "Coverage of Ministers under Old-Age, Survivors and Disability Insurance," *Social Security Bulletin*, 24(4): 18-22, Apr. 1961.

and emotional characteristics; changing one's relationships with family, peers, and friends; learning how to live with economic and environmental limitations, especially following occupational retirement; continuing to contribute positively to the larger community, and living a dynamic life of spiritual well-being and faith.[25]

Berg's "twelve rejuvenating techniques" for the renewal of older persons reflect the importance of personality development.[26] They are remotivation, physical conditioning, life-long education, creative resiliency, identification with the spirit of life and power rather than weakness, acclimation to death, accepting and creatively using leisure, spiritual renewal, reinforcement of independence through community, pre-retirement counselling, united action to meet common needs of older people, and senior power. These techniques are being used in the Point Loma Community Presbyterian Church of San Diego, California, under the leadership of Rev. Robert W. McClellan in an experimental program to cultivate them.

The church contributes in many ways to the kind of personality adjustment and development that enables one to live through the later years of life in calm composure and true enjoyment. Its potential contributions to this goal overlap with all the other contexts of services offered. For example, it can help modify the values of the society so that older people are respected as individuals with distinct personalities. As a result, older persons will have increased self-respect.

The church can impart such spiritual benefits to its constituents that an inner security will be developed in the face of come-what-may. They then will have increased self-confidence, based, of course, on their confidence in God, and will be able to face their problems more realistically and serenely.

The church can help develop social relationships which in turn assist the individual in the cultivation of personality

---

25. Abraham Maslow's "Hierarchy of Needs" is related to this. See his *Motivation and Personality,* Harper and Row, 1954, and other publications.
26. Kenneth L. Berg, *Senior Power—New Life for the Church,* D.Min. dissertation, San Francisco Theological Seminary, June 1974, and Robert W. McClellan, *A Study of the Need and Possibilities for Renewal and Fulfillment of Older People in Church, Synagogue and Community,* D.Min. dissertation, San Francisco Theological Seminary, 1976.

traits until he or she becomes a more gracious person, poised in any social situation.

The Christian church can inspire goals and values for which one can live in order to receive the truly abundant life that Jesus Christ came to give (John 10:10). By emphasizing the importance of the individual as a person created in the image of God and as a soul for whom God gave His only Son, it can impart to the individual a significant sense of importance and worth. This will contribute to personality development and good personal adjustment, if done in a way which at the same time imparts an appropriate sense of humility.

THE CHURCH HELPS SOLVE PERSONAL PROBLEMS

The personal problems which confront the aging individual typically are entirely new to the older person. He or she is expected to manage the estate of a deceased brother or sister, to arrange for the collection of insurance or a pension, to dispose of real estate that has been in the family for a lifetime, to make a will, or to take care of legal affairs for which there is no preparation by past experience or training. The well-trained pastor can do much to help with many of these personal problems, and he can lead the older person to a lawyer, social worker, or other professional person who is qualified to help solve the specific problems. Pastoral counselling of older people often deals with problems such as those mentioned above, problems of money, problems of social relationships, problems associated with adjusting to retirement, and so on.

Persons who are fearful, relatively uneducated, on welfare rolls, or suffering other forms of deprivation often experience considerable difficulty in obtaining services that are rightfully theirs. A personal advocate — one who can accompany them to help them fill in forms, cut through bureaucratic red tape, and identify the individuals in agencies who can provide the help that is needed — may constitute one of the most helpful forms of assistance conceivable. Other retired persons who have time and are willing to volunteer their services to assist such people on a one-to-one basis can be mobilized through church-sponsored programs. Such volunteers, in turn, should have professional support and assistance for those occasions on which they also become stymied by the bureaucratic entanglements of social welfare systems, Social Security, Medicare, Medicaid, and other service programs. In addition to such personal advocacy, the church and its personnel can exert influence as advocates of desirable changes in political, educational, legal, welfare, and other social systems, as we shall see in connection with civic and political affairs below.

Widow-to-Widow programs within some congregations and across church lines in many communities help the bereaved to adjust to their grief and the changes required to rebuild life without a husband or wife. They contribute significantly to the personal integration and sense of worth of the providers of service as well as the recipients.[27] Benefits never flow exclusively in one direction in one-to-one programs.

The church can prevent many personal problems of the aging by encouraging them to retire *to* something rather than simply to retire *from* their work and the active world.[28] It can encourage them to develop old hobbies, resurrect leisure-time interests, and find new activities which will help them to learn what they have long desired to know, to do what they like to do, to make new friends while not neglecting the old, to live in and for the present as much as or more than in and for the past, and to forget themselves in loving service to others who are in need.

Older persons who are in fellowship with one another through the social activities of the church or its auxiliary groups also have the opportunity to get help from others in their group whom they respect and whom they can trust. As they help one another, they give each other many of the satisfactions of recognition and responsibility that most people desire.

THE CHURCH CAN HELP MEET PHYSICAL AND MATERIAL NEEDS

The church is not primarily a welfare agency with the

27. Phyllis R. Silverman, "Widowhood and Preventive Intervention," *Family Coordinator,* 21: 95-102, Jan. 1972.

28. John J. Kane, *Plan and Enjoy your Retirement,* Claretian Publications, 1972.

task of handing out material aid to people in need. Nevertheless, throughout history religious institutions have included a concern for people who are in need of material help. Groups within the church can put its teaching to "bear one another's burdens" into practice by helping the aging with actual burdens they are forced to carry. At moving time, older people need help that may not be forthcoming from relatives and friends if they live far away or are engrossed in other responsibilities. They often need help with heavy work around the home — the laundry, lawn-mowing, putting up storm windows, shoveling snow, and the like. Some need assistance with cooking and household tasks that can best be met through regular, dependable visitors, foster care residence with a younger family, or as a last resort moving into a retirement home.[29]

The general orientation the church ought to have is that people should be independent as long as possible. The provision of very modest services can often make the difference between living independently and becoming confined to an institution. Visiting homemakers services, meals on wheels, visiting nurse programs, transportation, low-rent housing, and other community services can be provided by churches if no other community agency is filling the need.[30]

When the church cannot meet the material needs of older persons directly, it can help them find community agencies and personnel to help meet those needs. When the pastor or other representative of the church realizes that an older person may have serious physical or mental ailments, that person can be encouraged and helped to visit a medical doctor or to find some other appropriate source of help.

---

29. Research demonstrates that twice as many aged Americans would prefer to get help from the church rather than from the government if special care outside the family becomes necessary (James W. Wiggins and Helmut Schoeck, "A Profile of the Aging: U.S.A.," *Geriatrics*, 16: 336-342, July 1961).

30. See Eric Pfeiffer, ed., *Alternatives to Institutional Care for Older Americans: Practice and Planning*, Center for the Study of Aging and Human Development, Duke University, 1973; and Richard A. Goodling, ed., *The Church's Ministry to the Homebound*, General Board of Education of the Methodist Church, 1967. For an excellent survey of design criteria for the provision of housing for the handicapped and elderly see Alexander Kira *et al.*, *Housing Requirements of the Aged*, Center for Urban Development Research, Cornell University, 5th printing, 1973.

In some churches employment agencies with lay leadership can help capable persons who are in their later maturity to find part-time or full-time work. Even unpaid positions in the church itself are often left unfilled when organized efforts could produce capable volunteers from its own membership. The matching of older persons who have skills with others who have particular needs, such as for household repairs, interior decorating, house cleaning, baking, and completion of income tax returns, can be a valuable service for both the provider and the recipient of such labor. A community-wide coordinating service to match volunteers with positions that need volunteer services can be of great help to people of all ages.[31] In some cities an agency associated with the United Fund or its equivalent provides this need.

A clothing exchange, free store, or similar means for transferring unwanted material goods to persons who need them can also provide an important service. In rural and suburban communities the exchange of garden produce can meet a similar need.

Possibly one of the most important material services that can be provided by an active and alert congregation is to identify needy people in the community. Project FIND discovered that large numbers of poor people have failed to learn about services available to them in their own communities.[32] Locating these friendless, isolated, needy, and disabled people and helping them to find appropriate resources either inside or outside the church can be a very worthwhile challenge for many churches.

In regard to many of these needs, as well as with reference to the problem of safety from accidents and from crime,[33] the church needs to fulfill its responsibility as the conscience of society by making people aware of the need for changes in basic social institutions. The implications of ethical values

31. In Milwaukee the Voluntary Action Center is aided by an excellent weekly newspaper column announcing specific needs for volunteer services: Shirley Wile, "Wanted: Volunteers," Milwaukee *Journal,* each Sunday edition.

32. Project FIND, *The Golden Years: A Tarnished Myth,* National Council on the Aging, 1970.

33. See Erich M. Franz, *The Elderly as Victims of Crime,* Milwaukee Urban Observatory, University of Wisconsin-Milwaukee, 1975.

extend to people in all of society as well as to individuals who are personal acquaintances of church leaders and members.

THE CHURCH SERVES IN NURSING AND RETIREMENT HOMES

Churches have established many retirement homes and will no doubt continue to do so in the future. These, however, should be looked upon as a place in which to live rather than as merely a place to die. They should be so named that older people will not think of them in the same category as mental institutions or county poor farms. Needless to say, the standards and staffs of these church-sponsored homes ought to be of the highest quality.[34]

When it becomes necessary for an aging person to enter a nursing or retirement home, members of the church staff sometimes are asked to help in dealing with the emotional problems of the aging person and of family members or relatives who are responsible for the placement. Spiritual comfort and pastoral care can make a great difference in the state of mind and emotional health with which one makes such a transition. Furthermore, counsel is sometimes asked as to which of alternative homes is the better. Knowledge about the staff, the patients, the building and facilities, the food, the regimen of life, and similar details can help in making such recommendations, and assistance can be obtained from other professional people and community service agencies which do not have a vested interest in any given home.[35]

---

34. The church's responsibility is sketched briefly in George F. Packard, "A Church Houses the Elderly," in Rosamonde Boyd and Charles G. Oakes, eds., *Foundations of Practical Gerontology*, rev. ed., University of South Carolina Press, 1973, pp. 232-236. Thorough outlines of goals, facilities, services, and administration of homes for the aged are presented in *A Guide for Lutheran Homes Serving the Aged*, Division of Welfare, National Lutheran Church Council, 1957, and *Sheltered Care for Older Persons*, The Methodist Church Board of Hospitals and Homes, 1955.

35. The Council on Urban Life in Milwaukee, Wisconsin, published a brochure for Citizens for Better Nursing Home Care entitled "Nursing Homes: How To Avoid if You Can; How To Select if You Must." Similar resources are available in some other communities; the clergy, social workers, medical doctors, and similar professionals should know of their availability.

Occasionally allegedly humanizing activities like reality orientation are conducted in such manner that patients are treated imperialistically for the convenience of the staff.[36] Sensitivity to the subtle ways in which such abuses of human dignity can occur is one of the best means for identifying its presence and constructively contributing to desirable institutional changes.

Many residents of institutional care facilities lack close relatives or have family members so distant that they can visit only rarely. Volunteer service programs like Project Compassion of the Lutheran Church–Missouri Synod and the Adopt-A-Grandparent program of students at the University of South Dakota can establish friendly visiting on a one-to-one basis to overcome loneliness and to meet other needs.[37] Many other service programs are possible in such institutions.[38]

When church leaders become aware that institutional care is deficient in quality, they have a moral obligation to use their influence and resources to improve the level of patient care and restore human dignity to the clients.

THE CHURCH MEETS SOCIAL
AND RECREATIONAL NEEDS

The need for social fellowship and group participation, for many people at least, is not fully satisfied in the family and other informal groups. Many churches have organized activities specifically for older people, not to function only during the church school hour but also during the long days of the week between Sundays. Excursions, visits to museums,

---

36. Jaber F. Gubrium, "Death Worlds in a Nursing Home," *Urban Life*, 4(3): 317-338, Oct. 1975; Gubrium and Margret Ksander, "On Multiple Realities and Reality Orientation," *The Gerontologist*, 15(2): 142-145, April 1975; Gubrium, *Living and Dying at Murray Manor*, St. Martin's Press, 1975.

37. *Adopt A Grandparent*, Coyote Student Center, University of South Dakota, Vermillion, S.D. 57069, published in 1975 for the 1976 USA Bicentennial.

38. A. Luther Molberg, "Service Programs for the Aged Through Social Institutions," *Lutheran Social Concern*, 12(2): 40-45, Summer 1972. The adoption of a specific nursing home by each congregation as a means of linking its residents with the larger community and meeting their needs for visitors, transportation, and other service opportunities is recommended in "Adopt-a-Nursing Home," *Synagogue Aging*, Jan. 1976, p. 6.

concerts, plays, senior citizen camping, arts and crafts programs, travelogues, and nature tours are but a few examples of their ventures. Other churches refer older members to community organizations that satisfy many of these interests. These Golden Age clubs and similar groups, even when not sponsored directly by the church, often use church facilities and receive assistance from church personnel.[39]

Ideally, recreational programs for the aging should be run by the older persons themselves to as great an extent as possible. Members of the church or its auxiliaries can find opportunities for service to their own age group as well as to others through the church, as will be emphasized in the next chapter. Older persons cultivate a sense of fellowship with one another as they engage in corporate activities, such as worship. As they develop new friendships and new responsibilities, their needs for personal recognition are satisfied, they enjoy pleasant relaxation in social groups, and they keep their minds alert as they think about the new ideas they are gaining.

As much as possible older people should be integrated into existing groups, and services for them should be a normal part of the entire life of the church. It is often difficult to enroll them in new groups that are identified — rightly or wrongly — as just for "old people," for many are reluctant to admit that they are old. They feel they will always be "young at heart" or "young in spirit," so why should they be singled out for membership in an old folks' group? Being a part of the church fellowship contributes more to their happiness than being kept apart from it.

When organizing group activities for older people in the local church, the interests, hobbies, and backgrounds of group members should be known, and several principles should be heeded. The group should elect its own officers and plan its own programs. The program should be kept flexible and should change as the interests of the group change. Community resources should be used. The program should be person-centered, not activity-centered. Interests should be discovered through such devices as checklists and observation. Leaders

---

39. For resource materials and program ideas see Toni Merrill, *Social Clubs for the Aging*, Vol. 1, Charles C Thomas, 1973.

should not be over-protective of older adults in program activities. Responsibility should be delegated so as to be shared by all, and a patient, democratic attitude should be manifest instead of autocratic leadership that emphasizes speed.[40]

Even older persons who are homebound can be helped to retain a sense of belonging to groups in which they formerly were active as members visit or a visitation committee does its work, as they are supplied with study and worship materials used in their group, as they receive greetings on special occasions, and as special programs are given on occasional visits of groups from the church.[41] A church newsletter, or even a special newsletter designed explicitly for shut-ins, can be very helpful. Much of the work on such a paper can be done by persons who are homebound themselves.[42]

One category of people who deserve special attention in most churches and communities are widowed persons. In some respects they constitute a "forgotten minority." The problems associated with bereavement and loss, their feeling that they alone experience anger and guilt, and the practical problems associated with adjusting to living alone in a new life style are great. More than half of all women past the age of 65 are widows; they greatly outnumber the men, a substantial proportion of whom remarry after widowhood. Partly with the help of the Widowed Persons Service of Action for Independent Maturity, a division of the American Association of Retired Persons, a growing number of communities have established

---

40. These suggestions come from a group led by Catherine Wahlstrom at the International Conference on the Church and Older Persons in 1953 as reported by Viola K. Braun, "Older Adults Need Fellowship," *International Journal of Religious Education*, 30(3): 22, Nov. 1953. Many public service agencies have produced guidelines or booklets for leaders of groups for senior citizens. One good example is *Handbook for Leaders of Senior Citizens Clubs*, Illinois Dept. of Public Aid, Section on Services for Aging, 618 E. Washington Street, Springfield, IL 62706. See also Minna Field, *The Aged, the Family and the Community*, Columbia University Press, 1972, especially chap. 8, "Social Work with the Elderly," pp. 157-200.

41. See Goodling, *op. cit.*

42. A shut-in known only as Kathleen edits *The Shut-In*, a newspaper for shut-ins with games, puzzles, humor, a pen pal section, religious articles, and a message from Father Gene Jakubek, organizer of the Help program devoted to helping the elderly, lonely, and poor (Ione Quinby Griggs, "Newspaper for Shut-ins Spreads Help, Good Spirits," *The Milwaukee Journal*, May 7, 1975, Green Sheet, p. 4).

widowed persons groups in which such persons associate with each other and help one another.[43]

The NAIM Conference also conducts group discussions, special programs, forums, and local chapter activities to help widowed persons. This primarily Catholic organization provides assistance and an opportunity for service to people of other religious affiliations as well. Taking its name from Luke 7:11, THEOS is a Christian fellowship group which serves young and middle-aged widowed persons and their families. Its name implies the Greek word for God and also is an acronym for "They Help Each Other Spiritually." By 1976 it had 30 chapters in 7 states and Canada.[44]

In *Man, the Unknown,* Alexis Carrel said that for the old leisure is even more dangerous than for the young. The time of the aging individual should be "filled with mental and spiritual adventures" to enrich his declining years.[45] The church can do much to meet this need of its older constituents.

THE CHURCH CAN INFLUENCE CIVIC AFFAIRS AND POLITICS

Many civic projects on behalf of the aging deserve the active support of the church. Social and recreational associations, a community center, meals on wheels to feed shut-ins, other services for the homebound, and similar activities are worthy of the support of the church as it attempts to implement its principles of justice, kindness, and love.

The church staff or members who are volunteers may become aware of abuses of human dignity in nursing homes, hospitals, foster care facilities, welfare agencies, the funeral industry, or other community institutions. To ignore such abuses

---

43. A list of these appears in Edward Wakin, *Living as a Widow,* Claretian Publications, Jubilee Paperback CP-280, n.d. (ca. 1975); this is an excellent book with many practical suggestions for widowed persons and people who ought to understand them better.

44. Information on the NAIM Conference and its local chapters can be obtained from its headquarters, 109 N. Dearborn St., Chicago, IL 60602. The address of THEOS Foundation is 11609 Frankstown Road, Pittsburgh, PA 15235.

45. *Man, the Unknown,* Harper & Brothers, 1939, p. 186.

is to put a stamp of legitimacy upon them; genuine love demands active steps to correct such flaws.

Similarly, the church can encourage the passage of federal, state, and local laws to support the financial security, independence, and well-being of older people. Numerous areas need constructive social change in contemporary society. Here are a few examples. Many widowed people live with persons of the opposite sex without the benefit of marriage because they would lose substantial amounts of Social Security income if they would marry. Medications cost a great deal more for people in general because of laws which prohibit the substitution of generic equivalents for brand-name subscription drugs. Thousands of people who paid large sums of money into pension funds will never collect on their pensions because the investments either have not been vested in them personally or have not been secured against the failure of a holding corporation, bankruptcy of a business, or default of a labor union.[46] Government regulations pertinent to the coverage of costs in nursing and convalescent homes allow the management to benefit from the continuing disability of the patient, thus providing a vested interest in maintaining dependence instead of rehabilitating and restoring the patient to health.

These are a few examples of the numerous areas which cry out for major changes to correct weaknesses in the social and political structure of American society. Careful study of the facts, current laws, their interpretations and applications, and alternative proposals for their correction, together with identification of those who benefit through perpetuating the status quo, are a part of the process of bringing about constructive changes to enhance the personal dignity of all people.[47] Changes also are needed with regard to compulsory retirement legislation and practices, the false assumption that anything pertinent to spiritual well-being is obviously sectarian

---

46. See Dan M. McGill, *Preservation of Pension Benefit Rights,* Richard D. Irwin for the Pension Research Council, 1972.

47. This is not the same as being involved in "party politics" with the assumption that every position of one particular party is correct. We do not advocate that the church become identified with any political party, but rather that it be identified with the cause of righteousness and justice, regardless of which party it may thereby support in a given venture.

and therefore cannot receive any attention in government-funded programs, and the need to cultivate increased opportunities for independent living during later adulthood.[48]

Possibly the basic underlying structural weakness behind all of these problems is the low prestige associated with being a "senior citizen." Changing this constitutes a significant challenge that can be met only through instigated or induced social change.[49]

In order to be successful in their efforts to bring about change in civic and political affairs, churches need to cooperate with each other and with other agencies and groups which have similar perspectives on the particular issues of concern. The Better Business Bureau can be helpful on issues of consumer fraud and standards for charitable giving, and the United Fund headquarters can be helpful in problems that arise pertinent to social agencies and their programs. On political matters especially, a series of shifting coalitions is likely to emerge by which some groups that cooperate with each other on certain issues will be on opposite sides on others. Most political issues are that way; there is no completely clear "Christian" position on them because of the intermingling of pertinent values. A focus on certain details leads to one conclusion, while a focus upon other details may lead one to insist that the opposite position is "the Christian view." A high degree of charity and empathy is necessary to enable people of contrasting political positions to respect each other and to live in Christian love even when they disagree.

Church leaders and members should also remember that older people still are citizens who deserve the opportunity to remain active in political life.[50] Some may need transportation services to get to the polls. Others can participate in precinct activities, and some may join the Gray Panthers or a local senior action coalition to defend the rights of the aging. A church can demonstrate its belief in human dignity by pro-

48. Robert P. Wray, "Community Services: Help for Longer Independent Living," *Perspective on Aging*, May/June 1975, pp. 1-3.

49. Alvin L. Bertrand, "Adjustment to Aging," *RE: Arts Liberales* (Stephen F. Austin State University, Texas), 1(2): 29-36, Spring 1975.

50. Bernard E. Nash, "The Rights of Older Persons—To Be Political," *Lutheran Social Concern*, 12(2): 51-52, Summer 1972.

viding a meeting place for such activities, announcing rallies, and giving other forms of support.

THE CHURCH CAN COOPERATE WITH OTHER ORGANIZATIONS

Not only in politics, but in many other regards, cooperation with other churches and community agencies is highly desirable in the church's ministries with and for the aging. Many community programs have been made possible only because congregations, parishes, and synagogues with very diverse religious orientations cooperated. One of the most remarkable developments of the 1970's has been the establishment of interfaith coalitions and agencies in several regions, states, and metropolitan areas.[51]

The National Interfaith Coalition on Aging was established in 1972 as a result of the stimulus given by the section on spiritual well-being of the 1971 White House Conference on Aging. It draws together representatives of national religious bodies in order to develop awareness and to vitalize the role of the church and synagogue with respect to their responsibilities for improving the quality of life of the aging, to identify and to give priority to programs and services for the aging which can be implemented through religious bodies, to stimulate cooperative and coordinated action between the religious sector and other organizations and agencies which provide programs and services related to the welfare and dignity of aging people, and to encourage the aging to continue contributing to society as active participants in community life. One of its major activities has been a research project to identify programs with and for the aging which are under religious auspices. It also has produced informative cassette tapes, papers, and a working definition of spiritual well-being

---

51. Besides committees in several regional and state councils of churches, these include the Institute on Religion and Aging in Indianapolis, Interfaith Commission on Aging of the Missouri Council of Churches, Metropolitan Kansas City Interfaith Coalition on Aging, Illinois Interfaith Coalition on Aging, Pinellas County Interfaith Coalition on Aging in St. Petersburg, Florida, and Southern California Interfaith Coalition on Aging. For addresses see Clingan, *op. cit.,* pp. 23-24 .

which is making its impact felt in numerous religious bodies and programs.[52]

The Pinellas County Interfaith Coalition on Aging directed by Helen D. Drylie in St. Petersburg, Florida, is one example of what can be done through a local coalition. As of May 1975 it had a membership of 105 congregations from 22 denominations. It has sponsored a blood bank and the Shepherds Center with four locations for senior citizens. It has trained over 200 volunteers; has sponsored health days for screening people for diabetes, glaucoma, pulmonary function, and hypertension; has produced a county directory of church congregations and services available to the elderly together with other pertinent information needed by persons over 60; has provided assistance for completing Medicare forms; has sponsored a telephone reassurance service named the Samaritan Callers; and has furnished programming assistance to church and community organizations interested in improving their services with and for the aging.[53] Such cooperative endeavors make a much greater impact on the community and its people than could all of the individual congregations acting alone. They also make possible the purchase of multimedia materials, a library of resources for programs, aids to leaders, and other specialized services and materials which would be too expensive for individual congregations alone.

Cooperative programs and projects by churches with such secular agencies as the National Council on Aging and local chapters of the American Association of Retired Persons also can be mutually beneficial. The Church Relations Program of NRTA-AARP has several types of resources to aid churches in their ministries for the aging.[54]

More intensive forms of cooperation, like joint sponsorship of a community center, health clinic, or social service agency for senior citizens, are desirable in some communities. Normal procedures of careful planning, clear contractual arrangements, specification of lines of authority, and operational

---

52. For information write to Rev. Thomas C. Cook, Jr., NICA, 298 S. Hull St., Athens, GA 30601.

53. *Pinellas County Interfaith Coalition on Aging Newsletter,* 2(1), May 1975.

54. Rev. Earl Kragnes, Coordinator, 1909 K St., N.W., Washington, D.C. 20049.

details are important as means for retaining wholesome relationships and providing efficient services.[55]

THE CHURCH CAN ADAPT
ITS PHYSICAL FACILITIES

All too often, adapting a church building to meet the needs of older and handicapped persons has meant only such narrowly defined ventures as placing hearing aids in selected pews. Actually, facilities of this kind are often unused because they are so located that persons using them feel singled out and conspicuous.

More important, however, are locating rest rooms so that they can be reached conveniently by the aged and infirm; avoiding long flights of steps; the use of non-glare lighting, skid-proof floor wax, radiant heating, pews from which it is easy to arise; convenient location with respect to transportation; ramps for wheelchairs; and similar considerations.[56] By instituting such changes, the church can become a more convenient, useful, and comfortable place for older persons.

THE CHURCH CAN CONTRIBUTE TO RESEARCH

An increasing number of social and behavioral scientists are giving attention to gerontology, the study of aging. The church can help them gather information to test hypotheses and develop theories about the aging and their problems, help propose solutions, and take part in the evaluation of the results of action programs. The church can help researchers to gain access to older persons who would not be available otherwise and to secure cooperation from suspicious older people who, without church support, would be reluctant to give the personal information that is sometimes needed for scientific

55. One example suggestive of problems to avoid involved the Salvation Army in San Francisco. See Elinore Lurie, "Sai On: Organizational Difficulties in Establishing a Cooperative Protective Residence," Appendix XIII in Richard A. Kalish, *et al., On Lok Senior Health Services: Evaluation of a Success* (On Lok Senior Health Services, 1490 Mason St., San Francisco, CA 94133, 1975, $6.50).

56. F. Grover Fulkerson, "Older Adults in the Church Building," *International Journal of Religious Education*, 30(11): 12-14, July-Aug. 1954.

studies. Without those persons, the samples of people studied might be seriously biased and non-representative.

Some churches may even be encouraged to set up experimental educational or social programs which can be observed carefully by researchers over a period of time to determine their effects. As scientists and churchmen cooperate with one another, both will benefit, but the greatest benefit of all will come to the older people they both serve.

Churches can conduct or cooperate in community surveys which include analysis of the number, characteristics, and needs of the aging, existing programs for them, program objectives and effectiveness, leadership, and general evaluation.[57] Such studies can contribute to the improvement of both church-related and non-church activities for older people. As a result of these surveys, the church will often be led to introduce programs and activities for the aged into its own work and at the same time stimulate community action on their behalf.

Research, community surveys, and evaluative studies tend to be opposed by insecure lay and professional leaders in the church who know that their congregations and programs are not perfect.[58] Fearing exposure, bad publicity, or even loss of their positions, they prevent studies of the situation and, as a result, they often contribute to accelerated deterioration and a vicious cycle of institutional disease. Wise leaders do the opposite. They acknowledge imperfection, cooperate with researchers to find it as well as to identify strengths to be maintained, and use research findings as a tool for the church to correct its flaws and to improve its work.

THE CHURCH CAN CORRECT AND OVERCOME ITS DEFICIENCIES

It is very easy for critics of the church to identify ways in which it has made mistakes and fallen short of its potential in

57. See "Planning a Program" in Synagogue Council of America Project on Aging, op. cit., pp. 13-17, and "Test Your Congregation," Synagogue Aging, Nov. 1975, pp. 1-2.

58. See David O. Moberg, The Church as a Social Institution, Prentice-Hall, 1962, pp. 13-16.

ministries with and for the aging. Koller's summary constitutes both a summary description and an indictment:

> Religious organizations have been moderately successful in including older persons in their activities. However, as a resource effective in meeting personal and social needs, religion has been found wanting.[59]

Among the deficiencies identified in the 1971 White House Conference on Aging are the lack of comprehensive programs of services to coordinate spiritual ministries with other areas of human concern, duplication of effort by churches attempting to keep up with their ecclesiastical neighbors, shortage of trained personnel, and deficiencies in the preparation of the clergy. "Charities" that serve only middle and upper-middle class people instead of the poor are also a problem, as are ulterior motives, exploitation of the aging, concentration on institutionalized individuals rather than on the 95% of the aging who reside outside of institutions, limitations upon older people's freedom of choice when programs are planned for them instead of with them. The Conference also pointed to the omission of "the religious factor" from programs and agencies which serve the aging, focus by churches upon social and material needs so that spiritual needs are overlooked, the problems associated with "institutionless religion" as cell groups, house churches, and new non-institutional forms of religion become more popular, and confusing the "church universal" with the "institutional church." Finally, the Conference noted the failure to include preventive components in programs, dealing instead with problems only after they arise to the level of awareness, the subtle and unobtrusive vicious circles by which the problems of recipients of church-related services are accentuated by those who come to help, and lack of overall strategies in dealing with the aged.[60]

These deficiencies can be overcome only by painstaking attention to the theological basis of the church, the realities of aging, the developmental processes involved in the latter stages

---

59. Marvin R. Koller, *Social Gerontology*, Random House, 1968, p. 141. Compare Sanford M. Shapero, "The Vintage Years: General View and Jewish Challenge," *Journal of Religion and Health*, 14(2): 130-141, 1975.

60. Moberg, *op. cit.*, 1971, pp. 40-44.

of life development, community needs and realities, and whole-some principles for service like those which are shared in this book. By remembering that its primary responsibility is to minister to spiritual needs, the church will maintain a holistic perspective in all that it does. As a result, people in the totality of their beings, not merely disembodied, ghostlike "souls" nor solely materialistic bodies, will receive its attention. Although it is the conscience of society, the church must heed its own conscience also, for it is itself a part of human society.

THE CHURCH CAN CREATE OPPORTUNITIES FOR SERVICE

As we have seen earlier, people of all ages need to continue to be useful, to feel wanted, and to be creative. The church can help people who suffer from the societal discrimination of ageism, with its pressures to disengage from work and with-draw from other areas of active participation, to realize that they still can contribute to the well-being of others. Many of their contributions can be made through volunteer services in the church itself, as we shall see in chapter 9. Others can be donated through various community agencies and the personal neighborliness of helping individuals and families.

The church can help to coordinate community resources with human needs. The coordinating activity can itself be a volunteer service by a person employed on a part-time basis who has had experience in working with people, as in social agencies, education, industrial management, or similar professions.

Many community agencies need volunteer help. Some community-wide programs can be related to the projects and activities of a church or a coalition of churches. A Foster Grandparents project to give loving care to deprived children, the SCORE program by which retired executives use their experience to counsel leaders of small business on management problems, and RSVP (Retired Senior Volunteer Program) by which older Americans are given opportunity to provide serv-ices needed in their communities are all coordinated through

ACTION, a federal agency to promote volunteer services.[61]
These senior volunteers serve in schools, libraries, correctional
institutions, hospitals, nursing homes, local government agencies, courts, and other community service agencies to help
people of all ages.

Through positive support for volunteer service programs,
the church can help many persons overcome the initial hurdles
of taking the first step toward helping others. When they receive appropriate training and adequate supervision, most volunteers conclude that once they are involved in a program
they enjoy it greatly. They also experience the fact that "It is
more blessed to give than to receive" (Acts 20:35).

CONCLUSION

It may seem to the reader who is new to this subject that
the suggestions and subsidiary implications in this chapter
are visionary, impractical, ivory-tower speculations. In fact,
however, every one of these is being practiced in some place
or other.

A survey of Texas clergymen from 55 churches in the
greater Dallas area revealed that there are special programs for
the aging in 29 of the 55 congregations and parishes. These
include volunteer work, informal studies, arts and crafts, activities in the local community, telephone reassurance, companionship therapy, seasonal activities, demonstrations and ex-
hibits, service projects, camping, trips and tours, nutrition
groups, recreation, language classes, social programs, and other
projects. Specially trained personnel are assigned to the senior
adult program by 18 of the 55 churches responding.[62]

In a similar research project covering 60 churches, mainly
in Texas but also in other states, it was discovered that there
is a clear relationship between the size of a church's membership and the presence or absence of creatively intended activities for older members. Churches of over 1,000 members have

---

61. Each state office on aging can identify regional and local offices of
these programs, or one can write for information to ACTION/RSVP,
Washington, D.C. 20525.
62. Kay Tidwell, "The Church and the Senior Adult," unpublished research
project for Education 595, Dr. Lorraine Clark, Instructor, East Texas State
University, April 1974.

a substantially higher proportion of social, educational, recreational, homebound worship and communion, volunteer opportunities, and handicraft fairs activities than those which are smaller. Those of 200 or fewer members are very unlikely to have such activities, and of the two intermediate size categories, those with 501-1,000 members are about twice as likely as those of 201-500 to have such activities.[63]

A survey of 23 United Presbyterian Churches in the San Diego, California, area revealed that 11 have no programs specifically designed for persons over the age of 60. Two have taken leadership in providing housing for senior citizens. A wide variety of other activities was identified, including Golden Hours social programs, Bible classes, sewing clubs, friendship clubs, special visitation, emergency transportation and food, a monthly breakfast, a monthly potluck with a program mainly for fellowship purposes, a weekly bus tour, arts and crafts, and theater parties with transportation provided.[64]

Although a great deal has been done in many churches and although there is rich potential for programs to serve older people in nearly every congregation, so much remains undone that a comparison of the potential with its realization constitutes a major challenge. A Southern Baptist Conference on Aging in Nashville, Tennessee, October 23-25, 1974, presented a major workshop on the problems of the aging and the need to deal with that challenge in the nation's largest Protestant denomination. It concluded that there should be a structured approach to problems of aging in the denomination and that its goals should be to stimulate systematic planning for helping church members to give personal aid and understanding to the aging, to stress the place of love for the aging in the gospel, to provide continuing education for the aging

---

63. Kathleen Bush, "A Study of Enrichment Programs Provided by Churches for the Aging," research paper for Education 595, Dr. Lorraine Clark, Instructor, East Texas State University, April 1974.

64. Robert W. McClellan, *An Analysis of the Valuing of Persons over Sixty in the Churches of the San Diego Presbytery*, Research Paper, D. Min. Program, San Francisco Theological Seminary, Sep. 1974. For a description of an extensive and creative program of ministries within a single congregation, see the D. Min. Project Report by J. Hilton Olive, *Ministry to Mature Adults, Fifth Avenue Baptist Church, St. Petersburg, Florida*, New Orleans Baptist Theological Seminary, May 1975.

and for those who minister and relate to them, to develop models for aid and ministry to the aging, and to serve as special advocates for them. The 32 suggestions for local churches, 19 for the denomination, 12 for state conventions, and 5 for associations for the most part can be applied in other denominational groups as well.[65]

The suggestions in this chapter are already in effect in many places and are desired by many older people. Some are a natural outgrowth of the work of the church even when no special consideration is given to the aged as such, while others are a part of explicit, deliberately planned programs designed to meet the specific needs of the aged. Few churches have the personnel and other resources to put all of these suggestions into immediate practice, but all can introduce some of them as integral parts of their total program of worship and service to God and man.

To begin implementing the suggestions of this chapter is not costly except in terms of sacrificial love and consecrated time on the part of church leaders and workers.[66] In fact, in terms of humanitarian and spiritual values, *not* to do so is tremendously expensive. Indeed it can be argued with considerable justification that a high level of financial expense is itself an indication that a program is failing to meet the very important need of active older persons to have something significant and useful to do with their skills. When older persons are used as volunteers in church programs, activities with and for the aging will be within the financial means of their church.[67]

---

65. *Report of the SBC Study of the Problems of the Aging*, Executive Committee of the Southern Baptist Convention, 460 James Robertson Parkway, Nashville, TN 37219, 1975, $1.00.

66. Ed., "Church Services to Elderly Need Not Be Costly," *Christian Century*, 77: 251-252, Mar. 2, 1960.

67. Robb, *op. cit.*, p. 138.

NINE

What Older Persons Can Do for the Church

Popular presentations often imply that the sole end of life is to live comfortably during old age. This philosophy can lead to abject dependence and absurd selfishness.[1] Older people wish to feel useful, to continue contributing actively to the welfare of others, to feel wanted because of their contributions. This fundamental need to demonstrate love by giving is as basic a right as to be loved and wanted, to find recognition and meaning, and to feel fulfilled and satisfied. Meeting this need will help to gratify the others as well.[2] An important outlet for this is the church and its auxiliary organizations and programs.

This chapter indicates representative service opportunities for older members of the church. Not all apply to every older person; there are important differences in personalities and abilities among them, but every aging person who is willing can find several places of service in the church.

OLDER PERSONS CAN CONTRIBUTE TO WORSHIP

Aging members can participate actively when they are called upon to lead in public prayer, to tell the congregation how the Lord has led them through life and brought them through trials, or to share other experiences and insights.

Some older people, when given opportunity for public

---

1. See John R. Voris, "Let Senior Citizens Serve Others!," *Christian Century*, 77: 251-252, Mar. 2, 1960.
2. Anne K. Reisch, "The Rights of Older Persons—To Grow and Give," *Lutheran Social Concern*, 12(2): 48-50, Summer 1972.

testimony, do not seem to know when they ought to stop speaking. Wise leadership can help control that problem, but it can also be solved by giving them more regular and more frequent occasions to speak. If they are called upon only rarely, they may feel that they must express all that is on their minds. If more opportunities are given to speak in their own groups and in such other situations as educational or midweek activities of the church, they will usually say less on any one occasion.

Through both active and passive participation in the services of the church, people of all ages develop a sense of fellowship and belonging that is important to their personal adjustment and hence to their spiritual and social well-being. The integration of people of all ages can help to cure the societal plague of ageism, so the mere presence of the aging is an educational and liberating influence.

OLDER PERSONS CAN ENGAGE IN PERSONAL DEVOTIONS

It may appear to be a purely personal matter, but piety is a source of spiritual strength that indirectly spills over to others and as such becomes a means of fulfilling the church's goals.

Reading the Bible and meditating upon its contents is a major source of peace and comfort. The use of devotional literature prepared by the church, such as that prepared by various denominations for use in daily meditations, Bible reading, and prayers, can provide comfort and can assist in seeing the practical implications and applications of the teachings of the Bible.[3] The answers to many perplexing problems are found as one searches the Scriptures in the faith that they contain a personal message from God.

Many people are assisted in their religious devotions by symbolic objects (works of art, pictures, candles, etc.), by having a specific place of worship in the home (a "prayer closet"), or

3. Available devotional and inspirational literature published for the use of older people includes Glenn H. Asquith, *Lively May I Walk,* Abingdon Press, 1960; Asquith, *Sixty-Five and Counting,* Herald Press, 1975; Alfons Deeken, *Growing Old and How to Cope with It,* Paulist Press, 1972; Reuel Howe, *How to Stay Younger While Growing Older,* Word Books, 1974; Mildred Vandenburgh, *Fill Your Days with Life,* Regal Books, G/L Publications, 1975.

by a "family altar." Even though God does not dwell in temples made by hands, tangible symbols help many older people whose senses of communication are dull to cultivate an experience of the presence of God, of His watchcare over them, and of a heightened sense of the fellowship of all believers. These are then, subconsciously if not consciously, communicated to others who associate with them.

Many pastors and laymen have visited ill and infirm "saints of God" who were in great pain and suffering only to come away with far greater encouragement and help to their own souls than they felt they had imparted to the shut-in person. Examples such as this clearly demonstrate the great value there is for the church in the personal piety and devotion of its older members.

OLDER PERSONS CAN PRAY

Not only can the aging pray for themselves and their own needs, as is implied above, but they also can intercede with God on behalf of others. Even the shut-in on his or her death bed can develop through prayer a sense of participation in interpersonal relationships with God and with the innumerable host of fellow believers of the past, present, and future. The Christian confined to the sickroom or homebound by infirmities can still be a co-worker with God and other people by engaging in intercessory prayer.

The older Christian who lives in intimate fellowship with his Lord is never laid on the shelf. As long as one retains consciousness and is not in such extreme suffering that all thoughts except those of pain are squeezed from the mind, one can be active in the service of God, the church, and people through prayers on their behalf.

OLDER PERSONS CAN PARTICIPATE
IN GROUPS FOR THE AGING

This may seem to be a purely selfish and self-centered activity, but in helping to establish and support such groups the aging help others as well as themselves. They are given an increased sense of usefulness as they help others find a sense of worth. They ease their own loneliness as they help to alleviate the loneliness of others. They find work for themselves as they seek jobs for other senior adults. They make new friends as they help others develop friendships. They find pleasure and joy as they try to make others happy. Their own personal problems are mitigated as they help others find solutions or assistance for their difficulties. Their own burdens are lifted in the process of lifting the burdens of others.

OLDER PERSONS CAN TEACH

Many aging people can serve God and the church by teaching adult or children's classes in the church school.[4] Some can sponsor scout groups and teach craft classes. Many are also able to teach indirectly by reminding others of past experiences of the church when experimental programs were introduced. Their knowledge and skills often are a valuable source of insight into the history and the practical problems of the church, constituting a service graciously donated "as unto the Lord."

When church school teachers are young adults with growing children and other pressures, older members can help them prepare materials used in class activities, serving as assistant or associate teachers; thereby, they serve both the children and the younger adults.

OLDER PERSONS CAN VISIT

Various studies have established the fact that the fellowship within the church and efforts by lay members to build up the membership are more effective than at least the initial visit of the pastor.[5] Older members can play a major part in the missionary outreach and evangelistic emphasis of the local church. Their testimony of satisfactions achieved through their faith and the church can be a major influence attracting others into the church fellowship.

4. Harold H. Hazenfield, "Older Adults Can Serve the Church," *International Journal of Religious Education,* 30(5): 16-17, Jan. 1954.

5. One of these is by Roy G. Francis, Charles E. Ramsey, and Jacob A. Toews, "The Church in the Rural Fringe," *Minnesota Farm and Home Science,* 12(2): 8, 13, Feb. 1955.

Many older adults can assist in an organized visitation program of the church. They can visit the sick to comfort them. Many can visit prospective members and newcomers to orient them to the community and to invite them to the church.

Some can help cultivate a sense of fellowship in the congregation by visiting regular church members. Reports of their visits can be of great help to the pastor, relieving him of the responsibilities of visiting guests who are members of another church and came simply out of curiosity, reducing the frequency of his visits with shut-ins, and thus releasing time for other aspects of his ministry.

When older people converse, they often reminisce about the past. The younger generations tend to dismiss this activity as if it is only the insignificant rambling of people who have lost a sense of time and place, or they may even consider the behavior as senile or maladjusted. Research has demonstrated, however, that reminiscing is very healthy.[6] It is so wholesome and necessary to good mental health that gerontologists now encourage older people to conduct a life review. The life review is conducted in many ways. Expressing nostalgia and regret, story-telling about the past, reminiscing, assembling of family albums, scrapbooks, and genealogies, being interviewed for students' assignments or scientific research, and constructing personal or family life histories are some of the forms it can take. The process develops and sustains self-esteem, resolves grief, relieves stress, integrates the personality, rights old wrongs, provides serenity, gives a feeling of accomplishment, and serves generally as a constructive defense mechanism. When done so that results are shared with younger people or children, it facilitates intergenerational continuity, and it gives a better sense of historical time, connection with traditions and one's own past, and a model for one's future in the human life cycle.[7]

6. Allen Pincus, "Reminiscence in Aging and Its Implications for Social Work Practice," *Social Work*, 15(3): 47-53, 1970; and Charles N. Lewis, "Reminiscing and Self-Concept in Old Age," *Journal of Gerontology*, 26: 240-243, 1971.

7. Robert N. Butler and Myrna I. Lewis, *Aging and Mental Health*, C. V. Mosby Co., 1973, pp. 43-45; Barbara G. Myerhoff and Virginia Tufte, "Life History as Integration," *The Gerontologist*, 15(6): 541-543, Dec. 1975; Robert N. Butler, "The Life Review: An Interpretation of Reminiscence in the Aged," in Bernice L. Neugarten, ed., *Middle Age and Aging*, University of Chicago Press, 1968, pp. 486-496.

Volunteer visitors can encourage reminiscing. By being good listeners they contribute to the mental and spiritual health of older people. At times an interweaving of life histories by the visitor and the person visited will occur, each stimulating the other into further piecing together of one's own life story. While giving, the giver also receives the therapeutic benefits that come from interrelating the puzzling events of life and making sense of what seemed earlier to be a meaningless existence.

Visiting people with terminal illness poses special problems. Most such patients recognize, or at least suspect, the predicted outcome more clearly than their relatives and medical attendants believe they do, but delicacies of tact and common sense should not be ignored. Many of them wish to handle "unfinished business" of asking forgiveness for past mistakes, passing along words of advice to family members, arranging for disposition of property, completing their own life review, and turning or returning to religious faith. Perceptive visitors can help in many of these developmental tasks; their most important role may simply be providing their presence and a listening ear. Merely having somebody present in the closing hours of life is itself of great comfort to the dying person.[8]

Visiting those who have been bereaved may take on its highest level of significance for the healing of grief during the weeks and months following the immediate shock of separation from the departed family member or friend, rather than merely in the hours between death and the funeral. Previously widowed persons frequently can offer the best psychological and practical help, so a widow-to-widow program by which a one-to-one relationship to provide continuing assistance for widows and widowers over a year or more following bereavement together with group activities has been established in many

---

8. Among the many excellent resources to promote understanding of dying and bereaved people are Elisabeth Kübler-Ross, *On Death and Dying,* Macmillan, 1969; Edwin S. Shneidman, ed., *Death: Current Perspectives,* Mayfield Publishing Co., 1976; Orville G. Brim, Jr. *et al.,* eds., *The Dying Patient,* Russell Sage Foundation, 1970; John Hinton, *Dying,* Penguin Books, 1967; Diana Crane, "Death and Dying," in David Calhoun, ed., *1974 Britannica Yearbook of Science and the Future,* Helen Hemingway Benton, Publisher, 1973, pp. 96-111.

communities.[9] Friendship is the most important service provided, but through it also comes help with finances, finding a job, dealing with family members, legal problems, and emotional support in a period of intense loneliness. Where that kind of service is unavailable, churches might be the most appropriate initiators and sponsors, with older persons as their primary source of volunteer personnel.

OLDER PERSONS CAN IMPROVE AND MAINTAIN CHURCH PROPERTY

Many churches are badly landscaped and have grounds that are poorly tended. The lawn looks unkempt alongside those of residences in the vicinity. Flowers are not cultivated properly. Shrubbery often is not trimmed when and as it ought to be. Many aging people, feeling incapable of teaching or of visiting on behalf of the church, can be helped to realize that gardening and lawn-tending on the church premises is a significant service.

Many churches also need remodeling, painting, additional storage cabinets, or perhaps more classrooms. Many older people, retired from their regular occupations, have abilities that can be used to meet these needs. They may be used either as volunteers or as paid part-time workers.

The typical church nearly always needs minor repairs on squeaky chairs, bulletin boards that are marred and unsightly, coat racks that are broken or loose, upholstered chairs that have become dirty or badly worn, broken toys in the nursery, and many other things. Here, too, the time, talents, or hobbies of many older people can be used to good advantage.

In some churches older people serve as custodians of the church property. If the right person is found, he or she will consider such work to be a special service to God, not merely another job. When that occurs, the pride and interest in the task will make the church facilities much more attractive, usable, and effective than might otherwise be the case, and if the work is only part-time, the income supplementing Social Security can lift a person out of poverty.

---

9. See Phyllis Rolfe Silverman, "The Widow-to-Widow Program: An Experiment in Preventive Intervention," in Shneidman, *op. cit.*, pp. 356-363.

OLDER PERSONS CAN DO CLERICAL WORK

The aging who have clerical, teaching, and other white-collar or professional experience often can use their abilities for writing and editing a church paper or the church bulletin, keeping detailed church-school records that can greatly improve follow-up work by the staff, addressing and mailing church announcements, compiling missionary records and scrapbooks that can be used by church-school teachers and leaders of auxiliary organizations, building historical archives which record the establishment and growth of the church and its community, maintaining a church library, conducting surveys or other research, and similar activities.

Many of these avenues of service by older people can save the pastor long hours of work, both by making it unnecessary for him or his secretary to do it and by saving time in finding desired material at the time it is needed for producing a church anniversary history, writing the obituary of a long-time member, or seeking an incident or illustration for a sermon from the archives of the church.

OLDER PERSONS CAN CONDUCT CHURCH BUSINESS

Churches often buy and sometimes dispose of property. Many of them have building programs that take hours of extra work by the pastor and other leaders. If competent retired people are members in the church, they can relieve the clergy and other personnel of much tedious detail work that takes energy away from other responsibilities. The aging can serve as members of a "Volunteer Christian Corps," as Trueblood suggests, after their retirement from secular occupations. A few are qualified to serve as business managers for the church.[10]

OLDER PERSONS CAN BE COMMUNITY SERVICE VOLUNTEERS

Church-related and church-sponsored activities like those

10. Elton Trueblood, *Your Other Vocation,* Harper and Brothers, 1952, pp. 53ff. For one account of a person who did this, see "Pastor's Right-Hand Man," *Christian Life,* 17(8): pp. 51ff., Dec. 1955. In some denominations older adults are permitted to become clergymen after a period of preparation. The most systematic program assisting such a change of vocation is in the Episcopal Church.

mentioned in chapter 8 need personnel, and most churches lack financial resources to operate such programs exclusively with paid staff members. Volunteers are needed to help meet physical and material needs, to conduct social and recreational programs, to help people find resources to solve their personal problems, to focus the church's influence on civic and political affairs on the local, state, and national level, and to study the community. The exemplary program of friendly visiting sponsored by the International Ladies' Garment Workers' Union since 1967 is but one of many models of what can be done. Its staff of Friendly Visitors consists of retired garment workers who are paid for their services to retired persons in institutions.[11] The National Center for Voluntary Action maintains a clearinghouse on volunteer services for older persons[12] and has produced materials for use in directing volunteer programs, recruiting volunteers, and preparing them for their work.

Sometimes a volunteer service program takes on characteristics different from those originally intended. For example, in one project it was anticipated that aging Blacks would serve most effectively in a neighborhood one-to-one volunteer program by running errands, taking telephone calls, writing letters and reading to persons who themselves could not, visiting the lonely, doing light housekeeping chores, taking the infirm out of doors into the sunshine, and offering comfort, solace, and support to persons who were sick, bereaved, or undergoing traumatic personal crises. Because of environmental circumstances, problems of staff leadership, their own characteristics and propensities, and other factors, they instead became helpers in group activities of organized programs. Nevertheless, this in itself was an important task which brought personal rewards to both the volunteers and those whom they served.[13]

Cooperating in research is an indirect form of volunteer service. The aging have often been observed to be more cooperative in such work than people in earlier periods of life.

---

11. *Friendly Visiting to the Aged in Institutions,* ILGWU Retiree Service Department, 201 W. 52nd St., New York, NY 10019.

12. 1785 Massachusetts Ave., N.W., Washington, D.C. 20036.

13. Audrey Olsen Faulkner, "The Black Aged as Good Neighbors: An Experiment in Volunteer Service," *The Gerontologist,* 15(6): 554-559, Dec. 1975.

The topic of conversation typically is one of great interest to them, as to anyone — themselves. They also are given a renewed sense of personal dignity from the recognition conveyed during the interview that their information and opinions still are important. Even very old persons in their eighties and nineties and many who are identified as senile by people caring for them have been interviewed successfully when they have been approached slowly, letting them observe the interviewer first and assuring them of their ability to respond to the requests made of them.[14]

Significant leadership in efforts to overcome discrimination against older people is provided by such groups as the Gray Panthers under the leadership of Margaret ("Maggie") Kuhn, the National Council of Senior Citizens, the American Association of Retired Persons, and the National Caucus on the Black Aged. In many communities there are senior action coalitions which cooperate with chapters from these national associations in efforts to promote the well-being and interests of older people. If a church does nothing about the societal attitudes and actions which demean the aging and deprive them of their dignity, then it is capitulating sinfully to the status quo, for knowing what is right to do and then failing to do it is sin (James 4:17). Both through individual participation and as representatives of church groups, aging members can contribute to constructive social change in regard to ageism and the place of older people in society. This is one aspect of their not being conformed to this world, instead letting God transform their minds and conduct (Romans 12:2).

People who are institutionalized also can volunteer their services. For example, at the Philadelphia Geriatric Center a resident welcoming committee made up of volunteer residents was created to provide newly admitted persons with needed emotional support and orientation. Weekly group meetings also provided the committee members with a vehicle for discussion and exploration of their own problems. This group experience has had considerable therapeutic value and has

---

14. Joseph Zelan, "Interviewing the Aged," *Public Opinion Quarterly*, 33: 420-424, Fall 1969; Mary Gwynne Schmidt, "Interviewing the 'Old Old'," *The Gerontologist*, 15(6): 544-547, Dec. 1975.

been of as much help to the volunteers as to the others who have received their aid.[15]

Similarly, homebound shut-ins can serve others through telephone reassurance programs, prayer circles, missionary sewing projects, and many other types of service if only they are given opportunity through appropriate coordinating leadership.

The potentialities for service programs in the typical community are as broad as the range of human needs and the creativity of sympathetic people who seek ways to satisfy them. Whether for relatively simple services like helping to complete Medicare forms and write letters or for programs demanding more organizational structure like telephone reassurance and foster grandparents ventures, volunteers play the crucial role of delivering the services.[16] Churches and religious faith, in turn, provide much of the motivating force for such activities. Even when they are not the explicit sponsors, churches play a very significant role in community programs by their spiritual and psychological support which encourage members to participate.

OLDER PERSONS CAN HELP WITH NUMEROUS "MINOR" TASKS[17]

The aging can help in routine church tasks by offering (or being asked) to help usher, regulate the temperature, decorate the church with flowers, direct traffic in the church parking lot, or prepare and serve food for social gatherings. Or they may help in such jobs as counseling young people in their selection of vocations, serving in the church's music ministry, speaking to various church groups on relevant topics, including the customs of days gone by, representing the congregation at denominational and ecumenical conferences and assemblies,

15. Susan Friedman, "The Resident Welcoming Committee: Institutionalized Elderly in Volunteer Services to Their Peers," *The Gerontologist,* 15(4): 362-367, Aug. 1975.

16. For an excellent brochure on projects appropriate for religious groups see *The Church/Synagogue and Aging,* Church Relations Office, NRTA-AARP-AIM, 1909 K St., N.W., Washington, D.C. 20049.

17. See Marion P. Obenhaus, "Lights Under a Bushel," *International Journal of Religious Education,* 30(10): pp. 6ff., June 1954; and David O. Byler, "Utilizing Older Adults in the Music Ministry," *The Church Musician,* 10(7): 11-12, 14, July 1959, for many suggestions.

and representing the church at meetings of civic organizations in the community. In these and countless other ways they can provide the small and seemingly insignificant services which are seldom noticed when they are performed well but which usually are very obvious when they are left undone.

CONCLUSION

As the services of the aging are used in the church — and they will not be used unless there is wise leadership that invites and encourages them to be of service — the church will benefit and the older persons themselves will prosper.

Intelligent study of the needs of the church and of the interests and abilities of its senior members can result in the matching of needs and abilities. Then both the church and its older members will benefit, the roles of the young and the aging in the church will be modified, and the entire church program will take on renewed vigor and gain increased respect in the community. The influence and service of the church can be greatly extended with almost no monetary cost through voluntary lay workers. In 1958, for example, 45 lay men and women donated 15,620 hours to the Senior Citizen Project of the San Francisco Council of Churches,[18] and many other groups have reaped similar benefits.

In the early history of Christianity the apostles told the church to select seven men to relieve them of the task of "serving tables" and taking care of the daily distribution of material goods so that they could spend more time in prayer, the ministry of the word, and preaching (Acts 6:1-6). Similarly today it is appropriate for Christian pastors to use lay persons to the fullest advantage for routine duties in the church so that the clergy can engage in their ministry of teaching, preaching, praying, studying, and pastoral care. It is only logical that capable older persons who have much time on their hands should be used extensively in this type of service.

As the older person loses his or her life in sincere service to God, the church, and other people, he or she is more likely

---

18. Mrs. Milton Schiffman, "Report for 1958, Senior Citizen Project, San Francisco Council of Churches," *Maturity,* 6(1): 15-16, Mar. 31, 1959. The minimum monetary equivalent of this donated time was $39,050.

to find the "abundant life," the life that is characterized by good personal and social adjustment. It is indeed more blessed, that is, more conducive to happiness, to give than it is to receive.

Old age can be "the last of life for which the first was planned," a time of happiness and contentment, or it can be the most miserable period of life. Those who give the most in old age in turn receive the most. Even shut-in persons who may not leave home until the body is prepared for the grave can continue to give, and so can the older people who are physically and mentally in the best of health.

Both the teachings of America's religions and the values of her social scientists include the goal of making old age a time of happiness and joy, a stage of good personal and social adjustment, an age of high morale, and a time of life satisfaction, rather than a period of mental anguish, social maladjustment, and dissatisfaction. Many programs of churches, aided by findings of scientific studies such as those reported in this book,[19] are contributing to the attainment of that goal.

---

19. A wealth of research findings with soundly-based interpretations and implications is available in the 17 Background Papers prepared for the 1971 White House Conference on Aging (Government Printing Office, Washington, D.C., 1971). See also the resources mentioned in the footnotes and in Appendix III of this book.

TEN

The Clergy and Older People

Ministers, priests, and rabbis play pivotal roles in the ministries of religious organizations for and with older people. Their example, attitudes, activities, suggestions, and recommendations are more important than any other single influence within a church. If they support ministries for older people, their congregations are very likely to establish and sustain such ministries. If they oppose such ministries through benign neglect or direct confrontation, their congregations are likely to have none.

We recognize that there are constant pressures upon the clergy to establish programs for a large number and broad range of specialized categories of people and needs; they cannot do everything. Our emphasis in this chapter will be upon their facilitating and enabling roles in the context of the normal work which effective professional church leaders will be doing anyway; ministries with and for the aging in a congregation actually can relieve the clergy of some burdens that they are expected to carry.

PREACHING AND TEACHING

References to old age and aging processes emerge naturally in the sermons, meditations, and homilies of the clergy. The Scriptures, which typically are their basis, abound with references to the various stages of the life cycle and include many passages telling people to respect their elders, meet their needs, and heed their wisdom. Symbolic pictures of old men are conveyed by references to the patriarchs of the faith and even the anthropomorphic images of God. The commandment to honor one's father and mother is reflected in many Bible passages which are mentioned from the pulpit. Sermon illustrations and the applications of biblical principles to everyday life similarly include many references to generational differences and interrelationships.

If a religious leader has not given careful attention to his or her own process of aging, fears and anxieties may lurk in the unconscious, emerging in subtle reflections of attitudes which are detrimental to the well-being of older people and harmful to effective ministries with them. The cultural diseases of ageism and gerontophobia easily afflict the clergy and other professional leaders. Caught from the attitudes prevalent in our youth-oriented society, these tend to be self-perpetuated and to spread rampantly unless active steps are taken to correct them or to treat the illness. In other words, it is very easy for the clergy to be fully conformed to the world around them instead of allowing God to transform their hearts and minds from within (Romans 12:2).

Many attitudes are more easily caught by a congregation from its pastor than deliberately taught. The most effective teaching and preaching pertinent to aging and older people is that which occurs week in and week out rather than that which is the focus of an annual sermon on the subject, good and desirable as that is. References to pastoral visits, requests for prayer on behalf of older members, messages at funerals, and supportive comments about the programs of the congregation and ministries of individual members with and for older people can all make a significant contribution.

Both from the pulpit and in more explicitly educational contexts the clergy can teach the importance of independent living for the aging, the need to reform social structures which impede it, how to use spiritual resources for daily strength as well as in the crises which occur during aging,[1] and similar truths. The process of conscientization in this realm of life and

---

1. See, e.g., Warren Wiersbe, "You Can Make Your Retirement a Religious Experience," *Senior Power*, 1(1): 20-23, 30, 1975 (reprinted from *Moody Monthly*, Feb. 1975), and Ross Snyder, guest ed., "In the Aging Years: Spirit," special issue of *Chicago Theological Seminary Register*, 63(4), Sep. 1973.

thought can be viewed as one of "gerontologizing" people of all ages by sensitizing them to the presence, characteristics, needs, and resources of the older generation. Motivating people to contribute their love through volunteer service multiplies the impact of a church, and everything wholesome it accomplishes for children, youth, and young adults has a preventive impact which reduces the problems of aging.

There is some evidence that older people tend to reduce their instrumental activities and increase their expressive relationships. In other words, they become more interested in being than in doing, and they move away from endeavors oriented toward production and move toward those in which they can express themselves emotionally because their acts are ends in themselves, rather than means for the accomplishment of other goals.[2] Their contacts with clergy tend to be less for specific church business and more for spiritual nurture than when they were middle-aged. This suggests that there should be less minister-parishioner conflict among them than at other adult ages.[3] Satisfaction scores on the pastoral role of working with the aged in a study of 654 American Baptist clergy, however, were considerably lower than those for working with young people and teaching adults. The clergy with expressive role orientations derived greater satisfaction from ministering to the aged than did those who had an instrumental orientation.[4]

ADMINISTRATIVE LEADERSHIP

As the clergy survey what can be done by the church for older people and what they, in turn, can do in and for the church, they are likely to feel that such ministries constitute a full-time job for which they have no time whatever.

One of the most important roles that the clergy can play

2. Phillip E. Hammond, "Aging and the Ministry," in Matilda White Riley et al., Aging and Society, Vol. Two: Aging and the Professions, Russell Sage Foundation, 1969, pp. 293-323.

3. Ibid., p. 307.

4. Charles F. Longino, Jr., and Gay C. Kitson, "Parish Clergy and the Aged: Examining Stereotypes," Journal of Gerontology, 31(3): 340-345, May 1976.

in ministries for older people is developing supportive service ministries by lay people. Indeed, a strong case can be made for the position that equipping lay people for ministry is the primary task of the clergy (Ephesians 4:11-16). With appropriate encouragement and a minimum of pastoral leadership, highly creative programs can be developed to meet the needs of individuals and groups in the congregation and in the community. In some cases these can have an entirely volunteer orientation; in others a professional person employed part-time to direct the activities and, especially, to mobilize the resources available in relationship to the needs is a better approach.

Sensitivity of the clergy to these needs and opportunities will often make the deciding difference. Furthermore, once systematic programs of visitation, social services, home care, and the like are established, the pastor is relieved of many direct responsibilities because other people are helping to satisfy those human needs. Rather than constituting a drain upon the energies and time of the professional clergy, such ministries with and for the aging can relieve the pastor of a considerable amount of work and multiply the church's contributions to spiritual, social, psychological, and material well-being.[5]

PASTORAL CARE

A large proportion of the clinical pastoral work of the clergy is devoted to older people and those who are immediately concerned with their care. One of the things most desired by elderly people from the church is visits in their own homes.[6] Visiting elderly shut-ins, hospitalized persons, residents of convalescent homes, widows, other bereaved persons, and the families trapped in problems relevant to the care of aging members consumes a large block of the typical pastor's working time.

Much of the ministry of pastoral care is one of comfort,

---

5. For practical suggestions see the Rev. Calhoun W. Wick's guidebook, *The Management Side of Ministry,* Wick Press, 1976, esp. pp. 23-26, 80-81. (This excellent handbook for clergy is available at $5.00 from St. Michael's in the Hills, 4718 Brittany Rd., Toledo, OH 43615.) See also Sister M. Laurice, OSF, "What Can a Minister and a Congregation Do to Help Meet the Needs of the Aging," Missouri Interfaith Commission on Aging, n.d., ca. 1975.

6. Hammond, *op. cit.,* p. 304.

reassurance, helping people to forgive themselves, coping with anxieties, and providing the assurance of God's loving concern for human needs. Some of it, however, involves direct pleas for advice, such as the question of whether or not to place grand-mother in a retirement home. The pastor is often caught in the middle between the contrasting opinions and wishes of the persons involved and somehow needs to bring peace to a con-flict situation. The task of serving as a bridge between a dying person and an alienated spouse or child, of helping the dying patient to make relatives accept the inevitability of death, and of helping the patient gain psychological closure may be thrust upon the pastor.[7] Respect for the dignity of all people, even during alleged senility, is an important attitude and one gen-uinely consistent with religious principles.

Ministers who wait for people to come to them to request spiritual help generally find that most people ignore them. Through a regular pattern of visiting or, better yet, coordi-nated visitation activities by lay members, needs for special spiritual care may be identified, thus enabling preventive work prior to the eruption of major conflicts. Being readily accessible is one step in this direction, as is the constantly reiterated announcement of such availability.

Effective use of the telephone for counseling can save time and multiply the number of people helped. Even a telephone recording system, available at very modest cost, can be a major step in the direction of increasing the quality of pastoral care, provided such messages are followed up promptly. It can also help to relieve the pastor of telephone calls late in the night and at other inconvenient moments.[8]

Spiritual care for people who are in nursing homes is an area of special concern because many pastors tend to forget members, parishioners, and others who are in them and often overlook their needs. Sometimes, such members are located at a great distance from their home church, and the clergy in that locale do not wish to raise ethical questions by visiting mem-

---

7. *Ibid.*, p. 321, and Anselm L. Strauss and Barney G. Glaser, "Patterns of Dying," in Orville G. Brim, Jr. *et al.*, eds., *The Dying Patient*, Russell Sage Foundation, 1970, pp. 145-147.

8. See August W. Dowdy, Jr., *Phone Power*, Judson Press, 1975, for an excellent manual on use of the telephone in ministry.

bers of other congregations or parishes. Nursing and medical staff generally are not attuned to noticing and reporting spiritual needs. The concept of "total patient care" typically omits concern for explicitly spiritual needs.

In a few progressive nursing homes, such as Murray Manor, the clergy are requested to record the spiritual needs and progress of patients on their charts following each visit and to acknowledge their visits with the nursing staff. They also have the opportunity to meet with the chaplain of the home and to participate with the administrative staff in patient care conferences to help design the plan for care.[9] In such institutions a much more holistic perspective of patient care prevails than in the more typical homes in which clergy are viewed almost as intruders.

The clergy are often called upon shortly before and after death to deal with spiritual needs of the dying person, to comfort those who are bereaved, and to help prepare for funeral services. An understanding pastor who is a good listener and is able to bring the benefits of religious faith and sacramental rituals clearly to bear upon these difficult situations can make a major contribution to the well-being of all parties involved.[10] If, however, the timing of a chaplain's or priest's visit is not planned well, the patient or relatives may become unnecessarily frightened and upset.[11] The funeral often precedes the pangs of grief; their greatest impact typically is in the second week of bereavement, so the best time for pastoral visits is in the week following the funeral and at intervals during the first year of bereavement.[12]

9. Jaber F. Gubrium, Living and Dying at Murray Manor, St. Martin's Press, 1975, pp. 41, 65-78.

10. Arthur Foote, "Death and the Religious Counselor," in Betty R. Green and Donald Irish, eds., Death Education: Preparation for Living, Schenkman Publishing Co., 1971, pp. 97-100; Alois Müller, "Care of the Dying as a Task of the Church," in Norbert Greinacher and Alois Müller, eds., The Experience of Dying, Herder and Herder (Concilium No. 94), 1974, pp. 126-130; Robert Perske, "Death and Ministry: Episode and Response," Pastoral Psychology, 15(146): 25-35, Sep. 1964.

11. Barney G. Glaser and Anselm L. Strauss, Time for Dying, Aldine, 1968, pp. 192-193.

12. Colin M. Parkes, Bereavement: Studies of Grief in Adult Life, International Universities Press, 1972, pp. 158-161, 169-171.

Grief because of bereavement or other losses can cause considerable pain and misery. Along with medical doctors, ministers and other professional people should help grieving individuals to cry and to share their tears. The sharing of guilt helps to eliminate its irrational aspects and to work out a sense of forgiveness. Hostility and anger may be expressed toward those who share the grief; such reactions should not be taken personally but should be recognized as a part of the healing process.[13] Feelings of resentment and accusation against a minister or priest who offers help in time of bereavement are common during the stage of intense mourning in which the grieving person is likely also to express anger and reproach against God, society, the physician, family members, and oneself.[14]

All of the basic principles of pastoral care and counseling apply to these ministries; it is impossible to survey them here.[15] The specifics that are involved reflect varying theologies as well as different theories of the psychological and social nature of human need. Through reading, continuing education, association with other clergy, and use of experience in such a manner as to make it a genuine basis for learning, the clergy can grow in wisdom and in the ability to deal with the pastoral needs of their people.

PREPARATION OF THE CLERGY

Many clergy realize that their educational preparation and training for ministries with the aging has been deficient. Only 22 of 109 Milwaukee clergy who were surveyed to identify their felt needs in relationship to ministries to the aging indicated that they had specific and adequate preparation to help them understand the experiences and feelings of people as they grow older; 17 had only inadequate preparation, and 70 reported no specific preparation. Nearly all (95%) of those

13. Edwin P. Gramlich, "Recognition and Management of Grief in Elderly Patients," in Virginia M. Brantl and Sister Marie Raymond Brown, eds., *Readings in Gerontology,* C.V. Mosby Co., 1973, pp. 105-110 (originally published in *Geriatrics,* July 1968).

14. Grace Loucks Elliott, *To Come Full Circle: Toward An Understanding of Death,* published by the author in New York City, 1971.

15. One resource based upon the personality sciences and professional counseling skills is Edgar N. Jackson, *Parish Counseling,* Aronson, 1975.

who felt their past training was adequate believed that they worked very well or well with older people, compared to 85% of those who had no specific preparation and only 59% of those with inadequate preparation. Of the 109 respondents 106 were pastors of Catholic parishes or Protestant congregations; nine of the 106 pastors were in churches in which over half (50%) of the membership was age 65 and over, 26 had 35% to 49%, and 30 had 20% to 34% of their membership in that age category, yet 43 had no specific activities for older adults. The greatest need they identified was for knowledge of community resources to serve the aging, followed in order of priority by their desire for suggestions for innovative programs; meeting spiritual needs; how to meet other needs; how to help middle-age people prepare for retirement; information about the aging process; assistance for ministries for the sick, dying, and bereaved; relationships between the generations; and in lowest position, problems with their own attitudes and fears of aging.[16]

Theological education ought to include explicit attention to aging for many reasons. A large proportion of time is involved in the work of the typical clergy for visiting, counseling, and helping parishioners who are aging. The later period of life tends to be one of many severe crises and personal problems. Church programs are expanding to meet such needs, so their leaders are expected to understand and support them. Ministers themselves have assimilated a great deal of misguided folklore and many myths about the aged and the aging process. They need to be prepared for radical developments in medical technology, social security, pension plans, and other areas of life in our rapidly changing society. The widespread, unintentional neglect of the aging, even among persons in the helping professions, and the large numbers and growing proportion of the population who are past the age of 65 are further reasons for including aging in the education of the clergy. Above all, theological values in the Judeo-Christian ethic which admonish us to be our brother's keeper, to honor our parents, to love our neighbors, to sustain personal and social justice, and to

16. David O. Moberg, "Needs Felt by the Clergy for Ministries to the Aging," *The Gerontologist*, 15(2): 170-175, April 1975.

follow the example of God whose benefits fall upon the evil and unjust as well as upon those who are "good" demand a direct concern for aging in theological schools.[17]

Theological seminaries can prepare clergy to meet the increasing demand for well-balanced social and recreational programs for older parishioners by placing their students in retirement homes for part of their training. Volunteers for assistance in such programs can come from the church. The theological orientation of a church will, of course, influence the nature and scope of its services to the leisure-time and other needs of older people.

Opportunities for such training are gradually being incorporated into the curricula of theological seminaries. In 1975 Dr. Derrel Watkins, Professor of Social Work at Southwestern Baptist Theological Seminary, conducted a survey of seminary involvement in gerontology and specialized training of personnel for serving the aging for the National Interfaith Coalition on Aging. Of 99 theological seminaries in the U.S.A. which returned questionnaires, 27 indicated that they offer one or more courses in gerontology in their departments of pastoral ministry, religious education, social work, or ethics, and 79 schools reported having courses with gerontological content. Forty-eight schools required one or more courses which include such content; in the other schools an estimated one-fourth of the students were taking elective courses with some gerontological content. It is likely that the 75 seminaries that did not respond at all had an even poorer record, but only further checking can verify that hunch.[18]

A wide range of opportunities for continuing education is available to clergy. It includes formalized programs of Clinical Pastoral Education in the chaplaincy services of many major hospitals, conferences and workshops offered through continuing education departments of colleges and universities, workshops sponsored by councils of churches or ad hoc groups which sense a need in the community, books and magazine articles on relevant topics, and specialized short courses in

17. Moberg, "Aging and Its Implications for Theological Education," *Journal of Pastoral Care*, 24(2): 127-134, June 1970.
18. Watkins, "Seminary Instruction in Gerontology," *NICA INFORM*, 1: 2-3, Aug. 25, 1975.

theological schools, universities, and gerontology institutes. For those who cannot participate personally in such educational programs, cassette tapes are often available. Anyone who has a genuine desire to upgrade his or her training for ministries with the aging can find so many in-service opportunities for doing so that the greatest problem confronted is that of priorities.

Having such a wealth of opportunities and being pulled in so many different directions, some clergy simply fit into the comfortable rut of going about the daily, weekly, and seasonal round of activities with little thought for evaluation of outcomes as a means of improving the quality of their work. Many of them are trapped by the cultural disease of ageism into thinking that only what is done for children, youth, and young adults is of lasting value to the church. As a result, they cut off opportunities to minister to aging people; without realizing it, they thus cut off many opportunities to influence middle-aged and younger people as well. Evidencing genuine concern for people of all ages, on the contrary, has beneficial results for the total well-being of a church as well as of its individual members. Theological seminaries need to give more systematic attention to these facts.

There can be growth in this area even apart from formal training programs. The wise pastor will profit from the experiences of others through wide reading, discussions with other clergy to share each other's insights, and continual efforts to evaluate and upgrade the quality of pastoral care.[19]

RETIREMENT OF THE CLERGY

As is true of the historical development of many professions, little direct attention was given to retirement plans for

---

19. Many excellent suggestions are found in Paul B. Maves and J. Lennart Cedarleaf, *Older People and the Church*, Abingdon-Cokesbury Press, 1949, pp. 50-58, especially in chapter 6, "Principles and Methods of Pastoral Care," pp. 108-135. See also Harlow Donovan, "Pastoral Needs of Older Women," *Journal of Pastoral Care*, 10: 170-176, Fall 1956; Thomas B. Robb, *The Bonus Years: Foundations for Ministry with Older Persons*, Judson Press, 1968; Robert N. Butler and Myrna I. Lewis, *Aging and Mental Health*, C.V. Mosby Co., 1973. An excellent resource for leaders of educational programs in the church is Roy B. Zuck and Gene A. Getz, eds., *Adult Education in the Church*, Moody Press, 1970 (see especially David O. Moberg, "The Nature and Needs of Older Adults," pp. 56-72).

the clergy until relatively recently. Each was expected to work out his own arrangements in his own way, and the parishes or congregations which had employed them felt little or no responsibility for their needs during retirement. One of the consequences of this was that many churches refused to employ a minister who was past the age of 45. They were afraid that he might not be able to move to another congregation and might settle down, expecting to continue as minister until death, which they feared would come only long after his effective service had ended.

Many denominational bodies now have effective retirement plans for their clergy. The opportunity of ministers to have Social Security coverage also has helped to alleviate some of the worst problems of economic poverty during the later years. New developments in Roman Catholic religious congregations and orders also have made it necessary for them to think systematically about the retirement of their brothers, sisters, and priests. It can no longer be assumed that their retirement will be taken care of automatically through the employment and income of younger working members; a bureaucratic system of pre-retirement preparation programs is emerging. As pre-retirement programs have been established, it has been found that some of the difficulties associated with the "emptiness syndrome" experienced by many middle-aged members of religious orders also are dealt with, so these have a wholesome impact upon keeping people productively employed in their place of service.[20]

Numerous active roles are possible for the clergy after their retirement from the ministry. Many of them serve as interim ministers for short periods of time, bridging the period between the departure of a regular minister and the coming of a new one. Some of them have been very fruitful in using their wisdom and accumulated experience to bring peace between warring factions within a congregation or to initiate an

---

20. Brother Henry Ringkamp, S.M., *Religious Pre-Retirement and Retirement Programs*, Central Catholic High School, San Antonio, Texas 78215, Summer 1975. See also Sister Duchesne Herold, S.S.M., *New Life: Preparation of Religious for Retirement*, Catholic Hospital Association, 1973; and Tom Hickey, *et al.*, "Catholic Religious Orders and the Aging Process," *The Gerontologist*, 12(1): 16-21, Spring 1972.

awareness of the need for new ministries. Others serve as part-time visiting clergymen, leaders of ministries for senior citizens, resident pastors of retirement centers, and chaplains of hospitals or nursing homes. A retired pastor of one of the authors of this book, the Rev. Arthur Ellison, has undertaken an unpaid volunteer ministry of intercessory prayer for his past parishioners, remembering them individually by name as he prays.

CONCLUSION

The most important single person in all ministries of the church with and for the older person is the pastor. The basic attitudes of people in the congregation are shaped and modified by the minister's own attitudes through the ministries of preaching, teaching, and pastoral care. If those attitudes are defective, tainted with the cultural disease of ageism, the social-psychological illness of gerontophobia, and neglect of elderly shut-ins,[21] the sickness is likely to be caught by leading members. If, on the contrary, a wholesome spirit of genuine love and understanding of the aging (as well as of other age groups) characterizes the pastor, all will benefit as that love rubs off.

Through the roles of teaching, preaching, pastoral care, and administrative leadership, the minister or priest plays a primary part by providing services as well as by the stimulus given to ministries by other people of all ages. If it is assumed that every organized group within the church should have a service project that reaches out to other people in the congregation and the community, then older people and other often-forgotten minorities like the poor, mentally retarded, hospitalized, and physically or socially handicapped will be the beneficiaries.

The clergy play an important role in providing educational experiences for others who can minister to the aging, and they themselves have many opportunities for improving

_____

21. Older persons who can no longer attend church or contribute to its financial needs attribute such neglect to crassly materialistic goals, feeling they are not visited because the pastor and church no longer benefit from such contacts (Esther E. Twente, *Never Too Old*, Jossey-Bass, 1970, pp. 65, 221).

their own knowledge, wisdom, and skills for such ministries. By coping realistically with their own future retirement and death, they will be preparing themselves for more effective ministries with and for the aging.

The theological orientation of the clergy and the church is of great importance to their ministries with the aging. As Herbert C. Lazenby, S.T.D., past President of the American Association of Homes for the Aging, has said,

> ... Christian Social Service and action, which I think are roles of the church, point themselves to the God who is man's keeper, to the Lord, who is man's redeemer, and to the Holy Spirit, who is the ultimate Healer and Liberalizer of the world. Christian social action which loses sight of basic motivation to declare the handiwork of God is truncated unless it speaks of church as community.... The first business of the church is with God....
>
> In many ways this time of life is a time of exile and the church has nothing to offer the world if the world and the church become so indistinguishable that the church is thought of as just another do-good group or another social agency.[22]

Although much of the focus of this book has been upon material, physical, social, and emotional needs and problems of aging people, together with what the churches can do to meet those needs, all of these must be seen in the context of the primary responsibilities and task of the church. If the centrality of spiritual ministries is not maintained, other ministries eventually will suffer, for they are fruit that comes from the spiritual root. The teaching of Jesus Christ to seek first God's kingdom and righteousness (Matthew 6:33) applies to people collectively, as in a church, as well as individually. When that is done, the other needs will also be provided.

---

22. Lazenby, "Mandate to the Church," unpublished paper prepared for Provincial Conference on Aging, El Rancho del Obispo, Healdsburg, Calif., Feb. 1965, p. 7. For a social scientist's interpretation of the theological basis for and practical implications of Christian social responsibility, see David O. Moberg, *Inasmuch: Christian Social Responsibility in the Twentieth Century,* Eerdmans, 1965.

Appendix I

A Definition of Spiritual Well-Being

The term "Spiritual Well-Being," which was inherited from the 1971 White House Conference on Aging, received rigorous study by a select interfaith consultation of religious leaders and scholars in February 1975. The resulting definition with its accompanying interpretive commentary was adopted as a working definition by the National Interfaith Coalition on Aging at its annual meeting in April 1975, and serves as a basis for the National Intra-Decade Conference on the Spiritual Well-Being of the Elderly to be held in 1977.

The statement is intergenerational in its conception, so it should be equally useful at any stage of the aging process from the beginning of life to its end. Serving as a reference point or standard from which and to which any person or group may go in applying it to one's respective tradition or activity, the definition and commentary are copyrighted by NICA, but readers are encouraged to quote from it and to reproduce it with appropriate acknowledgment. Those who do so should send copies to NICA, 298 S. Hull St., Athens, GA 30601.

SPIRITUAL WELL-BEING

— a definition —

Spiritual Well-Being is the affirmation of life in a relationship with God, self, community and environment that nurtures and celebrates wholeness.

Commentary

SPIRITUAL WELL-BEING IS THE AFFIRMATION OF LIFE...

The *Spiritual* is not one dimension among many in life; rather, it permeates and gives meaning to all life. The term Spiritual Well-Being, therefore, indicates wholeness in contrast to fragmentation and isolation. "Spiritual" connotes our dependence on the source of life, God the Creator.

What, then, is Spiritual *Well-Being?* We cannot regard well-being as equated solely with physical, psychological, or social good health. Rather, it is an *affirmation of life*. It is to say "Yes" to life in spite of negative circumstances. This is not mere optimism which denies some of life's realities; rather, it is the acknowledgment of the destiny of life. In the light of that destiny it is the love of one's own life and of the lives of others, together with concern for one's community, society, and the whole of creation, which is the dynamic of Spiritual Well-Being.

A person's affirmation of life is rooted in participating in a community of faith. In such a community one grows to accept the past, to be aware and alive in the present, and to live in hope of fulfillment.

...A RELATIONSHIP WITH GOD, SELF, COMMUNITY, AND ENVIRONMENT...

Affirmation of life occurs within the context of one's relationship with God, self, community, and environment. God is seen as "Supreme Being," "Creator" of life, the Source of Power that wills well-being. All people are called upon to respond to God in love and obedience. Realizing we are God's children, we grow toward wholeness as individuals, and we are led to affirm our kinship with others in the community of faith as well as the entire human family. Under God and as members of the community of faith, we are responsible for relating the resources of the environment to the well-being of all humanity.

...THAT NURTURES AND CELEBRATES WHOLENESS

Human wholeness is never fully attained. Throughout life it is a possibility in process of becoming. In the Judeo-Christian tradition(s) life derives its significance through its relationship with God. This relationship awakens and nourishes the process of growth toward wholeness in self, crowns moments of life with meaning, and extols the spiritual fulfillment and unity of the person.

Appendix II

Suggestions for Further Study

The importance of aging as a phenomenon within society is increasing steadily. The problems associated with old age have vast dimensions; the evidence on every hand indicates that, if present trends continue, they will become more acute with time.

Research findings concerning the relationships of religion and church experiences to adjustment or well-being in old age have been examined in this book. These have led to the conclusion that religious faith and experiences play an important role in the personal adjustment and life satisfaction of millions of older people. For this reason, among others, knowledge about the older person and the church can be expected to become a major area of gerontology, the science of aging.

From the perspective of gerontological research, this book can be seen as providing an orientation and framework for further studies which could contribute much to science while also helping to heighten satisfactions of people in the later years and to alleviate many of their problems. To be sure, there is a relative paucity of knowledge upon which to base such research. Pollak's declaration a generation ago still has substantial validity. He said that in the field of religion

> ...changes affecting the participation of older people...have received so little attention that the fund of relevant knowledge is hardly sufficient to serve as a basis for making specific research proposals. For the time being, therefore, investigatory efforts... will have to be largely exploratory.[1]

The situation has improved since that time, but not as greatly as most social scientists, churchmen, and older people would desire.

---

1. Otto Pollak, *Social Adjustment in Old Age*, Social Science Research Council Bulletin 59, 1948, p. 153.

Growing out of the work that has been done to date, this appendix suggests a series of subjects on which research is desirable to clarify the relationship between religion and adjustment in old age, to analyze the influence of the church, to evaluate its effectiveness, and to learn more about the services it delivers to older people and on their behalf.[2] These will serve a double purpose: (1) they indicate some of the limitations of the knowledge summarized in this book, and (2) they can stimulate the building up of knowledge for the mutual benefit of scientists, churchmen, the elderly, those who will some day be old, and members of the helping professions. The categories are provided as a means of organizing the items; all of them overlap in a complex web of interrelationships.

FACT-FINDING AND DESCRIPTIVE STUDIES

1. *Comparative research on additional groups of older church members and non-members.* People living in their own homes and other settings should be analyzed to supplement the findings presented in chapter 4. This should include research on people in the various subcultures and regions of our own nation as well as in other lands.

2. *International and cross-cultural comparisons.* Are the findings of the relationships between religion and adjustment in old age reported in this book limited to our own culture? Different results may emerge, for example, from research in eastern nations, in those which have a state church, or in those with one dominant religious faith or institution. Research on this subject could be related to other, more extensive studies of the advantages and disadvantages of the pluralistic free-church situation in contrast to established-church societies.

3. *The impact of urbanization and suburbanization upon the church and its older members.* Comparisons of older people in rural, urban, and suburban churches and of rural-to-urban migrants with

---

2. Although everything in this book has made a contribution to the contents of this chapter, several of the items presented here have been adapted from suggestions made by Paul B. Maves, "Aging, Religion, and the Church," chap. 19 in Clark Tibbitts, ed., *Handbook of Social Gerontology,* University of Chicago Press, 1960, pp. 698-749; Phillip E. Hammond, "Aging and the Ministry," chap. 10 in Matilda White Riley *et al.,* eds., *Aging and Society, Vol. 2: Aging and the Professions,* Russell Sage Foundation, 1969, pp. 293-323; and John E. Cantelon *et al., Religion and Aging: The Behavioral and Social Sciences Look at Religion and Aging,* Rossmoor-Cortese Institute for the Study of Retirement and Aging, University of Southern California, 1967.

non-migrants might provide a basis for determining the results of the constant population shifts in our nation and predicting consequences of future changes. Problems thus indicated could become a focus for corrective action by the churches.

4. *Expectations of and desires in the church.* What do older people expect to receive in and from the church? Do they think it has been more inclined toward satisfying or failing to satisfy their needs (see chapters 6 and 7)? Do they expect it to contribute to their well-being or to be irrelevant to it? Do they personally perceive themselves as satisfied with their religious faith? How does their level of personal satisfaction relate to their generalized interpretation of expectations from the church, and what are the implications of these findings for church action?

5. *The status of older people in the church.* There is some evidence that older people in the church generally tend to be in a position of subjection and subordination. Yet it is possible that they are often "the power behind the throne" even when they do not hold positions of leadership in old age. If so, they may have much more influence in our religious institutions than is generally conceded. The extent to which this is true, the reasons why it is or is not so, and its consequences are worth investigation both for its own sake and for its implications for gerontological research in other institutions and segments of our society. The place of older people who serve in church activities other than leadership positions is also a worthy subject of study.

6. *Religious beliefs of older people.* In chapter 3 some evidence is presented that religious beliefs of the aging as a whole tend to deviate somewhat from those of younger people. Detailed historical, sociological, and psychological analyses of the scope of these differences, and especially efforts to discover the reasons for them, could help to answer the question of whether these observed differences are primarily an outgrowth of the aging process or are a result of divergent experiences and varying exposure to religion in childhood, youth, and earlier adulthood.

THE INFLUENCE AND IMPACT OF RELIGION AND THE CHURCH

7. *Personal satisfaction received from religion and the church.* Additional empirical investigations of the role of religion in times of personal crisis could contribute to our understanding both of the role of the church in modern society and of the social-psychological mechanisms of behavior of older people. What changes in self-

conception result from changes in status in the church in old age? How does religion help alleviate feelings of loneliness, anxieties about death, and the loss of a sense of usefulness? How does it help the older person maintain or regain a feeling of self-respect, companionship, and faith? Probing into these subjective areas may not be possible except through long and skillful exploration of individuals selected for their ability to verbalize inner feelings more freely than the average older person.

8. *Religious influence in the lives of older people.* To what extent does religion touch every area of life — economic, marital, occupational, political, social, etc. — and what is its influence? Are some areas more significantly related to the personal adjustment and life satisfaction of the individual than others? How can the most good be done for older people with the least expenditure of effort?

9. *Religious conversions of older people.* Under what circumstances do religious conversions of the aged take place? Are they largely an outgrowth of the frustrations and problems of old age? Knowledge of their frequency, compared to conversions in similar populations and at other ages, would help to confirm many stereotyped ideas of church workers or to break them down. Evangelists and the clergy would profit also from knowing which types of evangelistic outreach and appeal are most effective among older people.

10. *The relevance of theology.* How does theological perspective affect ministries with and for the aging? Do fundamentalists differ from theological liberals in their attitudes and behavior? How does a sacramental form of theology, in comparison to non-sacramental theological perspectives (especially among the clergy), affect ministries for the shut-ins and those who are dying? How do theological beliefs among older people inffuence what they expect from the clergy and the church?

PERSONAL ADJUSTMENT AND LIFE SATISFACTION

11. *Religion and personal adjustment in the various stages of the cycle of adjustment.* As an individual passes through the stages in the cycle of adjustment, it is possible that religion has different meanings and significance at the various social and psychological phases.[3] The assumed contributions of religion to personal adjustment may operate with either accelerating or decelerating speed as time elapses after the individual's initial or most outstanding experi-

3. Cf. Ernest W. Burgess, "The Growing Problem of Aging," in Clark Tibbitts, ed., *Living Through the Older Years,* University of Michigan Press, 1949, pp. 17-18.

ences with religion. The dynamics of the life-long process need to be analyzed by longitudinal studies.

12. *Fluctuations in the personal adjustment of older people.* The reliability of the Chicago Attitudes Inventory (chapters 3 and 4) as an instrument to measure personal adjustment in old age has been fairly well established. Yet it is possible that the personal adjustment of an individual as measured by it and similar instruments may vary somewhat with environmental and experiential factors. When it is cloudy and dreary, for example, many elderly people long for sunshine. In certain kinds of weather, arthritic pains are more severe. Similarly, after a discouraging experience in the church, the individual may be despondent. How stable are the feelings of well-being of older people in relation to environmental influences and personal experiences?

13. *Self-selection of religious faith and activity.* It is possible that older people who are religious are better adjusted in old age than those who are not because those who already are well-adjusted are more likely to become or remain religious. In other words, being "well-adjusted" and being "religious" may be common effects of some other cause, and the two may not be directly connected in a causal way to each other. If poorly adjusted persons do become deeply religious, what changes, if any, take place in their lives? If any well-adjusted individuals could be found who have given up their religion in old age, the effects of this change could be studied. The controlled study of the selection of certain types of religious activities by older people and their rejection by others would make a significant contribution to our knowledge and would have both theoretical and practical significance.

14. *The role of adaptability in old age.* Adaptability may be the key to the observed relationships between religion and personal adjustment or life satisfaction in the later years. The adaptable person may be the one who remains happy while the unadaptable one becomes maladjusted as a result of the loss of occupational, social, and economic status that so generally characterizes getting old in our society. If religion increases the adaptability of the older person, that may be the factor responsible for the better adjustment of religious people.

15. *The "faith of our fathers" and personal adjustment in old age.* Is the best personal adjustment in older people today found among those who conform to the types of religious faith and practice that they were taught during their childhood and youth? If so, what does this mean for a generation reared in a different religious atmosphere?

16. *Leadership in the church and satisfaction in later maturity.* Sociometric analysis could be used to single out the true leaders in a church, regardless of whether or not they are office-holders. The effects of loss of office could be analyzed comparatively for both the "power behind the throne" and those who actually were office-holders. The process of losing office in the later years of life and its effects upon personal adjustment at various stages in the process is also worthy of study.

17. *Religious conflict and personal adjustment in old age.* What are the subjective and objective results of the competitive striving of younger and older church members? How do church splits affect the participants when they reach old age, whether soon or long after the divisions? How many older people have been driven away from the church and religion as a result of internal conflict in the church? How many have emerged from them with strengthened faith and improved personal adjustment?

18. *Social class differences in adjustment.* It is common knowledge that there are significant differences between people at the various social and economic levels of the social stratification system. It is probable that the position of older church people in the class structure is related to their personal and social adjustment in the later years of life. In fact, it is even possible that the concepts of "personal adjustment" and "life satisfaction" are class-oriented and that new measuring concepts and tools will be needed to discover differences of well-being between the members of differing social classes.

19. *Comparisons of church participation with other social participation.* It is possible that the relationships observed between church participation and good personal adjustment in old age are a result of social participation itself and would accrue to individuals involved in any type of organizational affiliation and activity. What implications follow from findings either in support of or contrary to this hypothesis? Do lodges, clubs, senior citizen centers, and other voluntary associations perform the same functions for older people as the church? Are the results of social participation the same for the married as for widowed, divorced, separated, and single persons?

20. *The relationship between non-Christian religions and personal adjustment in old age.* Most of the findings reported in this book relate to the Christian religion in American society. Judaism in its various forms, Buddhism, Hinduism, and other religions could be analyzed both from the philosophical-theoretical viewpoint and from the perspective of the practical hypotheses that would emerge from theological analyses. Such studies ideally should be made in varying types of social settings, as, of course, is also the case with Christianity.

SERVICE DELIVERY BY THE CHURCH

21. *The church and the needs of old people.* Much evidence of the work the church can do for older people is given in this book. As the needs of the aged become increasingly clear, it may be discovered that some needs which the church is not meeting now can best be satisfied by it and that some services it is now providing could be offered much more effectively, economically, and efficiently by other institutions. Research can help to provide the answers.

22. *The role of the elderly in serving the church.* The literature of gerontology soundly documents the fact that older persons can carry out many functions in the church and other community agencies (chapter 9). Research is desirable to specify more fully what additional things older persons can do in and for the church. Demonstration projects are needed to evaluate the most effective means of matching older persons to the needs, perhaps in the capacity of church aides with assignments that will maximize their experience both in terms of contributing to the church and to their own personal adjustment.

23. *Older church members and young people.* As is very well known, thousands of young people are having a difficult time in coping with life and gaining a personal sense of identity. As a result, the use of drugs and alcoholic beverages is increasing among them, and there are high rates of deviancy, juvenile delinquency, and crime. Many believe that older persons could be used more frequently and effectively to help younger persons adjust to their life conditions. Research is needed to discover how older church members can be used in this capacity with respect to both younger church members and youth in general.

24. *The church and forced relocation.* A major problem facing many older persons is the necessity to give up their homes and move to a new place of residence. This forced relocation is brought on by many pressures, such as inability to maintain oneself in independent living, loss of a mate, highway and building construction, and urban decay. That forced relocation requires serious adjustments on the part of older persons, sometimes with negative effects on their health and personal well-being, has been conclusively documented. We need to know what community agencies in general and the church specifically can do to assist elderly persons who are forced to cope with this serious problem.

25. *Educational programs in the church.* Many church leaders lack knowledge concerning the educational needs of older persons and the role that the church can play in providing such education. Specifically we need to know what kinds of educational programs

can best be provided by the church and thus supplement those that are available in the community. More should be known about how best to coordinate church education programs with community education endeavors. Information about the roles older church members can play in educational activities, their needs, and their desires is much needed by religious educators and other church leaders responsible for such programs.

26. *Older church members and community service.* Thousands of retired older persons have the time, energy, and talent to give of themselves to assist fellowmen who are in less fortunate circumstances. A useful research and demonstration project would be an evaluation of the effectiveness of a church-sponsored program to bring together individuals in need and those elderly persons who can serve so that homes can be repaired, fences painted, yards cleaned, etc. Other services that could be provided more systematically than they are now are home visits, picnics, automobile rides, etc. The church is in an excellent position to offer these services, as is indicated by the resounding success of such programs. The need to expand and evaluate them is self-evident.

27. *The impact of the church's assistance in delivering quality medical care to all Americans.* It is a well-established fact that millions of Americans, especially poor and older persons, are not receiving adequate medical care. As a result, American medicine is in a transition marked by an intensive effort to deliver medical care to these people. It would be very useful to have research concerning what the church can do to encourage older persons to utilize existing medical services and, once they do, to comply with medical instructions.

28. *The role of the church and religion in community mental health centers.* An area of much-needed research concerns the role of the church and religion in community mental health centers. Their purpose is to prevent and treat mental disorders, primarily by keeping afflicted persons in their own homes or community insofar as this is practical. These centers are staffed by professionals and community residents in an attempt to provide comprehensive care for the center participants. Research and demonstration projects are needed concerning the role of religion and the clergy in this setting.

29. *Innovations in programs of care for the elderly.* As more programs professing to be holistic are developed for the aging, the church and religion can be expected to expand its role in many of these activities. For example, what can and ought the church to do in programs such as those that have been organized to care for the elderly mentally infirm? One kind of therapy mentioned earlier is Reality Orientation Training, in which a team of professional and

allied medical personnel attempts to keep the patient living as normal a life as long as possible by reinforcing the reality of the patient's world. Because the church is important to a large proportion of the mentally impaired persons, whether they are in a community or hospital setting, it can contribute to their treatment. We need to know much more concerning the specific contributions the church can make in this regard and how it can best carry out this function.

30. *Attitudes of older people toward the clergy.* Some studies suggest that more people turn first to the clergy when they face personal and family crises rather than to any other profession in the local community. Is this still true? Does it apply to all categories of people, or only to certain of them? What do these findings imply about the role of the church in the lives of older people? Do the attitudes vary with the age of the minister? Does this have implications for the retirement of the clergy, their education, pension plans, and other practical details?

31. *Clergy attitudes.* The attitudes of ministers toward older people, those who are in nursing care facilities, the shut-in elderly, and other categories should be studied to discover the range of attitudes among the clergy and the implications of their attitudinal perspectives for effective ministries with older people. How do they view the assets of aging members? How do they interpret the problems of older members? How widespread is gerontophobia among them? How do their attitudes, ageism, and unconscious stereotypes relate to their actual role activities and the results of their work with the aging?

32. *The impact of aging theories upon the church.* The clergy and other church leaders who work with the aging do have some theoretical orientation, whether they have ever labeled or identified it verbally or not. This may involve the disengagement theory, activity theory, some version of Gubrium's socio-environmental theory which tries to bridge the gap between the two, labeling theory, continuity theory, the aging as a minority, the identity crisis theory, or exchange theory, to mention some of the more prominent perspectives. Identification and study of the indicators which reflect adoption of one or another of these theories (or some combination of them) is a significant challenge for gerontologists. The development of research to determine the impact of such perspectives upon the work of individual clergy, church programs, and organized groups within the church constitutes a significant challenge for further work. Many of these theories can be tested scientifically through research on religion and churches.

EVALUATION RESEARCH

33. *The measurement of spiritual well-being.* In spite of considerable attention given to the concept of spiritual well-being at the 1971 White House Conference on Aging, there has been only one ecumenical attempt to define the concept uniformly (Appendix I). There is no measuring instrument to determine whether spiritual health is present or absent, nor can we determine its degree or strength. Although the central core of the concept possibly can never be directly studied empirically, various religious groups do have criteria by which they determine, with a reasonable degree of accuracy for their purposes, whether or not a person fulfills their qualifications of spiritual well-being. It therefore should be possible to identify objective indicators of it and to combine them into an appropriate measuring instrument.[4] Once such an instrument has been developed, the effects of programs within the church and care facilities for the aging (as well as for other age groups) can be studied to determine whether or not they actually improve the spiritual health of those who receive the services. This has the potential of becoming an important concept in studies of the Quality of Life and Social Indicators Movement.

34. *Evaluative studies of church programs.* Everything the church does has some effect upon its constituents. How does stressing programs for youth affect the older members? How do the various types of church-related programs designed specifically for older people affect them spiritually, socially, and psychologically? What is contributed to them by worship services, programs of the various organizations, and other activities that are church-related? Out of such studies can flow more effective programs of religious education. Longitudinal studies with both control and experimental groups measured "before and after" probably are the ideal method to use for this purpose. These should include analysis of the needs to be served, objectives of the programs introduced, and evaluation of the leadership responsible for carrying them out in particular community and institutional settings.

35. *Clergy effectiveness.* Studies of clergy should be undertaken to determine the personality traits, theoretical and theological orientations, perspectives on pastoral care, training, and other characteristics which are related to effective and ineffective work with older people.

---

4. David O. Moberg is currently working on this subject. Interested readers are encouraged to communicate with him at the Department of Sociology and Anthropology, Marquette University, Milwaukee, WI 53233.

36. *Qualitative studies of religion.* We need to know the nature of personal religious practices and piety among the aging and their impact upon the lives of individuals. What does religion mean to them? What types of these activities mean most to the greatest number of people? To what extent are churches facilitating the most meaningful and constructive forms of religious experience for aging members? Is there a wide gap, or are they directly "on target"?

CONCLUSION

The discriminating reader will undoubtedly observe that many of these suggestions for further research and study overlap. Any comprehensive, large-scale project of research on the church and the older person would have to consider most, if not all, of them, and it would of necessity have to be interdisciplinary in scope. Smaller studies could be made, of course, on any suggested topic.

These research themes are not an encyclopedic or exhaustive presentation of all projects that are possible. Rather, they are intended to be suggestive and stimulating to those who are interested in this field of knowledge as social and behavioral scientists, "social engineers," or church workers concerned with either theoretical problems or programs of action. The perceptive reader will easily identify dozens of additional subjects which are in need of careful research.

Appendix III

Recommended Reading and Resources

The works listed here are especially valuable for anyone involved in further studies related to the church and the aging, whether for the goal of academic studies and research, administrative work, or personal understanding of aging and the elderly. The footnotes throughout this book also can lead the reader to a wide range of publications which have rich contents. Journals mentioned in them can serve as a continuing source of recent materials, and other books relevant to the subject will be shelved in libraries alongside those which are mentioned here and in the footnotes.

Abernethy, Jean Beaven, *Old is Not a Four Letter Word*. Nashville: Abingdon Press, 1975. This paperback on "new moods and meanings in aging" is a useful essay for those who work with the aging as well as for the aging themselves. Its four parts deal with growing old as growing new, new opportunities in the later years, the life cycle vantage point and the personal life review, and new vistas stirred up by death which have an eternal perspective.

Aging, published monthly by the Administration on Aging, U.S. Dept. of Health, Education and Welfare. Subscriptions ($5.05 per year in 1976) from Supt. of Documents, Washington, DC 20402. This news magazine publishes feature articles and information about government-funded programs, state and area agencies on aging, community activities, special events, new publications, conferences, and pending legislation pertinent to aging.

Atchley, Robert C., *The Social Forces in Later Life*. Belmont, CA: Wadsworth Publishing Co., 1972; revised edition, 1977. This is possibly the best general introductory textbook in social gerontology. Its parts deal with the aging individual, age changes in situational contexts, and societal responses to the aging, including the role of religious and voluntary associations.

Butler, Robert N., and Myrna I. Lewis, *Aging and Mental Health: Positive Psychosocial Approaches.* St. Louis: C. V. Mosby Co., 1973. This textbook on the nature and problems of old age and the evaluation, treatment, and prevention of the problems is an excellent resource for professional people who work with the aging.

Clingan, Donald F., *Aging Persons in the Community of Faith.* Institute on Religion and Aging, 1100 W. 42nd St., Indianapolis, IN 46208, and Indiana Commission on the Aging and the Aged, 215 N. Senate Avenue, Indianapolis, IN 46202 ($1.00 plus shipping charges). This 80-page paperback was prepared by the first President and first Executive Director of the National Interfaith Coalition on Aging as a guidebook for churches and synagogues on ministry to, for, and with the aging.

Deeken, Alfons, *Growing Old and How to Cope with It.* Paramus, N.J.: Paulist Press, 1972, $1.25. This is an excellent discussion of the problems and process of growing old, coming to grips with old age, and how to grow old gracefully. Written by a Catholic priest, its perspectives are based upon a realistic understanding of the subject and the teachings of the Christian Scriptures.

The Gerontologist, published bi-monthly by the Gerontological Society, 1 Dupont Circle, Washington, DC 20036; subscriptions $20.00. This is the best all-around journal for professional people who wish to keep up with new developments in the field of aging. Its companion, the *Journal of Gerontology* (bi-monthly, $30.00 per year) has professional articles, including many from the biological and medical sciences, book reviews, and an extensive classified bibliography of current publications in the entire field of gerontology and geriatrics, usually covering over 500 references in each issue.

Hiltner, Seward, ed., *Toward a Theology of Aging.* New York: Human Sciences Press, 1975. Based on lectures at a Conference on the Theology of Aging, this stimulating collection deals with the need for theological reflection on aging, psychological, eschatological, and sociopsychological perspectives on it, Jewish and Christian values, and a preface to a practical theology of aging.

Maves, Paul B., "Aging, Religion, and the Church," chap. 19 in Clark Tibbitts, ed., *Handbook of Social Gerontology: Societal Aspects of Aging.* University of Chicago Press, 1960, pp. 698-749. This masterful survey deals with such topics as the impact of aging on churches, factors which complicate the study of religion and aging, theoretical considerations, Judeo-Christian teachings and attitudes relevant to aging and old age, history of the care of the aged by religious bodies, church programs for older people in and beyond the local parish, participation of older people in parish programs, and the meaning of religion, participation, and isolation.

Moberg, David O., *Spiritual Well-Being: Background and Issues.*
    Washington, DC: White House Conference on Aging, Feb. 1971.
    Government Printing Office Catalog #5247-0015, $.70. This 69-
    page paper used by the Section on Spiritual Well-Being of the
    1971 WHCA covers the nature and scope of spiritual needs,
    long-range goals for ministering to those needs, knowledge from
    pertinent research, the status of church, community, and govern-
    mental programs, deficiencies in those programs, and issues pro-
    posed for discussion in the WHCA. The 12-page bibliography is
    a valuable resource.

Modern Maturity, bi-monthly magazine of the American Association
    of Retired Persons, 1909 K St. N.W., Washington, DC 20049,
    $3.00 per year. (Free with membership in AARP at the same
    price of $3.00 per year.) This magazine of general news and
    feature articles oriented around the interests of retired people
    is an interesting, informative, and often inspirational resource
    for older people.

Morgan, John H., *Aging in the Religious Life: A Comprehensive
    Bibliography (1960-1975).* Wichita, Kansas: Institute on Ministry
    and the Elderly, Kansas Newman College, 1976, $3.95. This non-
    annotated bibliography and its introductory essay on "Aging and
    Religious Vocation: Toward a Non-Cataclysmic Perspective" is a
    valuable resource for all who are interested in aging and religion,
    not only for those who are members of religious orders.

Otte, Elmer, *Welcome Retirement.* St. Louis: Concordia Publishing
    House, 1974. This Crossroads paperback is a very helpful and
    informative guide to constructive ways of preparing for retire-
    ment. It includes an excellent chapter on spiritual health.

Post-White House Conference on Aging Reports, 1973. Joint Com-
    mittee Print, 93rd Congress, 1st Session, Sep. 1973. Supt. of
    Documents, U.S. Government Printing Office, Washington, DC
    20402. Stock number 5270-01994, $5.20. This describes adminis-
    trative responses to recommendations from the 1971 WHCA.
    Prepared for the Subcommittee on Aging of the Committee of
    Labor and Public Welfare and the Special Committee on Aging
    of the U.S. Senate, it includes the 15 recommendations of the
    WHCA Section on Spiritual Well-Being together with interpre-
    tive statements of the Administration's response and the study
    panel's reactions (pp. 555-577).

Riley, Matilda White, *et al.,* eds., *Aging and Society,* 3 vols. New
    York: Russell Sage Foundation, 1968-1969. Volume 1 is a com-
    prehensive inventory of research findings on all aspects of the
    subject, including religion. Volume 2 on aging and the pro-
    fessions includes a chapter on "Aging and the Ministry" by
    Phillip E. Hammond. Volume 3 is a sociology of age stratification.

SCA Project on Aging, *That Thy Days May Be Long in the Good
    Land: A Guide to Aging Programs for Synagogues.* Synagogue
    Council of America, Institute for Jewish Policy Planning and

Research, 1776 Massachusetts Ave. N.W., Washington, DC 20036, 1975, $1.50. This 95-page spiral bound manual includes a rationale for synagogue planning with the Jewish aging, how to plan and start a program, programs for serving the home-bound elderly, synagogue-based programs of senior clubs, adult education, and personal service clinics, ways of reaching out to the institutionalized elderly, films, offices, and agencies dealing with the aging, and national voluntary organizations. It is an excellent resource for religious leaders of all faiths.

Southern Baptist Convention, *Report of the SBC Study of the Problems of the Aging.* Executive Committee of the SBC, 460 James Robertson Parkway, Nashville, TN 37219, $1.00. This fine-print, 26-page summary condenses a massive amount of information, perspectives, and recommendations which are pertinent to lay and professional leaders in any religious body.

Tournier, Paul, *Learn to Grow Old,* translated from the French by Edwin Hudson. New York: Harper and Row, 1972. The famous Swiss psychologist and medical doctor interprets work and leisure, the need for a more humane society, the condition of the elderly, the place of a second career, the meaning and acceptance of old age, and faith.

Veatch, Robert, *Death and Dying.* Today paperback #CP-238, Claretian Publications, 221 W. Madison St., Chicago, IL 60606, 1974, $.75. This is an excellent survey of death as a taboo topic, the five stages of dying, the ethical issues involved, the nature of death, and the care of the dying.

Wakin, Edward, *Living as a Widow.* Jubilee Paperback #CP2-80, Claretian Publications, 221 W. Madison St., Chicago, IL 60606, $.95. This booklet can be used by either widowed persons or those who wish to understand them better. It deals with widowed people as a forgotten minority, grief, decision-making, and adjusting to a new life.

Index

219